George Augustus Lofton

English Baptist Reformation

George Augustus Lofton

English Baptist Reformation

ISBN/EAN: 9783743335790

Manufactured in Europe, USA, Canada, Australia, Japa

Cover: Foto ©Lupo / pixelio.de

Manufactured and distributed by brebook publishing software (www.brebook.com)

George Augustus Lofton

English Baptist Reformation

ENGLISH BAPTIST REFORMATION.

(From 1609 to 1641 A. D.)

BY

GEO. A. LOFTON, D. D.,

Author of Bible Thoughts and Themes, Character Sketches, Harp of Life,
A Review of the Question, Review of Dr. Thomas on
the Whitsitt Question, etc.

"Succession . . . . . is Antichrist's Chief Hold.

                                          Thomas Helwys.
Amsterdam   William Piggot.
                                       Thomas Seamer.
this 12th of March, 1609.   John Morton."

LOUISVILLE, KY.
CHAS. T. DEARING,
1899.

CONTENTS.

CHAPTER.		PAGE.
I.	THE ANCIENT BRITISH CHRISTIANS	9
II.	ANABAPTISTS OF THE XVI. CENTURY	18
III.	ORIGIN OF THE GENERAL BAPTISTS	29
IV.	ORIGIN OF THE GENERAL BAPTISTS—Continued	41
V.	ORIGIN OF THE PARTICULAR BAPTISTS	55
VI.	DISUSE OF IMMERSION IN ENGLAND	68
VII.	RESTORATION OF IMMERSION IN ENGLAND	79
VIII.	THE SO-CALLED KIFFIN MANUSCRIPT	91
IX.	THE OBJECTIONS TO THE SO-CALLED KIFFIN MANUSCRIPT	104
X.	WILLIAM KIFFIN	116
XI.	THE BAMPFIELD DOCUMENT	128
XII.	CROSBY'S WITNESSES	140
XIII.	CROSBY'S WITNESSES—Continued	152
XIV.	EDWARD BARBER AND PRAISEGOD BAREBONE	163
XV.	SOME OTHER BAPTIST WITNESSES	175
XVI.	SOME OTHER BAPTIST WITNESSES—Continued	187
XVII.	WHAT THE ENEMY SAID—DR. FEATLEY	202
XVIII.	WHAT THE ENEMY SAID—Continued	213
XIX.	WHAT THE ENEMY SAID—Concluded	226
XX.	SIGNIFICANT FACTS	239
XXI.	WERE THEY BAPTISTS?	250
	APPENDIX	262
	INDEX	276

PREFACE.

This work treats chiefly of that period of English Baptist History included between 1609 and 1641 A. D. This was the formative era of the Anglo-Saxon Baptists. The Baptist writers of the 17th century distinctly claim their movement as a "Beginning," or "Reformation." From 1609 to 1641 and for some time afterward the Anabaptists of England were organically as well as individually Separatists upon the principle of believers' baptism; but it was not until 1641 that they fully reached Baptist practice by the adoption of immersion. They were elementally based upon the old evangelical principles of Lollardism and Dutch Anabaptism which had produced English Congregationalism. In the early part of the 17th century Calvinistic Anabaptism seems to have been individually "intermixed" with Congregationalism; and it was out of this pure evangelical element that the work of Baptist Separation began, in 1633, to reform. The General or Arminian Baptists of England separated in 1609 and began their reformation in Holland—returning to England in 1611. Kiffin, King, Allen, Lamb, Jessey and others followed by Crosby, speak of this movement as a "separation," "beginning," a "reformation upon the same principles on which all other protestants built their reformation;" and these and all other writers of the period who touch the subject, expressly or impliedly, affirm that the English Baptists separated and reformed upon a higher plane of truth than even the Independents who while they took high ground and advanced position, never reached the ultimate logic of Scriptural reform. They never got out of infant baptism or sprinkling—compulsory religion; and hence the Baptists claimed that they never got out of Rome, nor reached the goal of a pure church or religious liberty—even in their Independency.

Hence the title of this work. The two first chapters are merely introductory, treating of the Ancient British Christians and such of the Foreign Anabaptists as from time to time penetrated the Kingdom, and who though migratory and unsettled, laid the foundation of Congregationalism or Independency in

England, and who furnished the evangelical base and theory of Baptist organism and reformation at a later date. Baptist history in England, according to General and Particular designation, begins within the period to which this work is confined; and such a period for many reasons made prominent in the body of this work, deserves special and elaborate treatment.

It is needless to say that this volume is the product of the great contention which has grown out of the "Whitsitt Question;" and though it is a treatment different in form from that of Dr. Whitsitt's Question in Baptist History, yet it is primarily dependent upon Dr. Whitsitt's work for its original suggestions and data. This work adds nothing to, nor takes anything from, Dr. Whitsitt's thesis of "1641." It only sustains that thesis; and it is only a question of time when all unbiased scholarship will accept the fact that the Baptists of England restored immersion in 1641. Others besides Dr. Whitsitt claim independently to have made the same discovery about the same time. Such were Drs. Newman and Dexter, learned and competent investigators; and more recently it has transpired that Prof. Rauschenbush, another scholar, came to the same conclusion, about the same time, in Germany. So of Prof. de Hoop Scheffer and others. Thomas Crosby, 1738-40, in the first history of Baptists, without giving the date, 1641, details all the facts of that date which show the revival of immersion by the English Baptists; and but for this mistake of our first historian who had the so-called Kiffin Manuscript before him, we should have escaped the present controversy. The more recent recovery of this manuscript by Dr. Geo. Gould of London, led Dr. Whitsitt to assert the discovery of the obscured date and to prove his thesis by ample collateral testimony that the Baptists of England recovered immersion in 1641.

The author of this volume has written considerably in defense of Dr. Whitsitt's view—basing his view upon Crosby's history; but he determined to make a more thorough investigation of the subject—visiting the British Museum and Dr. Williams' Library in London, the Bodleian Library in Oxford and the Libraries of Edinburgh and other places for the purpose. He now lays the result of his research before his readers; and while much of it has been a verification of the material on hand, he presents much new and additional testimony. More than fifty original authorities, Baptist and Pedobaptist, are here cited as a part of his collection and verification; and he has been elaborate, though not exhaustive, in detail and quotation, in order to give, as far as practicable, the full setting of his authorities and to show the exact position and history of the Baptists upon this question and upon related points within the reformatory period under discussion. The 1641 thesis is not merely incidental to this discussion, but the author's aim is to present that thesis as only related to a larger history of the Baptists which involves that thesis and a corresponding reformation which is inseparable from that thesis.

This work is not intended to be simply controversial but historical in fact and in spirit; and the author assures his readers that his investigation has been in an unpartisan search for the truth as in the fear and under the guidance of God. He solemnly determined to renounce the 1641 thesis, if the facts of history were against it; but among the 17th century authorities, Baptist or Pedobaptist, he could find nothing which did not confirm the thesis. After all it is only a question of history, and should be treated as such with a historic spirit and method which deal with facts and not fictions, with original sources and not subsequent traditions, with established research and not learned opinions which have found place in literature without data or special investigation. One good original authority is worth a hundred current traditions or opinions in any given historical question. Positions in history are not always true because some scholarly man holds them; and it is often too true, for this reason, that certain positions in history are taken for granted.

Besides the learned and able work of Dr. Wm. H. Whitsitt (A Question in Baptist History) the author is indebted to the great work of Dr. A. H. Newman (Hist. Antipedobaptism), which reaches down to the date at which this work begins, and to Prof. Henry C. Vedder's Short History of the Baptists, a very valuable production lately revised and enlarged. He also commends as most able and opportune the Baptist History of Prof. Rauschenbusch, only the 17th chapter of which he has seen, but which squarely adopts the 1641 thesis from Crosby. These late Baptist publications, bearing upon the subject under discussion, are written with scholarly ability and unpartisan courage, and should be read by every impartial Baptist. While the author feels indebted to these later writers, he has made an investigation of his own; and he bases his conclusions upon the original sources of the 17th century and upon the original history of the English

Baptists, based upon these same sources by Thomas Crosby, Evans and others.

The thesis of this work is not of the author's choosing, but one to which he has been driven by careful study contrary to his former predilections and training. He knows how to sympathize, therefore, with his brethren of a contrary opinion; and but for such opinion the question would be of little moment apart from the facts of Baptist history. For this reason however the author feels that he has made a valuable contribution to his brethren, (1) because he has contributed to a better understanding of Baptist history and position, (2) because he has reset the ancient Baptist landmark of constant *reproduction* instead of visible *succession*, which was unknown to the English Baptist churches. To the peace and fraternity of the brethren these pages are therefore dedicated; and with a broader and more enlightened view of Baptist history and polity, it is here devoutly wished that the Baptist denomination, founded by our Anglo-Saxon fathers in tears and blood, may rise to wider fields of usefulness and progress and grander achievements, as it stands upon the Word of God for its sole authority, depends upon Christ for its sole head, and follows the Holy Ghost for its sole guide.

An extra chapter and also an Appendix has been added, during the printing of this work, in order to meet the published objections and criticisms which, up to date, have been offered to the 1641 thesis of the Jessey Records and Kiffin MS. The Author begs a careful reading of Chapter IX. and the Appendix in answer to these objections; and he regrets that having to go to press he has not further time to notice further criticism in this work.

GEO. A. L.

NASHVILLE, TENN.,
March 13, 1899.

ENGLISH BAPTIST REFORMATION.

(FROM 1609 TO 1641 A. D.)

CHAPTER I.

THE ANCIENT BRITISH CHRISTIANS.

There are several traditions which make it probable that Christianity was planted in Great Britain early in the first century by propagandists from Asia and not from Rome; and with the exception of 558 years, from the time of Austin, 600 A. D., to the time of Henry II., 1158 A. D., there seems to be scarcely a period in English Annals in which we cannot find some trace of Baptist principles. Down to the time of Austin's invasion and massacre of the Welsh Christians, 603 A. D., it is maintained by some Baptist historians that those ancient British Christians were Baptists. The first English Baptist Historians, Crosby and Ivimey, incline to this view; but Evans, one of the latest and best writers on early English Baptist History, after a thorough investigation of the subject concludes that the assumption is based only on "probability." That they practiced trine immersion is clear; but the important question is: Did they practice infant baptism? The data upon which hangs the question consists in the *nature* of Austin's demands of the British bishops in 600 A. D., which, according to Bede, were these:

"To keep Easter *at the due time;* to administer baptism, by which we are *again born to God* [that ye *give Christendom to children* (Fabian)], according to the *custom* of the Holy Roman Apostolic Church; and jointly with us preach the Word of God to the English nation, &c."

But for Fabian's addition to Bede's account, namely, that "ye give Christendom to children," the question of infant baptism would not be involved. With this addition, including the *form* of Austin's demand, arises the doubt with reference to the practice of ancient Britons. Wall, Baxter, Murdock, Calamy and other Pedobaptist writers affirm that Austin demanded simply *uniformity* with the Romish time of keeping Easter, with the

Romish theory of sacramental baptism, and with the Romish manner of baptizing children in white garments, with milk, honey, etc. Against this view Ivimey, D'Anvers, Davye and other Baptist writers contend that the demand pertained exclusively to baptism, or the baptism of children, without reference to uniformity with Romish custom. According to Cathcart, the evidence on the question furnished by Bede (Eccles. Hist., Lib. II., Cap. 2) leaves the matter without positive determination. The fact that, at the time of Austin's demand, infant baptism had not then everywhere superceded adult baptism, as in succeeding centuries, is, according to Evans, an argument against the probability that the ancient British Christians practiced infant baptism; and yet there is much plausibility in the view of Wall, Baxter and others in spite of Evans' "probability."

The fact is that those British Christians up to and at the time of Austin kept Easter according, perhaps, to the Eastern Church time; and it is certain on this point that Austin was demanding uniformity with the Paschal time of Rome. He was also demanding conformity to the sacramental theory of baptism which, it would seem, these British Christians had not held; and if they were practicing infant baptism, which is in question, then he was demanding uniformity with the Romish custom of white garments, milk and honey, etc., as Wall and others maintain. The passage from Pelagius, a British Christian of the fifth century, quoted by Dr. Wall, in which he says: "That men do slander him, as if he denied the sacrament of baptism to infants, and did promise the kingdom of heaven to any person without the redemption of Christ, which he had never heard, no, not even any impious heretic or sectary say," in spite of Ivimey (Vol. I., p. 52) would seem to indicate the presence of infant baptism among the British Christians in the fifth century. Pelagius' statement is almost conclusive of the fact. Although the system of Pelagius denied the imputation of Adam's sin to infants, it never rejected infant baptism; and while it held that infant baptism did not bestow eternal life, it maintained that infants, in some sense, were excluded from the kingdom of heaven (though not from eternal life) without baptism. (Mosheim, Vol. I., p. 371, N. 47.) The passage cited from Pelagius fits the theory of Pelagianism precisely and it is possible that his view of infant baptism among the British churches explains the demand of Austin for conformity to the Romish idea of infant baptism.

Whatever the nature of Austin's demands, however, the British Christians rejected them, because they were independent of Rome's jurisdiction and had never had any connection with it. Nevertheless these British Christians seem to have maintained, after the manner of early Episcopacy, some sort of Romish polity. In rejecting the demands of Austin, according to Sir H. Spelman (Cathcart's Ancient British and Irish Churches, p. 257), the Abbot of Bangor, Wales, in the name of the British bishops and churches declared "that they were under jurisdiction of the Bishop of Caerleon upon Usk, who was, under God, their spiritual overseer and director;" and thus they formally declined the jurisdiction of the Pope of Rome. They observed Lent, Easter, and other Romish ceremonies according to their own time and way; their great schools were called "monasteries" and their teachers "monks"; they had abbeys and abbots; and though independent of Rome, they were somewhat after the fashion of Rome. British bishops were at the Catholic council of Nice in 325 A. D., and at the council of Arles and other convocations of Catholic bishops before the time of Austin in England. Like the Novatians and Donatists, who revolted from Rome and still retained her polity and infant baptism (250–389), these British Christians, though independent of Rome, were, at that time, very much like Rome.

In some of the essentials of faith and practice these ancient British churches—and so of the ancient Scotch and Irish churches—were Baptistic. St. Patrick, Cathcart thinks, was "*substantially*" a Baptist; but he was ordained a bishop in Gaul after the Gallican Catholic order of that day; and so he ordained hundreds of bishops in the Irish churches over which he seemed to preside as bishop of the whole. He, too, was evidently independent of Rome, as were the British churches, whether he ever practiced infant baptism or not; and it is possible that the British churches did not practice infant baptism at first, nor until it became prevalent. Crosby seems to think that for the first 300 years adult immersion alone prevailed among them; and if so they were at least Baptistic in the practice of baptism for that period, whatever their polity or practice in other respects. Like the Novatians, Donatists and Gallican Christians of the time, they were very likely at an early day modeled after the Episcopal order, though entirely independent of Rome.

The Christians of the Eastern type, who evidently evangelized

Britain, landing first, it is said, at Glastonbury, near Bristol, were probably of the same general stamp as Irenaeus, who labored in Southern France during the latter half of the second century. So far as known the ancient British Christians, as appeared in England, Ireland, Scotland, the Rhine Valley, Thuringia and other places, were never charged with Antipedobaptism, and this fact is almost decisive that they never opposed infant baptism and must have practiced it so soon as it became prevalent. Whether St. Patrick ever practiced it or not, though an immersionist, he was not a Baptist. He seems to have believed in baptismal regeneration; and his method of evangelization appears to have been to interest a chieftain or a king in Christianity and without waiting for much catechizing, to baptize him and his entire following. He baptized 12,000 in one night; and it is impossible to suppose that they were evangelically converted. In fact they seem as ferocious after as before baptism; and such men as Patrick, Columba and the like did not hesitate to call on these barbarian kings to fight their battles. In this as in most other respects they resembled the church of Rome both in polity and policy.

According to Cathcart (Ancient British and Irish Churches, pp. 277–286) there remained in Cornwall, Wales and other remote sections of England some of the ancient British Christians or churches which never conformed to the polity of Rome until the time of Henry I., 1109 A. D., when Wales was subjugated by this prince; and it was not until 1282 A. D., when Llewellyn, the Prince of Wales, was conquered and slain by Edward III., and when Wales lost her last vestige of liberty, that Rome at last completely triumphed over Welsh Protestantism and utterly extinguished what was left of it after the massacre by Austin, 603 A. D. Down to 1109, and onward to 1282, there were hidden, here and there in remote parts of the kingdom, fragments of the old independent British Protestantism which continued to refuse conformity to Rome, as in 600 A. D.; and possibly seeds of this anti-Roman Christianity remained in Wales down to the sixteenth century. Hence the fertility of that soil for early Puritan dissent and for Baptist principles and growth after the Reformation. It is claimed, with some degree of plausibility, that traces of the Baptist element are discernable very early, if not all the way through the history of Welsh Christianity, but without any reliable historical data. According to Joshua Thomas the first Baptist church ever known in Wales was formed at Ilston in 1649 A. D.; and there is no basis for the tradition of a Baptist church at Olchon, 1633. (Armitage, p. 599.) It is said that the Welsh Bards afford the best historic annals down to the fourteenth century, and they trace no line of Baptist "heretics" to that period. In fact down to the sixteenth century Wales was completely under the shadow of Romanism; and it is said that there was no Bible in the Welsh tongue until thirty years after Elizabeth established Protestantism in Wales by law. It is claimed that in Chester county a Baptist church dates its origin back to 1422. If so this church was historically unknown for 357 years down to 1649 when the first known Welsh Baptist church was established at Ilston; and it seems utterly impossible in that small country for such a church to have escaped the persecution and destruction of Rome or the notice of history. Such traditions are childish and misleading; and nothing can be gained by any people who advocate them in the face of authentic history. It is enough to claim traditional traces of Baptist footprints or principles in Wales through all these centuries of darkness and despotism; but it is absurd to claim organization or succession which cannot be established by history.

The first instance, in the history of England, of anything like an Anabaptist movement occurred in 1158, during the reign of Henry II. and 558 years after the invasion of Austin and the establishment of Romanism in Britain. An account of it is given by Dr. Henry (Hist. Great Britain, vol. viii., p. 338) and also by Rapin, Collier, Lyttleton, Denne, and others—also Evans (vol. i., p. 10). Thirty Hollanders at this time appeared in England, were arrested and tried before a council of the Clergy in Oxford and driven to extinction by persecution for opposing the dogmas of Rome. They were charged with rejecting baptism and the Eucharist, without any reference to infant baptism, although otherwise found to be orthodox as to the essentials of Christianity, such as the doctrine of the Trinity, incarnation, and the like. These people, though called Waldenses by Rome, were evidently Paulicians or Cathari who, like the Quakers, did not regard baptism and the Lord's Supper of perpetual obligation, and of course were intensely averse to infant baptism. This movement was called the "first revolt" in England from Rome, and it has been claimed as an Antipedobaptist movement, although these Hollanders were Anabaptists who neither baptized nor kept the Lord's Supper because of Rome's perversion of the ordinances. Nevertheless it was a step in the direction of Baptist Principles; and it is historically the first evidence of the Baptist element in England since the first three centuries if then. Even this was foreign and not native born; but, as we shall see, Baptist elements in England were long imported before Baptist principles or churches were ever restablished.

According to Roger Hoveden, Henry II., 1182 A. D., was, on account of State reasons, "very favorable to the Waldensian Sect in England"; and we thus become aware of the fact of their existence here at this period, just twenty-four years after the extermination of the Hollanders by the same king, already mentioned. Hoveden also shows that in the time of Richard I. and of King John there was no opposition to the Waldenses because of the wars which engrossed these kings. It has been claimed that these Waldenses were Dutch and French weavers who fled from persecution and were protected by the kings of this period on account of their industries; and hence it is held that Baptist principles were thus early and permanently planted in England. Upon the authority of Archbishop Usher it is stated that in the time of Henry III., 1235 A. D., the orders of the Friers Minorites came from France into England to suppress the Waldensian heresy. Crosby and Ivimey declare that in the time of Edward II., 1315 A. D., Walter Lollard, a man of great renown among the Waldenses, came into England and spread their doctrines "very much in these parts"; and that afterwards these Waldenses went by the name of Lollards, subsequently becoming confounded with the Wyckliffeites. It is to be noted here that Evans makes no mention of this history so far as it relates to the Waldenses; and there seems to be no historical details which give any clear idea of the character or extent of Waldensian aggression or influence upon England at the periods mentioned, except that it possibly laid the foundation for Lollardism in the kingdom. The Waldenses were at that time Anabaptists; and through them we discover at this later period another trace of Baptist principles in England before the evangelical movement of the Lollards and Wyckliffeites in the 14th Century.

Taking the opinion of Baptist historians, Ivimey seems to think that Wyckliffe and his followers were Antipedobaptists. Crosby is not satisfied that Wyckliffe clearly opposed infant baptism, but that some of his followers did. Evans is satisfied that there is no document which authorizes the conclusion that the great reformer himself rejected infant baptism; but he thinks the Lollards and the Wyckliffeites were opposed to infant baptism. In a sermon on baptism Wycliffe said that it was immaterial whether infants were "dipped once, or thrice, or water be poured upon their heads"; and in addition to his sanction here of the infant rite he thus, according to Dr. Whitsitt, made the first concession in England to pouring or sprinkling for baptism. It is evident that while Wyckliffe was a Baptist in the essential elements of Christianity and rejected the sacramental efficacy of baptism, he never renounced infant baptism as a legitimate rite; and what was true of Wyckliffe was no doubt true of his followers. Their opposition to the saving efficacy of infant baptism was construed into their opposition to the rite itself; and hence the charges of their enemies to this effect, from which however they were defended by others. Wyckliffe never left the Romish church, and he was strongly defended by many of its leading men and ministry against papal bulls and efforts to condemn and destroy him. Dr. Newman (History of Antipedobaptism, p. 342) has well said:

"Diligent research has failed to discover any case of Anti-pedobaptism among English evangelicals before the incoming of Anti-pedobaptists from the Continent (1530 onward)."

Nothing is said of the mode of baptism among the Lollards or Wyckliffeites; but if in this particular they followed the great reformer, the mode of the ordinance must have been a matter of indifference long before the advent of the 16th Century.

The English nation became widely affected with the evangelical principles of the Lollards or Wyckliffeites by the end of the 14th Century. The same was true in Scotland and Wales; and the movement projected itself into Bohemia and other Continental countries. By the year 1400 A. D., during the reign of Henry IV., both Church and State combined to crush out this growing and widespread "heresy" as Rome saw it. Sawtry, the first martyr burned in England, was committed to the stake; and Lord Cobham and others met a like fate in their devotion to the principles of Wyckliffe. By 1420 the Lollards were driven from the open field; and although still numerous and powerful in secret for many years, they were hunted and persecuted unto death in large numbers until they were practically crushed though not extinct by the 16th Century. A mighty and vigorous evangelical party, they were the forerunners of the Reformation in England of which Wyckliffe was the "morning star"; and as Dr. Newman says: "The deeply rooted principles of Lollardism lay at the base of the Puritanism and Independency of the later times." What become of Waldensianism in this movement does not appear; but no doubt in England as in Bohemia it merged with Lollardism or Wyckliffeism; and although anti-pedobaptistic at first it shaded off in this union into indifference upon this point, as indicated by its later history.

Thus it will be seen that the old evangelical life of the British Christians faintly projected into the middle ages of English Christianity, was finally crushed out; and, about the same time, the old evangelical life of the Continent made its way into England through the Waldenses, developed into Lollardism, then into Wyckliffeism in the 14th and 15th Centuries, and then rolled back upon the Continent with fresh vigor and renewed enthusiasm. Lollardism under the teaching and inspiration of Wyckliffe affected most profoundly the English mind with the fundamental doctrines of Christianity; and, as Dr. Newman said, "was the forerunner of all that was best in English Puritanism, from which, in an important sense, modern Baptists have derived their origin. "But," says he, "we have searched in vain for any satisfactory proof that it imbodied distinctively Baptist principles or practices." Again he says:

"Nothing in Wyckliffes published writings—and Lechler claims to have read through his extant manuscript works without finding anything—that would warrant the inference that he rejected infant baptism. The nearest approach to the Baptist position is his expression of opinion that unbaptized infants may be saved. But he did not even venture so far as to express a decided conviction that they would be. His rigid predestinarianism inclined him to the opinion that elect infants would be saved whether baptized or not; but he was not quite sure whether elect infants ever fail to receive baptism. The Lollards took a far more decided stand than Wyckliffe in favor of the salvation of unbaptized infants; but no one of them so far as we are aware denied the propriety or utility of infant baptism." (Hist. Anti-pedobaptism, pp. 55, 56.)

What was true of Wyckliffe and the Lollards was true of Tyndale and his followers. Tyndale was radically evangelical; he had much in common with Lollardism and Antipedobaptistism; but however he discarded its sacramental efficacy, he never gave up infant baptism. Like Wyckliffe he seems early to have conceded affusion as indifferent with immersion in the practice of infant baptism; but like Wyckliffe he never surrendered the propriety or utility of the rite, nor became an Anti-pedobaptist as some claim for him. Nothing beyond the old evangelical life and principles of Waldensianism (1315) projected itself into Lollardism, or Wyckliffeism, or Tyndaleism, or into the English mind of the 14th, 15th and 16th Centuries. Antipedobaptism was a foreign element in England in the 16th Century; and it never took hold upon the evangelical life of the English people until Puritan Congregationalism had reached its ultimate logic in Anabaptist position which was predicted by those who charged such men as Tyndale, Browne, Barrowe and Penry with Anabaptistery. Robert Baillie and others declared that Anabaptism was the true foundation of Independency; and it is pretty clear that Browne and Harrison caught their ideals from the Dutch Anabaptists of Norwich and other places in England. Antipedobaptism first created the ideal of Independency among the English; and then it engrafted upon this English tree the rich foliage of believers' baptism, then immersion and finally all the principles and practices of Christ's spiritual and liberty-loving religion. The conservative Englishman was slow to become a Baptist; but when the process of development was finished, he bestowed upon the name, Baptist, a prestige and a power in English history which have never been rivalled in the annals of martyrdom and progress, considering its small beginning and long opposition at the hands of all the world. The English Baptist reformation which really began in 1609 and was consummated in 1641 had its foundation in Congregational Puritanism which was the outgrowth of prior Anabaptist elements planted in English soil and incorporated with the Lollard movement.

ENGLISH BAPTIST REFORMATION.
(FROM 1609 TO 1641 A. D.)

CHAPTER II.
ANABAPTISTS OF THE SIXTEENTH CENTURY.

The real Anabaptist movement in England begins with the reign of Henry VIII., 1534 A. D., at which time Crosby says: "I find their principles about baptism more fairly stated." During the reigns of Henry VIII., Edward VI., Mary, Elizabeth and James I. onward, we trace the history of a people in England stigmatized as "Anabaptists" and persecuted in every conceivable form by imprisonment, banishment and death for holding doctrines essentially Baptistic or intensely Anti-pedobaptistic. There is no mistaking who they are in history. They are not merely traditional. Their views though variant are well-defined and formulated; and you can track them all the way through this century by their blood. Henry VIII. burned scores of them; two were burned by Edward VI.; Queen Mary who burned every class of non-conformists, burned ten Anabaptists in the year 1555 and large numbers at different times and places; Queen Elizabeth burned two; and James I. burned two and otherwise cruelly persecuted them during his reign. Among the martyrs were Joan Boucher, 1550, and Pieters and Terwoot, 1575, who left behind them their declaration of faith under the sign and seal of their own blood. These people maintained believers' baptism as opposed to infant baptism; a converted church membership as opposed to the corrupt Establishments of Rome and England; independency as opposed to hierarchy; soul-liberty as opposed to magisterial interference and force in matters of faith; the word of God as opposed to the traditions and commandments of men; a voluntary as opposed to a compulsory religion—for all of which and more they pleaded, lived and died with heroic devotion to Baptist principles.

They were sometimes Socinian, Pelagian, or at best Arminian in doctrine. Most if not all of them maintained that the humanity of Christ was not of the substance of Mary's body. They had many vagaries about oaths, war, majesty, and the like; but they stood by Baptist principles and peculiarities in the main with a martyr zeal and devotion which edicts of banishment and fires of persecution could not quench.

These Anabaptists of England during the 16th Century, with but little exception, were foreigners, chiefly from Holland, who fled from persecution and death in their own country to meet a like fate in England—whether at the hands of Papist or Protestant. According to Dr. Newman (Hist. Antipedobaptism, pp. 345, 346,) there was a large immigration of Dutch artisans to England in 1528; in 1560, there were 10,000 in England; and in 1568–73, the number reached 50,000. In London, Norwich, Dover, Romney, Sandwich, Canterbury, Colchester, Hastings and Hythe, there was a large Dutch population, most of whom were Calvinists; "but," says Dr. Newman, "a considerable portion of them were certainly Anti-pedobaptists, at first of the Hoffmanite and later of the Mennonite type." Thomas Fuller makes 1538 A. D., the date at which the name "Anabaptist" first appears in the chronicles of England; but in 1534 public notice was taken of foreign Anabaptists in England by a royal proclamation of Henry VIII. There was no such thing at this time as an English Anabaptist; and every record of these people during this century indicates that they were foreigners, chiefly Dutch, who made little if any impression upon the English who were the last of any people to adopt anti-pedobaptist sentiments. Where they departed from Romanism or Episcopacy, they adhered to other forms of dissent, such as Presbyterianism and Congregationalism; and yet Puritan Independency which was a Separatist movement against Presbyterial as well as the Papal and Episcopal abomination, was probably first learned by Robert Browne and Robert Harrison, 1578–80, from the Dutch Anabaptists of Norwich. Nevertheless these Separatists could not brook Anabaptism in its opposition to infant baptism, nor in its views of incarnation, oaths, majesty and the like; and hence the slow and difficult growth of the English towards Baptist principles and peculiarities. Though in 1575 the Anabaptists had increased "wonderfully" in the land yet according to Thomas Fuller (Ch. Hist. Cent. xvi., p. 104), "The English as yet were free from the infection." In the same year John Fox (Letter to Queen Elizabeth) pleading against the burning of two Anabaptists and for toleration of their so-called heresy, said:

"We have great reason to thank God on this account, that I hear not of an Englishman that is inclined to this madness."

During the reign of Elizabeth these Dutch Anabaptists continued to grow in numbers and influence, but towards the close of her reign notices of their existence in the kingdom became "few and insignificant." During the years 1560, 67, 68, 73, 75, the Act of Uniformity was enforced with cruel severity against them, especially in 1568 when large numbers of the Dutch fled before the cruel persecutions of the Duke of Alva to England, and when, according to Collier and Strype, many of the Dutch Anabaptists were said to be holding private conventicles in London and perverting a large number of citizens. In 1575, thirty Dutch Anabaptists were seized in one of these London conventicles held in a private house. Some recanted, most of them were banished, the balance were committed to the dungeon in chains and Pieters and Terwoot were burned. Towards the close of Elizabeth's reign, "with the decline of persecution on the Continent," says Prof. Vedder, "their numbers dwindled until they disappeared." At least, a "large proportion" of the Anabaptists as of the non-conforming Puritans and Separatists were driven from England by these inquisitorial proceedings to the Netherlands where at this time a larger measure of freedom was enjoyed. The predominating party of dissent at the close of Elizabeth's reign was the Puritan; and in the earlier part of the 17th Century down to 1633, as shown by Crosby, there were Anabaptists "intermixed" with their Congregational brethren from whom they separated in order "to form churches of those of their own persuasion." Down to that date, 1633, the intermixture was personal and not organic; and with the exception of the Helwys people, there were historically no Anabaptist organizations in England before 1609-11 until 1633 when the "intermixed" elements began to separate and organize for themselves.

Private Dutch conventicles, among the Anabaptists, held in London are mentioned by Collier and Strype, at an earlier date; and, in 1587, Dr. Some speaks of "several Anabaptistical conventicles in London and other places." Evans adds to this testimony that they were not "exclusively" Dutchmen, and that, according to Dr. Some, there were "some persons of these sentiments who had been bred in our universities." In 1589 Dr. Some charged the Separatists with being "essentially Anabaptists," and so John Payne had warned Englishmen against the "new English Anabaptists." It is possible now that people who were regarded as Dutch-English Anabaptists were confounded with the followers of Greenwood, Penry, and Barrowe who, like Milton at a later date, though merely Separatists, were charged with "Anabaptistry"; and hence it is difficult to tell, at this time, who were meant by the stigma of "Anabaptistry." The Anabaptist seed had been planted however in the heart of some of the English people by the close of Elizabeth's reign; and no doubt there were now Dutch-English Anabaptist conventicles which probably extended down to and into the 17th Century, which by reason of a common persecution became "intermixed" with the Puritans until 1633 when they began to separate. Among these who entertained Anabaptist "sentiments" were some who had been "bred at the universities"—as among the Puritans with whom they became "intermixed" by sympathy and similarity; and it was thus, at last, that the foundation was laid upon which was subsequently erected the Baptist reformation of the 17th Century.

Hanserd Knollys (Moderate Answer unto Dr. Bastwick's Book, etc., pp. 24, 25, London, 1645) is cited as authority for the probable existence, before 1641, of some such Anabaptist churches in London. It cannot be possible, however, that they were the Dutch-English conventicles, which had succeeded from the sixteenth century, of which Knollys speaks in 1645—of whose "saints" he had "experience," with whom he "walked," and who were ministered to by pastors "driven out of other countries"—and to whose evangelicalness in preaching, gathering converts and baptizing upon a profession of faith he testifies in highly Baptistic terms, as the ministry and churches of God. Knollys was an English clergyman until 1636, when he resigned his ministry from Anabaptist convictions. In the same year he was arrested by order of the High Commission Court, but escaped to Boston, Mass., which he reached in 1638. He became a member of the Dover, N. H., Congregational Church, where, in 1640, his Anabaptist sentiments led to a controversy; and in 1641 he removed to Long Island and thence, in the same year, to New Jersey. Afterward he returned to England, and in 1645 we find him pastor of a Baptist church in London. The "churches of God" and the ministry with whom he "walked" and had "experience" in London, prior to 1645, must have existed somewhere between

1641 and 1645, if they were publicly and privately preaching and baptizing *"with water"* as he describes. He could not have had such fraternal relations with them down to 1636, when he was an English clergyman; and he could not have had such observation of their practice from 1636 to 1641, when he was in America. Hence, the period to which he alludes and which involved such liberty, must have been after the abolition of the High Commission Court, 1641 and onward. Granting, however, that such churches and their "ministry driven out of foreign countries" existed before 1641 in London, and that Knollys knew and walked with them, they could have been no other than the Anabaptist churches of 1611–1633; and there is no proof in either case of immersion among them by the statement of Knollys that they baptized *"with water"*—the point sought to be proved by the citation. (See Cathcart's Baptist Cyclopaedia, "Knollys"; J. Newton Brown, "Hanserd Knollys," Bap. Quarterly, 1858.)

Great antiquity is claimed for some of the Baptist churches in England, dating back, it is said, into and beyond the sixteenth century. Prof. Vedder well says:

"The traditions of a remote origin cherished by a few Baptist churches rest on no documentary or archeological proofs, and are probably of comparatively recent origin. Nothing is more common than a claim of vast antiquity for institutions that are demonstrably only a few centuries old. The sole thing that we are entitled to affirm with regard to the Baptists of England is that traces of them appear in historical documents early in the sixteenth century." (Short Hist. Baptists, pp. 108, 109.)

Hill Cliffe, Eythorne, Bocking, Canterbury, the old French churches in London and Spittlefield, according to tradition, antedate the historic origin of the General and Particular Baptists in England; but such a claim is not set up by the writers of the seventeenth century, when the history of the English Baptists begins. Some of those writers lived in the communities where those churches are located and preached to their membership in the latter half of the seventeenth century; and yet those very writers claim the self-originated "beginning" of the English Baptists as belonging to the period now under consideration. It seems incredible that Baptist churches of such ancient origin and long continuance, as is claimed for these traditionary bodies, should have escaped the record of their persecutors or the notice of the first Baptist writers who lived in their vicinity and preached to them if in existence; and such a claim, based upon subsequent traditions, must be exceedingly unreliable. Doubtless in the localities of these churches there were formerly Lollard or Anabaptist conventicles as in many other communities in England. It is possible that Lollard or Anabaptist elements, as in London, remained in these communities, "intermixed" with the Puritans, and formed the basis of Baptist organizations in the seventeenth century. It is possible that these Baptist traditions have their foundation back in old Lollard or Anabaptist conventicles, or people, once existent in these communities; but historically no Baptist church in England can be traced beyond 1611–1633. Even if you could trace the origin and continuance of such churches back to the antiquity claimed for their beginning, there is nothing in the facts of subsequent history to prove their continuance in the practice of immersion, which is also claimed for them without any proof whatever.

This brings us to a consideration of the mode of baptism among the Anabaptists of England in the sixteenth century. At the beginning of their history, 1538, Thomas Fuller (Stow's Chron., p. 576) speaks of them as "*Donatists new dipt.*" According to Dr. Newman these Dutch Anabaptists were of the Hoffmannite first and later of the Mennonite type; and it is almost certain that both types practiced pouring or sprinkling. Hoffmann, the father of the Dutch Anabaptists, so practiced at the earlier date; and of the Mennonites or Doopsgezinden it is affirmed by Prof. Muller (Evans, Vol. I., p. 223) that their usual mode was sprinkling and at no time practiced immersion. So declares Prof. Scheffer (Quest. Bap. Hist., p. 47). So also Dr. Newman with reference to Menno himself (Hist. Antipedobaptism, p. 302, Note). The Mennonite Classic is the Martyr's Mirror. In the first part, written by Van Braght, 1660, he says (on Seventh century) that the word baptism means not only immerse, but also washing or sprinkling, which gives the Mennonite idea of his day. So Schyn, 1729. In the light of all this testimony it can only be supposed that Fuller was simply characterizing these Dutch Anabaptists, as Dr. Whitsitt says, under a "new name," that is, new Christened, under the alliteration of "Donatists new dipt." Historically they were not immersionists.

Fox has been cited, 1563, as saying that there were some Anabaptists at that time in England who came over from Germany:

"Of these there were two sects: The first only objected to the baptizing of children, and to the manner of it, by sprinkling instead of dipping."

The statement is found in Fox's Book of Martyrs, *Alden's Edition*, p. 338; also in *Worthington's Edition*, p. 338; but it has never been traced to the original Fox's Book of Martyrs, otherwise known as the Acts and Monuments of the Christian Church, London, 1563.

John Penry, of Wales, 1586, is cited as an Anabaptist preacher (!) and as possibly the first who preached believers' baptism openly and publicly after the Reformation and as probably "the first who administered the ordinance, by immersion upon a profession of faith, in and about Olchon." Penry was one of the well known martyrs of "early Congregationalism"; and for a full account of him I refer the reader to Dexter's "Congregationalism as Seen in its Literature," (pp. 246–252). Such a claim is a reproach to Baptist learning and history. Dr. Newman says:

"Undue stress is laid on the fact that Separatists like Penry were charged by their opponents with Anabaptistèry. All that they meant was that the Separatist position, if logically carried out, would lead to Anabaptistery which proved to be true a few years later. Penry was in thorough sympathy with Barrowe and Greenwood and was not a Baptist. There seems to be no historical foundation for the statement that he was an immersionist." (Review of the Question, p. 220.)

In the year 1551, William Turner (Preservative or triacle against the poyson of Pelagius, &c.) is cited as calling the Anabaptists in England, "*Catabaptists*" which is construed to mean immersionists. *Katabaptidzo* means to dip, plunge, or drown; passive, to be drowned (Liddell & Scott); and in the classical sense the word is generally if not always employed in the bad sense of overwhelming or drowning. In the ecclesiastical use of the word, which is not found in the lexicons, Catabaptist means one who is opposed to baptism, that is, to infant baptism, and a preventive and destroyer of it, a depriver and depraver of it by rebaptism. Zwingle in his Elenchus Contra Catabaptistas (Opera III., p. 392) clearly shows that this was the meaning of the word in the first part of the 16th Century. He calls the rebaptism of the Anabaptists, the "baptism of heresy" (*baptismus haereseos*), "deservedly called *pseudo* or Catabaptism" (*pseudo sive catabaptismus*); and then he defines rebaptism as *contra*baptism which is the equivalent for *cata*baptism, as against the custom of the church. Herman Schyn (Historia Mennonitarium, 1723) has been cited as applying Catabaptist to his brethren whom he calls "true Catabaptists," instead of Anabaptists because of the opprobrium attached to the latter word. In a later work (1729) he prefers the designation "Mennonite Christians," instead of "Baptists," "Baptismists," or "Catabaptists," because of the ambiguous meaning and use of the latter word in a bad sense by adversaries; and because it properly (*literally*) means immerse, "a rite," he says, "not in common use among most Mennonites, nor is esteemed necessary among all Mennonites"—excepting I suppose the Rhynsburgers and others who began immersion, 1620 A.D. The truth is that Schyn created a use of his own in applying the word Catabaptist to his people; and then afterwards objected to it for two reasons: (1) on account of its ecclesiastical or opprobrious sense, (2) on account of one of its literal or lexicographal senses which had no application to his people as affusionists and which was never applied to any people because of their mode of baptism—not even to dippers.

In all my research, I find that uniformly the word *Catabaptism* is used to express the "profanation" of infant baptism and never used to define the mode of baptism. John Godwin (Catabaptism, or New Baptism, Waxing Old, etc., London, 1645) evidently uses the word as synonymous with Anabaptism without reference to the mode. Frederick Spanhemius (England's Warning by Germanies Woes, etc., London, 1646,) on page 46, says:

"'Tis evident also, that they [the Anabaptists] are called Catabaptists, because they inveigh against Children's Baptisme, and will have it banished out of the Church of God as being not only unprofitable but altogether unlawful."

Dr. Featley (Dippers Dipt, London, 1647,) on page 26, says:

"The name *Anabaptist* is derived from the preposition ἀνὰ and βαπτίζω, and signifieth a rebaptizer; and at least such an one who alloweth of, and maintaineth re-baptizing: they are called also *Catabaptists* from the preposition κατα and βαπτίζω, signifying an abuser or prophaner of baptisme. For indeed every Anabaptist is also a Catabaptist: the reiteration of that Sacrament of our entrance into the Church, and seale of our new birth in Christ, is a violation and deprivation of that holy ordinance."

On page 240 he says again:

"An Anabaptist *deprives* children of baptisme, and a Catabaptist *depraves* baptisme. A Catabaptist may sometimes be no Anabaptist, such as was *Leo Copronymous*, who defiled the font at his baptisme, yet was not christened again: but every Anabaptist is necessarily a *Catabaptist*, for the reiteration of that Sacrament is an abuse and pollution thereof."

John Brinsley (The Doctrine and Practice of Pædobaptisme etc., London, 1645,) on page 97, says of the divers sects of Anabaptists:

"Amongst others, some *Catabaptists*, others Anabaptists. The former opposith the *Baptisme of Infants*, as a thing not meet and lawful etc."

Thos. Bakewell (Confutation of Anabaptists, London, 1644), speaking on page 75 of Anabaptists who are not pleased with the baptism of infants, says:

"Such *Katabaptists* were in Calvin's time, that did furiously cal upon them to be baptized againe."

For a complete refutation of the position that Catabaptism was applied to the Anabaptists because they were immersionists, I refer the reader to a critique of Dr. A. H. Newman upon the citation from Geisler of Fuessli (III., 229) (Eccles. Hist., V., pp. 355, 356)—also from Ottius' Annales Anabaptistici—of a passage for the purpose. (Review of the Question, pp. 227–229.) "The early anti-Pedobaptists," says Dr. Newman, "were with zeal against infant baptism, declaring it to be the invention of the Pope or the Devil." From this point of view they were stigmatized as Catabaptists. This is also the view of Dr. Whitsitt and of all the authors I have found to speak on the subject.

In this connection William Turner (1551) is cited again as favoring the view, at this time, that the Anabaptists in England practiced immersion from an expression in his book regarding the dipping of "old folke," as well as "childes," which is attributed to the Anabaptists whom he is represented as answering in their language, but which is his own language. His book, which was incited by the polemics of Robert Cooke, an Anabaptist (who afterwards modified his opinion on Pelagianism), seems to be in answer to the Anabaptist claim that one of his sermons, in some particulars, coincided with the theory of believers' baptism. He is referred to the ancient custom of baptizing Catechumen, and it is argued that "such a lyke custom was once our most holy religion;" but Turner retorted that "such a custom was not of Christ but of the Pope and the Catabaptists." (pp. 14, 15.) On pp. 96, 97, he argues against the Anabaptist position that baptism, like the Lord's Supper, should be deferred until the subject was old enough to believe and act for himself, upon the ground that baptism was a passive ordinance in which no one could baptize himself and not an active ordinance like the Supper in which every one must participate for himself. Hence he says:

"Childes may be as well dipped into the water in ye name of Christ (which is the outward baptism and as much as any one man give another), even as olde folke: and when as they have the promise of salvation, as well as olde folke & can receive the sign of the same as well: there is no cause why the baptisme of Childes should be differed."

Turner was an English Church immersionist and he was using his own language as to the subject of baptism, incidentally as to mode and polemically against the theory of believers' baptism. The mode was not in controversy, but the deferring of baptism until, as in the Supper, the subject should be old enough to act for himself; and Turner, from his own standpoint, as an English Church immersionist, takes the position that children have the same rights as old folks in the *passive* act of baptism as contradistinguished from the *active* participation in the Lord's Supper. There is here no intention whatever to refer to dipping as the mode of baptism among the Anabaptists, or to reply to them as urging the delay of baptism, as immersion, until children were old enough to believe and act for themselves, as in the Supper. At that time, 1551, the mode had begun to change from immersion to sprinkling, but there were many then who still clung to the ancient ordinance—among whom was William Turner, "Doctor of Physick"; and he is here incidentally alluding to immersion as practiced still among some of his own church without any reference to the mode among the Dutch Anabaptists, which was likely affusion after the Hoffmann type.

The above are about the only citations so far of any historical importance which might imply immersion among the 16th Century Anabaptists in England. They are so few and far between—so indefinite in particulars—that it would be impossible to draw any legitimate inference from them in favor of any such view.

The most that could be concluded from them, even if they were valid, is the probability that some of the Anabaptists did and some did not dip, although all of them held to the principle of believers' as opposed to infant baptism and to all the other dogmas and corruptions alike of Romanism and Protestantism. In the course of this work we shall see allusions to the Anabaptists of this period which indicate that they practiced sprinkling for baptism, but I shall not produce them here. It is to be regretted that so little is known of their mode of baptism; but with what we do know, it is to be regretted also that any of our old Anabaptist brethren every practiced any other mode of baptism than immersion. They were a heroic and glorious people and worthy of our ancestry in their sacrificial devotion to Baptist principles; and we can but devoutly wish that they had never varied in any doctrine or practice of the Scriptures. The matter now, however, is of no greater importance than being faithful to the facts of history; and it would be but sheer nonsense to maintain the fiction that the Sixteenth century Baptists were immersionists, any of them, if they were not. I should be far from denying them this claim if I thought they were; and I shall hasten to retract my error if my position is proved to be wrong. As will be seen under the head of certain "Witnesses," both Baptist and Pedobaptist, such as Kaye and Watts, it is probable that the sixteenth century Anabaptists sprinkled—that it is almost certain that those of the first half of the seventeenth century so did, according to a multitude of witnesses—and I refer the reader now to a careful perusal of the subsequent pages of this volume, which embraces the history of the English Baptists from 1609 to 1641 A. D., and which demonstrates the truth of a "reformation" as well as a "beginning" in their organization, ministry and baptism, as claimed by their writers in the Seventeenth century.

ENGLISH BAPTIST REFORMATION.

(FROM 1609 to 1641 A. D.)

CHAPTER III.

ORIGIN OF THE GENERAL BAPTISTS.

Thomas Crosby, the first Baptist historian, (Vol. I., pp. 265-278), gives an account of the origin of the first Baptist church in English history, organized 1609 A. D. It originated with John Smyth and his followers at Amsterdam, Holland, whither they fled in 1606 from persecution. They were a body of English Separatists gathered by Smyth, who had left the Established Church, in 1602, on account of his inclination to Puritanism and his opposition to the corruptions of the English Church. Smyth and his congregation at Amsterdam were the second English church of Separatists in that city, whither also Robinson and his congregation followed in 1607, and where the older congregation of Johnson and Ainsworth was already well established—all of the same faith and order, and in full fellowship with each other. Smyth and his people were still Pedobaptists and intensely prejudiced against the Anabaptists up to the close of 1608; but in the year 1609, having gradually developed along more Scriptural lines against certain Congregational forms of ecclesiasticism and worship, he reached at last the conviction that infant baptism was not in accord with personal obedience to Christ, and that the Separatists themselves had no other claim to the succession of a true church than their infant baptism through the apostate Church of England and thence through Rome.

He separated, for these reasons, from the Separatists as he had previously separated from the corrupt English Establishment, dissolved his own church and proceeded to reorganize anew upon the Baptist model, which is based upon a regenerate church membership and believers' baptism. He acted upon the presumption that the true church and right baptism were lost; and that with the Scriptures he had the right, with others in communion, to restore both. He recognized that there could be no succession of either through the apostate Church of England or Rome, or through the Separatists who had received their baptism in infancy from the Church of England; the Mennonites, or Anabaptists, were so grossly affected with errors that they had neither the true church nor baptism. Hence the church and baptism must be self-originated or anew by "recovery;" and so he baptized himself and then Helwys and Morton with the rest in communion, according to the united testimony of himself and his contemporaries, as shown in his work, Character of the Beast, and the writings of Clyfton, Robinson and others. His thesis was that there must be first at least two persons in communion through whom to begin baptism and organization anew; and that of the number one could baptize himself and then baptize others in this communion in order to set up anew Christ's church in order, offices and ordinances—all of which he claims he and his followers did.

In his Character of the Beast, in reply to Clyfton, his position is fully set forth. Smyth invariably assumes that the true church and baptism had been lost under the defection of Antichrist, and that he and his people had restored them according to the Scriptures. The Separation, having no other baptism than that of Rome through England, was equally apostate with its mother and grandmother.

"Therefor the Separation must either go back to England, or go forward to true baptism." (P. 2.)

Clyfton, in his Plea for Infants and Elder People Concerning their Baptisme, &c., (pp. 170–181), charges that the Anabaptists in rejecting the baptism of the Separation rejected the baptism of Christ, which had been preserved pure under the defection of Antichrist—just as the golden vessels of the Lord's house in the temple of Nebuchadnezzar under the captivity of Israel had been preserved and restored without being "new cast;" that the Anabaptists, in devising a new baptism, brought in a new covenant and gospel; that they "baptized themselves without warrant from the Word;" that if in extraordinary case baptism were lost and had to be restored, it would have to be done in an extraordinary way, as by another John the Baptist, or under a new commission; they were apostate from the faith and custom of their forefathers; the succession of baptism has been perfect and the gates of hell have never prevailed against the church. This in substance.

Origin of the General Baptists. 31

Smyth's replies are clear and conclusive. He says:

"If the gates of Hel shall never prevail against the church then ther hath always been a true Church, & Antichrist could never make the Church false: and so you of the Separation have sinned most shamefully in calling the Church of Antichrist false." . . "If my argument be not good against you of the Separation for erecting a new Church, no more is yours good against us for erecting new baptism." . . "The Covenant is said to be everlasting not in respect of the visible real existence in the world in an established Church, but in respect of the stability & firmness of it in regard of Sathan's malice which should not so abolish it, that it should never be recovered again." . . "There was no true Church in the depth of Antichristianism, & so no true baptism, for can anything be true in a false Church, but the Scriptures and the truths contayned therein. I deny therefor, that the Covenant, Church, or baptism was visible always: For it was invisible when the Church went into the wilderness: & therefor as you when ther was not a true church in the world, took upon you to set up a new church, &c.: So the Anabaptists (as you call them) doe not set up a new Covenant & Gospel, though they set up a new or rather the old Apostolique baptism which Antichrist had overthrown: & whereas you say they [the Anabaptists] have no warrant to baptize themselves, I say as much as you have to set up a true church, yea fully as much: For if a true church may be erected which is the most noble ordinance of the New Testament, then much more baptisme." . . "When all Christ's visible ordinances are lost, eyther men must recover them agayne, or let them alone: if they let them alone til extraordinary men come and tongs [tongues], as the Apostles did, then men are familists (for that is their opinion) or if they must recover them, men must *begin* so to doe & then two men joyning together may make a church (as you say): Why may they not baptize seeing they cannot conjoyne into Christ but by baptisme, Mat. 28:19, compared with Mat. 18:10, Gala. 3:27." . . "Now for baptizing a mans self ther is as good warrant, as for a mans churching himself." (Character of the Beast, pp. 57–59.)

Smyth says again, (ibid, 62–64):

"The true Church is only by a Spirituall Line of Fayth, and true baptisme by the Spirituall succession uppon the Spirituall Lyne of Faythfull men confessing the Fayth and the sinnes, which was typed by the Carnal Line of the Old Testament." . . "I deny that ever the English nation, or any one of our predecessors were of the Fayth of Christ. Shew

it if you can : but we came of a Pagan race til Rome the mother came & put upon us the false baptisme: and therefor although the Romans might plead this, yet England could not plead it: and so your dissimilitude cannot hold in that thing: and our case is simply Paganish." . .
"I do utterly deny that ever our forefathers of the English nation believed, and you can never prove it. For that which you say seeing we are Apostates, therefore it followeth that sometyme we or our ancestors had the truth, I wonder at you for so saying: for we are departed from the faith of the Scriptures, not from the faith of our ancestors, who never a one of them at any time believed *visibly* in a true constituted church."

Smyth squarely assumes that there had never been a true church having the true ministry and baptism in England. He does not mean that there had never been any true believers in England—nor that foreign Anabaptists had never at times been in the Kingdom—but that the English people had never had the truth of a visibly constituted Gospel Church. This utterly precludes the existence of Anabaptist churches in England at the time of Smyth, else he had not erected a new church and baptism; and as we have seen Smyth considered that there was neither gospel baptism nor church in the world, not even with the Mennonites, else he had adopted their baptism.

Helwys and Morton were in exact line with Smyth on the doctrine that there had been no succession of the true church, baptism or ministry and that they had to be recovered *de novo*. In the same way that Clyfton assails Smyth does Robinson attack Helwys. In his Works (Vol. III., p. 168) Robinson asks:

"If the church be gathered by baptism then will Mr. Helwisse's church appear to all men to be built upon the sand, considering the baptism it hath, which as I have heard from themselves, was on this manner: Mr. Smyth, Mr. Helwisse, and the rest, having utterly dissolved and disclaimed their former church state and ministry, came together to erect a new church by baptism ; unto which they also ascribed so great virtue, as that they would not so much as pray together before they had it. And after some straining of courtesy who should begin, and that of John Baptist, Matt, iii., 14, misalleged, Mr. Smyth baptized first himself, and next Mr. Helwisse, and so the rest ; making their particular confessions. Now to let pass his not sanctifying a public action by prayer, i. Tim. iv., 4, 5. his taking unto himself that honor which was not given him, either immediately from Christ or by the church, Heb. v., 4 ; his baptizing himself, which was more than Christ did, Matt. iii., 14; I demand into what church he entered by baptism? or entering by baptism into no church, how his baptism could be true by their own doctrine? Or Mr. Smyth's baptism not being true, nor he, by it, entering into any church, how Mr. Helwisse's baptism could be true, or into what church he entered by it?"

In all Helwys fight with Robinson and Brownism, in his Mystery of Iniquity and other writings, he makes no denial of Smyth's self-baptism, nor of his own baptism at Smyth's hands; and in both his works, The New Fryelers and the Mystery of Iniquity, as also in his advice to the Mennonites not to receive Smyth and his faction after their defection, he reiterates the doctrines and arguments of Smyth, before his last separation.

Ashton (Robinson's Works, Sect. xvii., p. 452) cites in a note a tract of Robinson, entitled, "Manumission," of which no copy has been found and to which Ereunetes, in the dialogue, thus refers:

"That John Robinson, preacher to the English, at Leyden, hath printed half a sheet of paper; who laboreth to prove that none may baptize but pastors or elders.'

"The question discussed," says Ashton, "in that tract was, Is it Scriptural and right for any person who can preach and whom God blesses in his labors to baptize others? Mr. Smyth and his friends contend for the affirmative, Mr. Robinson for the negative. The question had its origin in the fact, that on the Rev. John Smyth and the Rev. Thos. Helwisse becoming Antipedobaptists, they renounced their church connexions, and hence a difficulty arose how they could be baptized. They agreed together that Mr. Smyth should baptize himself, whether by immersion as the English Baptists now practice, or by affusion, as the Mennonites or Dutch Baptists did and do still practice, is not known; and then Mr. Smyth baptized Mr. Helwisse, and thus both became qualified to baptize others. They justified their baptism by contending that any church or teacher had a right to administer the ordinance; that it was not so far a church ordinance as to require its administration by pastors or elders; and that Christ had so ordered it in his last commission to the Apostles, Matt. xxviii. 19. Mr. Robinson endeavors to prove that baptism is a *church* ordinance; and that no one should administer it but a pastor of a church; except in the two following cases—by extraordinary calling, as John and the Apostles by divine authority—or where a church has no pastor, by a special calling from the church itself. Neither of the cases applied to

Mr. Smyth. He was not inspired and he belonged to no church. The question excited great interest in Amsterdam both among the Mennonites and the English Separatists. Mr. Underhill, the respected Secretary of the Hanserd Knollys Society, informed the editor that, when in Holland, he found among the archives of the Mennonite Church in Amsterdam a final application from some of Mr. Smyth's party to be admitted to the fellowship of the Church, but were refused til acknowledgment was made of their error, in maintainiug that baptism might be administered by individuals, apart from connexion with a church, or that a church might administer it among themselves, independently of pastors or elders."

Morton in his Description, 1620, pp. 154, 155, replies to Robinson's argument, as follows:

"In this thing we are partly called upon, and therefore shall manifest, that any Disciple of Christ, that hath received power and commandment from God to Preach and convert, though no Pastor, may also by the same power and commandment baptize, which I will first prove by the Scriptures, and then answer the objections particularly."

He uses the same arguments of Smyth and Helwys that the true church and baptism had been lost in Rome, and that the Separatists have no other claim for their foundation than their baptism received from Rome through the English Church. "But," says he, p. 161, "now I prove, the servant of Christ not yet being in the office of Pastor or Elder, may baptize, thus:

"Whatsoever is written aforetime is written for our teaching: but it is written aforetime that Disciples of *Christ*, though yet no Pastors, did Baptize: therefore we are taught being disciples of Christ, although yet no pastors, to Baptize when just occasion is given."

He instances John the Baptist, the Commission of the Apostles as disciples making other disciples, and not as officials, who should to the end of time teach and baptize—pointing to the time when Antichrist forbade it and set up infant baptism, a baptism of its own. On pp. 162, 163, he says:

"The Apostles have left their power and doctrine wholly behind them, nothing is dead but their persons; and therefore the doctrine of *Paul*, being now in the person of a believer: the Commandment is written for his instruction, bidding him go Preach the Gospell to every creature & to all nations (according as God enableth him, for he requirith not what we have not) Baptizing them: this commandment is now as powerful as it ever was."

I have quoted freely from Smyth—his friends and opponents—in order to show clearly the origin of the first General Baptist Church and the principle and practice upon which it was founded. By a gradual process of development thro' perhaps eight or ten years—separating first from the English Church and then from the Brownists—Smyth evolved the ideal of a Baptist church in the light of the Scriptures contrasted with the errors both of the Pedobaptists and Mennonites. As an English churchman he saw Rome the usurper of the "historic episcopate" in England; as a Separatist he saw the English Church as a corrupt hierarchy; and at last convinced of Baptist principles, he saw the Separation as only the legitimate offspring—the daughter of the English establishment and the granddaughter of the Romish apostate. Infant baptism was the "mark" or "character of the beast" in violation of Christ's fundamental law of church constitution; and being a clear-headed, honest and zealous man, he immediately reached the logic of believers' baptism and a regenerate membership as the sole basis of New Testament church organization. The Anabaptists around him held to this view, but Smyth seems to have worked out through gradual development the ideal of the gospel church in the light of the Scriptures; and however soon he discovered this principle among the Mennonites, or whatever they contributed to his knowledge and decision on the subject, they, too, were apostate from deeper and larger doctrinal standpoints. In England nor on the Continent could he and his followers find baptismal, organic or doctrinal succession, even among the Anabaptists, and much less through apostate Rome and her Pedobaptist daughters whose universal constitution was infant baptism—"the mark of the beast." He knew the beginning as well as the doctrinal depravation of the Mennonites—he knew the origin and history of infant baptism—and he well concluded that there was then not a true Scriptural church on earth and so declares himself in his Character of the Beast.

Reaching this conclusion he was not long in acting. The logic of the situation led him to dissolve his church and sever all connexion with the Separatists. Regarding baptism as the ceremonial constitution of the church, and that being lost, he struck upon the novel idea of baptizing himself and of then baptizing the rest of his company in communion, after each had made his confession of faith in Christ; and it was then through the act of baptism that the church was constituted. No public act, not even prayer, was allowed in the body, until baptism was performed and the church thus constituted. The work was done—the true baptism and church were recovered—and thus was organized and set up the first English church, after the Baptist model, which has had any succession to modern times. Beyond that English Baptist annals cannot historically go for baptismal or organic connexion with the Anabaptist sects who proceeded the English Anabaptists of the Seventeenth century. Dr. Joseph Angus (Baptist Handbook, 1898) well observes:

"The earliest General Baptist Churches of which any history is known were founded about 1611-14 by Thomas Helwisse, in London, Tiverton, Coventry, &c.; and the earliest Particular Baptist Church by John Spilsbury, at Wapping, in 1633. There are traditions of earlier churches. The Baptist Society at Shrewsbury is said to have been formed in 1627; that at Blackenhall (now at Hatch), near Taunton, in 1630 (Thompson quoted by Toulmin, Neal iii., p. 352). Even in 1457 there is said to have been a congregation of this kind at Chesterton (Robinson's Claude, ii., p. 54). The earliest books in defense of their views were written by John Smyth in 1608-9. More than seventy years earlier, however, literature supplies us with evidence of the existence and activity of Baptists in England. In 1548 John Vernon translated and published Bullinger's 'Holesome Antidote against the Pestilent Sect of the Anabaptists.' Three years later William Turner, Doctor of Physick, devysed a 'Triacle against the poyson—lately stirred up again by the furious Secte of the Anabaptists,' London, 1551. These are the earliest English Antibaptist books I know."

Dr. Angus goes on to give the usual historical citations regarding the Anabaptists of England as far back as 1538, "for a hundred years," he says, "before we hear of Baptist churches"; but he fixes the dates 1611-14 as the earliest at which any authentic history of Baptist churches, as such, begins. Really the first English Baptist church, so called, began its existence, in 1609, in Holland, and was transplanted to London in 1611— as we shall see—but it had no connection with the Holland Anabaptists. Mosheim seemed to think that the English Baptists had their origin from the German and Dutch Anabaptists; but as Taylor, in his history of the General Baptists (Vol. II., p. 70), and as the plainest facts show, affirms that Mosheim was clearly mistaken.

The great principle upon which Smyth and his followers acted, as the quotations from their writings show, was that true baptism and the true church having been lost, true disciples moved of God and having Christ, the Scriptures and the Spirit had the right to recover them. This also implied that any disciple empowered to preach was empowered to baptize and so begin a church anywhere and at any time circumstances required. Hence their theory involved the setting up of a new ministry as well as new baptism and church order; and upon this, as upon the other points of their thesis, their position was hotly contested by Robinson, Clyfton, Johnson, Ainsworth, Jessop and others. The position was carried to extremes by some of Smyth's followers; and hence in his last book, The Retraction of his Errors, Smyth inveighed against the theory when it was carried beyond the setting up of the church which could then establish its own ministry and perpetuate the ordinances without the need of self-origination. He still in his Retraction claimed that succession had been lost and properly restored, but that here the setting up anew of baptism, church or ministry ought to end; and he finally sought membership among the Mennonites upon the ground that they were orderly churches already existent at the time he organized the first English Baptist church. This was after further acquaintance with them and after imbibing their errors; and Helwys, still retaining Smyth's original position, antagonized his old leader and brought on a severe controversy with him. Smyth was correct as against the logical extreme of his position regarding the right to restore the church, its ministry and ordinances, after it was once accomplished; and he sought properly to correct it by contending that the right should not be claimed when once the church, its ministry and ordinances, had been established.

The principle upon which the first English Baptist Church was founded, were maintained not only by the immediate followers of Smyth, but by all the Baptists, so far as I have read, in the 17th Century. They all claimed that they had a new "Beginning" or "reformation" in England—even down to Crosby who wrote their history in 1738-40; and the right to self-origination, upon the ground that the true baptism, church and ministry were lost in the apostasy of Rome and her offspring, was a cardinal doctrine of all the writers of the 17th Century whom I have examined. Smyth, Helwys, Morton, Spilsbury, Tombes, Lawrence, Barber, Kiffin, King, Collins, Kilcop, Cornwell, Allen, Denne, Oates, Patient, Lamb and others—all both General and Particular Baptists—repudiated the doctrine of organic or baptismal succession, and defended the right to restore baptism, the church and the ministry upon the principle of self-origination. From the start they called believers' baptism "new baptism" recovered from the depths of the Romish Apostasy; and from 1640-41 and onward they give their baptism the additional title of being "new" by reason of the restoration of the "ancient practice of immersion." They are not only called "new rebaptizers" but "new dippers" after the latter date. There was but one thing in John Smyth which they rejected—his self-baptism; and in all else, except (with the Particular Baptists) his Arminianism, he set the pace for Baptist position in England; and though he went over to the errors of the Mennonites his immediate successors Helwys and Morton reasserted and continued the foundation upon which he built.

As already intimated, soon after the establishment of Smyth's church, the mother of the General Baptists, sometime in the year 1609, upon further acquaintance with the Mennonites and having become tainted with their Pelagian, or Socinian views, Smyth became convinced that he and his followers had erred in their attempt to restore right baptism and true church order; and with the majority of his congregation he sought admission into the Mennonite Church in Amsterdam which he now regarded as the true church having right baptism if not regular succession. This was his third separation; and he was now excluded from the Anabaptist organization which, with Helwys and others at the head, besought the Mennonites to be cautious about receiving Smyth and his faction. Helwys and his church, as already said, rigidly adhered to the original principles upon which they were constituted and denounced the "succession" theory upon which Smyth, in their view now, seemed to proceed, as a "Jewish Ordinance" and the "chief hold of Antichrist"; and it was not until after Smyth's death, in 1612, that Smyth's faction, in the year 1615, was finally admitted into the membership of the Mennonite Church, no difference whatever being found between the Dutch and the English either in the doctrine of salvation or in the design and mode of baptism. (Evans, Vol. I., p. 202). In the providence of God, however, Smyth, like Roger Williams, builded wiser than he afterwards thought; and unwisely, like Roger Williams, he abandoned and vainly attempted to tear down God's building.

Though still imperfect in doctrine and practice, the true idea of Christ's Church—based upon a regenerate church membership and believers' baptism—was now freshly and purely restored; and the grosser errors of Anabaptism, as it then existed, were largely eliminated. The foundation in principle, if not in practice, was thus laid for the future Baptist Denomination among the English people. Although the evolution through which we have passed to our present higher and more perfect position has been slow and sometimes convulsive, yet, in the providence of God, the eccentric and errant John Smyth was the humble instrument through whom God operated the scheme of restoration; and strange or mysterious as this beginning may appear, it is but another illustration of that all-wise Providence which left Israel in captivity and slavery, and then raised up Moses to lead his people through the wilderness to the promised land which he truly saw, but never entered. Joshua led Israel over Jordan; and so Helwys led the first English Anabaptist church—the mother of the General Baptists—to London and established it there, in 1611, and thus completed the first great step in the Baptist reformation.

The very fact, as we shall see in the next chapter, that Smyth abandoned his newly erected church and sought admission among the Mennonites, shows that he had come to agree with them in every particular of doctrine and practice. He now regarded them as embodying the true church; and while he had erected baptism and a church anew upon their model, he now regarded it as an error that he and his followers had not at first joined the Mennonites, and thus established the English organization under the form of regularity, if not of succession, which he still denied as existent, though charged to the contrary. Hence it is clear that whatever form of baptism the Mennonites maintained, that was the form originally adopted by Smyth. He now agreed with them, not only in the mode of baptism, but he had adopted all their doctrinal views of salvation, however heretical heretofore considered; and Helwys not only adhered to the original idea of Smyth's new baptism and church, but he still maintained that the Mennonites, or "New Fryelers," as he called them, were heretics, and vigorously wrote against them—and so against Smyth. Morton likewise agreed with Helwys in the original plan and doctrine of the newly erected church; and these two level-headed Anabaptists engineered this providential movement to a successful consummation. Neither of them, however, antagonized Smyth's mode or method of baptism; and neither did they antagonize the Mennonites as regards their mode of baptism, which, like Smyth's, as we shall see, was affusion.

The sum of the chapter is this:

1. Smyth held that, at his time, the world was in the depths of Antichristianism; that the *visible* church, with its ministry and ordinances, was lost; and that the spiritual or invisible church was still in the wilderness, without order, office, or ordinance.

2. Neither in the Churches of Rome, England, nor among the Separatists or Anabaptists could New Testament order, orthodoxy or purity be found.

3. By the dissolution of his Pedobaptist organization and by a self-originated baptism he and his followers as true believers, recovered the *visible* church, its ministry and ordinances, according to the commission of the Scriptures.

4. He afterwards became infected with the doctrinal heresies of the Mennonites; and while he did not recant his doctrine that succession had been lost, he adopted the view that among the Mennonites true baptism and church order already existed.

5. Helwys, Morton and the rest of their church retained and made permanent Smyth's original position as to the truth of Baptist position and history.

ENGLISH BAPTIST REFORMATION.
(FROM 1609 TO 1641, A. D.)

CHAPTER IV.
ORIGIN OF THE GENERAL BAPTISTS—CONTINUED.

In the year 1611, Helwys and Morton, with the Amsterdam Church, returned to England and settled in London. It was a very small body, but through much persecution and adversity it continued to exist and grow. In 1615 Crosby mentions Helwys and his people in London; and again, in 1622, he refers to the spirit and management of these "Baptists" as well represented by a published letter supposed to have been written by Helwys himself. According to Evans (Vol. II., p. 26), John Morton had succeeded by 1626 in organizing five other churches of this persuasion in London, Lincoln, Sarum, Coventry and Tiverton —all of them small bodies, aggregating about 150 members. According to Barclay (Inner Life, p. 95), there were besides these, which is doubtful, four other churches of the same order, numbering 11 in 1626. Dr. Featley in his epistle to Downam (Dippers Dipt) gives the General Baptists 47 churches in 1644. Baillie (Anabaptisme, The True Fountaine of Independency, &c., p. 49) gives them only 39, or 46 churches in all, including the 7 Particular Baptist Churches, in 1644. Neal (History Puritans, Vol. III., p. 543) states that in 1644 there were 47 Baptist churches in the country and 7 in London, in all 54. It is probable that Baillie is right, and that Featley's 47 included the 7 Particular Churches and also the one French Church in London, which was also a Particular Baptist Church, making 8, which, added to Baillie's 39 General Churches, would make Featley's 47. It is evident that Neal added the 7 Particular Churches to Featley's 47, making 54, by mistake.

Helwys died in 1626, after a pastorate of fifteen years, when John Morton stood at the head of this General Baptist movement. In 1630 Morton also died; and with the exception of the correspondence (1624-26) which Evans (Vol. II., pp. 21-51) records between the English Anabaptists and the Dutch Mennonites at Amsterdam, there is but little definite history of the General Baptist movement until after 1641, when both branches of the Baptist body became prominent in the religious and political annals of England.

From these early English Baptists emanated a few documents which immortalize them in history and literature. Besides the published works of Smyth and Helwys they left several confessions of faith which are the first statements of the English Baptists in doctrine and practice; and though imperfect in some particulars they are soundly Baptistic and worthy of our beginning as a denomination in England. Bating its modified Arminian view of salvation, the confession of 1611 is a substantially good document. I have a manuscript copy of Helwys' publication, 1611, against the "New Fryelers," or Mennonites, in which, besides orthodox views upon the humanity of Christ, the Sabbath and Majesty—contrary to the former teachings of the Anabaptists—he ably disproves the claim of "succession" to any sect of Christians and shows it to be Jewish and Antichristian. From the year 1614 and onward we discover published documents of these English brethren who disclaimed the name of "Anabaptists," in defense of "religious liberty" and against the corruptions and persecutions of the State Church which forever distinguish them and which gave the key note to all the subsequent contests of the Baptists for independency and freedom. Such are Busher's "Religion's Peace," 1614; "Persecution for Religion Judged and Condemned," 1615; "An Humble Supplication" to King James, 1620, etc. These documents clearly define the Baptist position upon almost any question which differentiates them from other people; and they constitute a rich heritage in the archives of Baptist literature.

These early English Baptists, however, did not altogether escape the errors of their Anabaptist brethren; and some of them laid the foundations of heresy which well nigh wrecked the General Baptists in the following century. An intimate relation, from the start, existed between the English and Dutch brethren. Besides false views of majesty, oaths, warfare and the like, the English became tainted with Mennonite Socinianism which has never been thoroughly eradicated from the General Baptist body. Though Helwys and Morton objected to many features which distinguished the Dutch from the English, yet from 1624 to 1626

Origin of the General Baptists.

these Mennonite peculiarities regarding the Deity of Christ, the weekly observance of the Lord's Supper, the lawfulness of oaths, warfare and majesty had become questions in the English body, and both parties to the contention were appealing to the Dutch brethren for recognition and unity. Such was the harmony between the two bodies that Elias Tookey with fifteen others who had been excluded or alienated from Morton's church in London (1624) sought union with the Amsterdam Church; and in the discussion of the differences between them, there appears to be nothing which would bar them from fraternal fellowship. After the death of John Morton, 1630, his wife returned to her father in Amsterdam; and with several others who probably returned with her she was received into the Monnonite church on her former baptism by John Smyth. (Evans, Vol. I., p. 223.)

This intimate relationship not only led the English into some Mennonite errors which permanently injured their original orthodoxy and narrowed their spirit and usefulness, but it indicated their agreement on the mode of baptism which was affusion. Prof. Scheffer affirms that this relationship continued until 1641, when it was suddenly broken off on account of the adoption of immersion by the English Baptists at that date; and this suggests an inquiry into the mode of baptism practiced alike by both parties.

1. It is the testimony of the best scholarship, of Smyth himself and of his contemporaries that he baptized himself and then baptized Helwys, Morton and the rest of his company. The quotation from his Character of the Beast, etc., pp. 58, 59, 1609, is conclusive and reads as follows:

"Whereas, you say that they [we] have no warrant to baptize themselves [ourselves], I say, as much as you have to set up a true church, yea, fully as much. For if a true church may be erected which is the most noble ordinance of the New Testament, then much more baptism; and if a true church cannot be erected without baptism . . . you cannot deny . . . that baptism may also be recovered. If they must recover them, men must begin to do so, and then two men joining may make a church . . . Why may they not baptize, seeing they cannot conjoin into Christ but by baptism? . . . *Now for baptizing a man's self there is as good warrant as for a man churching himself.* For two men singly are no church, jointly they are a church, and they both of them put a church upon themselves, so may two men put baptism upon themselves. For as both those persons unchurched yet have power to assume the church each of them for himself with others in communion; *so each of them unbaptized hath power to assume baptism for himself with others in communion.* And as Abraham and John Baptist, aud all proselytes after Abraham's example (Exod. 12:48) did administer the sacrament upon themselves, so may any man raised up after the apostasy of Antichrist, in the recovering of the church by baptism, *administer it upon himself in communion with others* . . . And as in the Old Testament, every man that was unclean washed himself; every priest going to sacrifice washed himself in the laver at the door of the tabernacle of the congregation; which was a type of baptism, the door of the church (Titus 3:5). Every master of a family administered the Passover to himself and all of his family. The priest daily sacrificed for himself and others. A man cannot baptize others into the church, himself being out of the church. *Therefore it is lawful for a man to baptize himself together with others in communion, and this warrant is a plerophery for the practice which is done by us.*"

As Dr. Newman (Hist. Antipedobaptism, p. 386) says: "Thus the fact of se-baptism seems to be fully admitted by Smyth himself." So conclude Drs. Armitage, Vedder, Whitsitt, Burrage and Evans, Baptists; and so Drs. Dexter, Muller, Scheffer, Ashton, Barclay, Robinson, Johnson, Ainsworth, Jessop, Wall and others—some of whom were Smyth's contemporaries and on the spot when and where the self-baptism was performed. Crosby, who believed that Smyth restored immersion in Holland, but who had not seen Smyth's writings, seems to doubt that the above quotation, which he found in Wall's Baptism Anatomized (p. 111, 112) was sufficient proof of Smyth's self-baptism; but Crosby, in order to his argument (Vol. I., pp. 98–99), mutilates and garbles the quotation without any satisfactory conclusion to himself. He drops the question and says:

"If he were guilty of what they charge him with, 't is no blemish on the English Baptists; who neither approved of any such method, nor did they receive their baptism from him." (Vol. I., pp., 99–100.)

There is no doubt that Smyth baptized himself.

2. What was the mode of his self-baptism which he transmitted to his followers? It seems clearly *affusion;* and this fact, in the absence of Smyth's writings, explains why Crosby, who believed that Smyth was immersed, does not solve the mystery

that Smyth's followers did not introduce immersion into England, 1611; and hence he dropped summarily the matter of his self-baptism by repudiating it as never having succeeded to the English Baptists. Crosby did not then know the secret since explained.

Robert Ashton (1851) in his edition of the Works of John Robinson (Vol. III., p. 461, Appendix) says:

"It is a rather singular fact that zealous as were Mr. Smyth and his friends for believers' baptism, and earnest as were their opponents in behalf of infant baptism, the question of the mode of baptism was never mooted by either party. Immersion baptism does not appear to have been practiced or pleaded for by either Smyth or Helwys, the alledged founders of the General Baptist denomination in England. Nothing appears in their controversial writings to warrant the supposition that they regarded immersion as the proper and only mode of administering that ordinance. Incidental allusions there are, in their own works and in the replies of Robinson, that the baptism which Mr. Smyth performed on himself must have been rather by affusion, or pouring. Nor is this supposition improbable, from the fact that the Dutch Baptists, by whom they were surrounded uniformly administered baptism by affusion."

Prof. Rauschenbusch positively affirms that Smyth practiced affusion.

Dr. B. Evans, 1864, in his History of the Early English Baptists, cites in proof Dr. Muller, who "fully agrees" with Ashton. He shows from the records of the church at Amsterdam, that Smyth, after being excluded from the English Church, with some twenty-four of his faction sought membership in one of the Mennonite churches of Amsterdam. It was probably a Waterland church, whose mode of baptism was *affusion* or *sprinkling*. "The said English were questioned about their doctrine of salvation and the ground and the form (mode) of their baptism; and no difference was found between them and us," said the Mennonite ministers appointed to examine Smyth and his party. "This statement is singular," says Evans, "as the members of this community were not immersionists;" and to satisfy these Mennonites, with whom he sought union, Smyth and his friends acknowledged and repented their error of *self-baptism* as contrary to the order of Christ. (Evans, Vol. I., pp. 208, 209.) After Smyth's decease, in 1612, his faction was received into full fellowship in this Mennonite church—the unbaptized portion of it being admitted by *"sprinkling"* and not immersion, according to Muller. (Evans, Vol. I., p. 223.) This is good inferential evidence that Smyth and the already baptized portion of his party had never been immersed—not only because a portion of them were sprinkled, but because it is impossible to conceive that, if Smyth was an immersionist, seeking the true church and true baptism now by "succession," he would have gone for the purpose to a "sprinkling" church for membership. Especially is this probable if, as Evans seems to think (for which he has no proof), there were some of the Mennonites who at the time immersed. Drs. Muller, Scheffer and others affirm that the Mennonites never immersed. According to Muller (Evans, Vol. I., p. 223): "The Waterlanders [to whom Smyth applied], nor any of the Netherland Doopsgezinden practiced at any time baptism by immersion." In this connection he says: "This mode of baptizing [sprinkling] was from the days of Menno, the only usual mode among them, and is still amongst us"—although pouring was sometimes practiced, especially at first.

But it is objected that there is a qualifying sentence in the paragraph, from which Muller's language is quoted, which implies that the English already baptized among the faction received into the Waterlander church were immersed and that therefore Smyth's baptism was immersion. The sentence reads thus:

"But they [the Waterlanders] cared only for the *very nature* of the baptism, and were therefore willing to admit even those who were baptized by a mode differing from theirs just as we are wont to do now-a-days."

It is replied that the Waterlanders found no difference between themselves and Smyth as to the "ground and the form (mode) of baptism." The Waterlander mode was "sprinkling." Therefore Smyth's mode was sprinkling. Hence the qualifying sentence can only be an expression of liberality which indicates that even if the already baptized portion of Smyth's faction had been immersed they *would* have been received—just as the Mennonites and Pedobaptists do at this day. Dr. Muller wants to leave the impression that there would have been no narrowness with the Mennonites about a difference in the *mode* of baptism, the *"ground"* of baptism being the same; but the context shows that there was no difference either in the ground or nature—nor the form or mode, between them.

After a thorough study of the matter, Evans (Vol. II., pp. 51, 52) says of the mode of baptism practiced by Smyth and his followers:

"We have to deal with it in the spirit of history, not controversy. Only as an historic fact do we touch it. Again and again has it been asserted that at this period immersion was not the mode adopted by these heroic confessors. The question is only of moment in the light of history. Beyond this its interest and value do not go. Truth is more important to us than theory. In this spirit we shall enter into this inquiry."

He then quotes Altute, who assumes that till the beginning of the seventeenth century the English Baptists only rejected the baptism of infants, but did not insist on immersion until introduced by John Smyth—a fiction already disproved by Evans and his authorities and so confuted in his following thesis. He cites again Ashton, the editor of Robinson's works and repeats the expression:

"Nothing (referring to Smyth and Helwys) appears in their controvercial writings to warrant the supposition that they regarded immersion as the proper and only mode of administering that ordinance, &c.,"

and who concludes, as seen heretofore, that Smyth baptized himself by "affusion," in whose "opinion," says Evans, "Dr. Muller fully agrees."

"But," asks Dr. Evans, "was it so? We cannot pronounce positively, but we are bound to confess that the probabilities are greatly in its favor. The harmony of opinion, and the anxiety for agreement, which their Dutch brethren manifested in the documents laid before our readers, would more than warrant this conclusion. Add to this the fact already stated by Ivimey, that, *on the formation of the first Particular Baptist Church in England, an individual was sent over to Holland to be immersed.* Now this could not arise from their being no Baptists in the country. We have seen that the very opposite was the fact. Other churches, too, as will be seen presently, existed in the country. Only from one or two causes could this condition arise: dislike to Arminian doctrines, or dissatisfaction with the *mode* of baptism. Which of these operated, it is difficult to say. Probably both had an influence in determining this course."

In all this Dr. Evans clearly inclines to the opinion that Smyth, Helwys and their followers were *affusionists*.

Dr. Evans, however, does not stop here. He points us to the fact that, so late as 1646, at Chelmsford, there still existed among the Anabaptists this Mennonite affusion as indicated by the presence of the *Old Men*, or *Aspersi*, as contradistinguished from the *New Men* or *Immersi* (Vol. II., pp. 52, 53). After commenting upon the introduction of the Particular Baptist Churches and the deputation to Holland for immersion, he concludes:

"Most will now see that the practice of the Mennonite brethren [*affusion*] was common [among the Anabaptists] in this country [England]. These New Men [*Immersi*] soon cast them [the Old Men or *Aspersi*] into the shade, and this practice speedily became obsolete. Immersion as the mode of baptism became the rule with both sections of the Baptist community. Indeed from this time [1646], beyond the fact already given [at Chelmsford] we know not of a solitary exception." (Vol. II., p. 79).

Thus in the spirit of history and not partisan interest Evans concedes the strong probability—"the conclusion more than warranted"—that Smyth and his followers practiced Mennonite affusion down to the formation of the first Particular Baptist Church and to the time of Blunt's deputation to Holland for immersion; and he goes further in saying that, as late as 1646, the Anabaptists were still divided between the practice of the Old Men or *Aspersi* and the New Men or *Immersi*—showing that immersion among the Anabaptists was a *"new"* thing in England at that date. Dr. Evans was an able and accurate Baptist historian; and he is cited in the interests of history, not controversy, and in evidence of a reformation which was gradual and somewhat slow in development.

In the Confessions of Smyth and Helwys the articles on baptism, separated from the facts of history, would not strongly indicate that they did not regard immersion as the Scripture form of Baptism. They never use the word immersion, however, in their writings or confessions; and in the 14th article of the 1611 Confession which defines baptism, this language is used: "Baptism, or *washing with water*, is the outward manifestation of dying unto sin and walking in newness of life; therefore in no wise apperteineth to infants." Smyth in his Latin Confession (Art. 14) says: "That baptism is the external sign of remission of sins, of dying and being made alive, and therefore does not belong to infants." In his confession presented to the sprinkling Mennonites (Art. XXXVIII) he speaks of baptism as being "buried with Christ into death, (Rom. 6:4; Col. 2:12);" and in his English Confession he represents baptism as the outward witness of the inward baptism of the believer "in the laver of regeneration and renewing of the Holy Ghost, washing the soul from all pollution and sin." Baptism as a *"washing with water,"* according to the 1611 Confession, agrees with the general Pedobaptist form of expression applied to sprinkling or pouring in that day and since; but the symbolic allusions in all these articles to immersion—such as dying to sin and walking in newness of life—would seem to imply the Baptist idea of the ordinance, though the word immersion is never used. The only explanation of such usage, in conflict with the apparent facts of history, is that most of the Anabaptists of that day—the Mennonites especially—while they regarded immersion as a Scriptural mode of baptism, they regarded affusion as an alternate method and practiced it as sufficient baptism; and hence in defining the ordinance as a "washing with water," they had no hesitation in attaching the burial and resurrection symbolism of Rom. 6:4; Col. 2:12 as the ideal baptism without regard to mode.

In his Character of the Beast, pp. 3, 4, inveighing against infant baptism, Smyth says:

"When the Apostle (1 Pet. 3:21) saith that the baptism of the Spirit is the question of a good conscience unto God, &c., Heb. 10:22, when the baptism which is inward is called the sprinkling of the heart from an evil conscience: seeing therefore infants neither have an evil conscience nor the question of a good conscience, nor the purging of the heart, for all these are proper to actual sinners: hence it followeth that infants baptism is folly and nothing."

Here Smyth defines inward baptism by *sprinkling;* and hence the outward baptism which he always calls a "washing with water" was in his mind defined by affusion. On page 54, after showing that the *matter* of baptism is a believing subject and the *form* a washing with water into the name of the Trinity, he says:

"Water is not the matter of baptism, but only the instrument of baptism: For as fire is the instrument of burning, so is Water of washing: the matter of burning is the fewel that is burnt, so the matter of washing is the party washed."

A Baptist believing in immersion would define water as the element in which, but not the *"instrument"* by which, a man is baptized: and "sprinkling" or "washing" for baptism is now utterly out of the question in any sense with Baptist definition. Helwys in his Mystery of Iniquity and Morton in his work entitled, A Description, both repeatedly keep up Smyth's use of the word "washing" as the definition of baptism; and in all their discussion with Robinson, Ainsworth, Johnson, Jessop and others who practiced sprinkling, they invariably used the word "washing" for baptism as their opponents did. They spoke of the folly of "washing infants" as a definition of infant baptism— just as they defined adult baptism; and it is clear that they meant just what their opponents did by the mode of baptism which was affusion. Such was the usage of the sprinkling Mennonites with whom they were associated and who did not hesitate to use Rom. 6:4; Col. 2:12 as expressive of the ideal effect of baptism in washing away sin. Smyth, Helwys and Morton use Heb. 10:22 in the sense of *baptizo*, both as to the baptism of the heart by the sprinkling of blood and the washing (*leloumenoi*) of the body with pure water.

As Dr. Newman says:

"The use of the Biblical language about burial and resurrection in connection with baptism proves absolutely nothing as to the practice of a writer."

The opponents of Smyth, Helwys and Morton, though aspersionists, employed the same symbolism. Edmond Jessop (A Discovery of the Errors of the English Anabaptists, &c., p. 62, 1623), says of Col. 2:12:

" In which words (I say) he settled downe expressly, that the baptisme which saveth, the baptisme whereby we put on Christ, the baptisme whereby our hearts are purged and sanctified, and the sinnes of our flesh done away, whereby we are buried with Christ and doe rise with him, even that which is through the faith and operation of the Spirit, is one and the same, with the circumcision of the heart."

Jessop is speaking of the sacramental effect of baptism as a washing away of sin, the effect of which is to unite us with Christ in his death and resurrection and which, with the Pedobaptists, is expressed just as well by affusion as immersion. He meant no more by his definition than the Puritan Catechism,

"To Sions Virgins," 1644, when it asks the question: "*How are we buried by baptism with Christ?*" and answers it as follows:

"When he was buried by baptism, sweating water and blood, he was buried by baptisme, being under the wrath of the Father all his woes were over him, then were the elect buried with him in his death, when many came aforehand to bury him, in being manifested to believers when they are baptized by the Spirit dying unto sin and rising unto newness of life."

This Catechism is defending sprinkling as the mode of baptism against immersion; and it has no hesitation in adopting the burial and resurrection significance of baptism as expressive of spiritual washing which kills the soul to sin and unites it with Christ in his death and resurrection. The Mennonites, Smyth, Helwys, Morton, abound in the expressions, "believe and be baptized," "put on Christ in baptism," "buried and risen with him in baptism," and the like; and yet they in no way differed from the sprinkling Puritans in usage or practice, except in the application of such symbolism to unbelieving infants.

Hence the word immersion was never put into an English Baptist Confession, until 1644, for the reason, as we shall see, that immersion was never adopted by the English Baptists until 1640–41. It was not put into the Confessions of Smyth and Helwys, 1611, because they practiced Mennonite affusion and called it, as the Puritans did, a "washing with water." The argument that they took immersion for granted because it was the normal or universal mode is purely gratuitous, since in 1609–11 sprinkling or pouring was the mode around them; if they were immersionists in conflict with the other modes of baptism, their failure to employ the word, immersion, would be astounding. Certainly they could have incurred no danger from persecution in using the word, immersion, in their Confessions and writings, if that was the prevailing mode; and the omission to use it is *prima facie* evidence that they did not practice it, aside from the fact of history that they were affusionists.

The so-called "Ancient Records" of the Epworth, Crowle and West Butterwick church, 1558–9, published by Dr. John Clifford in 1879, have been thoroughly exposed as a forgery by Dr. Dexter in his work entitled: True Story of John Smyth, the Se-Baptist; and it has now been repudiated by all true Baptist scholarship. The fraud was evidently invented to escape the odium of Smyth's self-baptism which, after all, had it been immersion, is no worse than the self-originated baptism of Spilsbury or Roger Williams begun without a baptized administrator to accomplish the same thing that Smyth purposed. Somebody had to begin the administration of the ordinance; and whether self-baptized or not, Smyth, in the providence of God, was right in principle if not in method and form of his baptism. The great wonder is that scholars like Drs. Clifford and Angus, in the light of history, should have been misled by such a forgery as the "Ancient Records." As already said, Smyth and his followers were Separatists, intensely opposed to Anabaptism, after reaching Holland, down to 1608; and in the light of their own literature, and according to Robinson and Ashton (his editor), Ainsworth, Johnson, Jessop and other contemporaries, to say nothing of Evans, Müller, de Hoop Scheffer and Barclay in more recent times, it is utterly improbable to suppose that Smyth was already a Baptist, immersed in the river Don at midnight, 1606, by John Morton, or that he was ever immersed at all.

The tradition that Smyth was immersed under the claim of being the founder of the General Baptist denomination, has naturally been followed by a number of writers of later date, such as Thomas Wall (1691), Giles Shute (1696), Daniel Neal (1722), and still later by Taylor, Ivimey, Adshead, Punchard, Blackburn, Masson, Price, Wilson and others who have been cited in favor of the view that Smyth was immersed, or immersed himself. No testimony has been adduced by one of these writers to prove Smyth's immersion; and it is pretty clear from the writings of Smyth and his contemporaries—especially by the later revelations of Ashton, Muller, Scheffer and others—that he not only baptized himself, but did it by "affusion." If, as claimed by Masson, Price and others, Smyth and Helwys had made the issue with the Puritans on the mode as on the subject of baptism, the fact would have appeared in their writings and in the writings of their opponents. Prof. David Masson, M.A., LL.D. (Life of John Milton, Vol. II., p. 540) represents Smyth in his separation as not only "rejecting the baptism of infants altogether," but as "insisting on immersion as the proper Scriptural form of the rite." On p. 544, he assumes that the "Helwisse's folk" differed from the Independents "on the subject of Infant Baptism and Dipping." In a recent interview Prof. Masson seems to imply that he drew his opinion from the utterance of Leonard Busher

ORIGIN OF THE GENERAL BAPTISTS.   53

(1614) and from Dr. Featley's "Dippers Dipt" (1644) and Edwards' Gangraena (1646) as conclusive that Baptists had been "Dippers" from John Smyth onward; but it is evident that, in his great work, Prof. Masson had only incidentally examined Baptist history from 1609 to 1641, and was unacquainted with the documents and writers which overthrow his thesis—as we shall see.

The only man of the time who in this reformatory movement gave a single utterance in favor of immersion was Leonard Busher (1614), who defined baptism as "dipped for dead in water." The isolation of that utterance indicates the universal prevalence of sprinkling or pouring; and it seems to have been lost in the universal silence of the waters which were undisturbed by adult dipping. Crosby's explanation, as will be seen in another chapter, that immersion prior to 1640-41 had been *"disused"* even as an infant rite, and was *"restored"* as an adult ordinance about that date, gives the reason for the silence. He shows that the "ancient custom of immersion" had never been "revived" in England since it was "disused" down to that time, and since it was not known if the Anabaptists had *begun* it; and the fact is confirmed by the voluminous testimony of writers who discuss the subject from 1640-41, and onward. Busher's utterance is like a flash of lightning and a clap of thunder on the midnight sky of believers' baptism, which had lost its lustrous symbolism; and the sky did not relume from the long night of "disuse" until Blunt caught the distant echo and flash of Busher's peal, and proclaimed and put in practice his plea for immersion. Then the storm of controversy arose against the practice as something "new" and which nullified all other forms of baptism; and the contest raged until the end of the seventeenth century. Busher's definition was certainly apart from any practice of his day.

It is probable that the Helwys-Morton people, in spite of persecution, increased in membership down to 1640-41, by the number of churches ascribed to them in 1644; but it is likely that this increase from 1640 to 1644 was far greater than from 1611 to 1641. Ivimey's assumption, based upon the testimony of Dr. Some, that as early as 1589 there were many churches of this order in London and the country—or that such churches succeeded to the seventeenth century—is without historical foundation. The early origin and continuance of Baptist churches in England seem to have a definite, however limited, history; and it is not likely that any Anabaptist churches before 1641 in England escaped the eye of history at the time. What Baptists at that date did not generally know of themselves, their enemies did; and it is improbable that any Anabaptist conventicle, in any locality of England, could have had an ancient origin and long continuance without some record of its persecutors. The claim of antiquity for the existence of any Anabaptist church before 1611–1641, other than those recorded between those dates, is simply traditional and unreliable; and if such a claim could be established, it does not deny the absence or "disuse" of immersion among them applicable to the great body of Baptists, as we shall see, who restored immersion in England, 1640–41. Such long and unbroken existence as is claimed for the churches of Canterbury, Eythorne, Hill Cliffe, Bocking, and others, in an enemy's country and under the perpetual surveillance and intolerance of the ecclesiastical and civil powers, seems improbable without any authentic record of the fact—as already said. The Baptist and other writers of the 17th Century know nothing of these or any other immersion bodies before 1640–41; and if such bodies in England had come down to that date the invariable charge and defense of *self-originated* baptism after that date would have been absurd. So of the charge and defense of "Separation" and "reformation." There is no possible explanation of the *terms* of the 1640–41 controversy regarding Baptist baptism, except upon the theory of a "revival of immersion" at the hands of the whole Baptist body; and a hundred writers, both Baptist and Pedobaptist, contending over the subject for sixty years—all over England—ought to have known if any immersion body in the Kingdom had come down to 1640–41, and had not joined in the restoration of the ordinance claimed to be *"lost."*

ENGLISH BAPTIST REFORMATION.
(FROM 1609 TO 1641 A. D.)

CHAPTER V.
ORIGIN OF THE PARTICULAR BAPTISTS.

Thomas Crosby, the first English Baptist historian (Vol. I., pp. 147-149; Vol. III., pp. 40-42), chronicles the origin of what are called the first Particular or Calvinistic Baptist churches in England, as distinguished from the General or Arminian Baptists. He points to the year, 1633, as the date at which the Particular Baptist movement began, as follows:

"In the year 1633, the Baptists who had hitherto been intermixd among other Protestant Dissenters, without distinction, and so consequently shared with the Puritans all the persecutions of those times, began now to separate themselves, and form distinct societies of those of their own persuasion."

He seems to imply that this was the origin of the first *Baptist* churches in England; but whatever his reason for thus expressing himself, the origin of the Particular Baptist churches was synchronous with the movement of 1633. He gives no data for the assertion that the Baptists were individually "intermixed" with the Puritans up to that date; but if his assumption is correct, they must have agreed with the Puritans in doctrine and practice, except infant baptism. If there were such "intermixed" Baptists they were unorganized and had no churches of their own, but were in fellowship and co-operation with the Congregationalists. They were different in kind from the General Baptists who retained till 1641 the fellowship and peculiarities of the Mennonites; and as the Particular Baptists retained the mixed church or communion idea and their Calvinism inherited from their ancestral relationship with the Puritans, so the General Baptists retained, for the same reason, the peculiarities of the Mennonites—especially their Pelagian, Socinian, or Arminian tendencies. The Particular Baptists were free from the Mennonite errors in doctrine and practice; but with their otherwise Baptistic doctrines and practices, they inherited from their Puritan ancestors the mixed church and communion fallacy, of which the Jessey church was the mother.

For his account of the Particular Baptists Crosby cites the so-called Kiffin Manuscript, or the Jessey Records, as his authority, from which he collects the following facts: On the 12th of September, 1633, there was a secession from the Jacob-Lathrop (Independent) church of the people he calls " Baptist," hitherto "intermixed," upon the ground chiefly, according to Crosby:

"That baptism was not rightly administered to infants, so they looked upon the baptism they had received at that age as invalid: whereupon most or all of them received a new baptism."

According to the Records the 1633 secession was based rather upon dissatisfaction "with the churches owning the English Parishes to be true churches;" and "denying the truth of ye Parish Churches," and having "become so large that it might be prejudicial," they "desired dismission that they might become an entire church and further ye communion of those churches in order amongst themselves." This dissatisfaction with regard to the Parish Churches arose in 1630, according to the Jessey Records, in the Jacob church because of those who had their children baptized in the Parish Churches; and notwithstanding the compromise " Covenant" adopted in that year as a peace measure, this dissatisfaction continued until the split in 1633 for the reasons expressed above. The secession of 1633 was mainly an Independent movement which arose partly from necessity and which aimed at rebuking affiliation with the Parish Churches and which looked to the furthering of " communion " with other Independent churches which were " in order " and did not so affiliate. There was an Anabaptist element among the secessionists, such as " Mr. Eaton and some others " who "received a further baptism," but the Records do not sustain Crosby's statement that "most or all of them received a new baptism." Hence this 1633 secession could not have been wholly a body of Anabaptists, or " Baptists," at the time of their separation, though subsequently they became such; and it is proper to keep the Records in view since Crosby bases his version upon them. Only a few of the secession were Anabaptists, at the start, who received a "further" or a "new baptism," that is, believers' baptism as opposed to infant baptism; but this does not appear to have been the main reason for the bulk of the separation. As between Smyth and the Brownists at his separation—or as between the General Baptists and the Mennonites in their relation—the question of baptismal mode was not mooted, so between the Particular Baptists and the Puritans in their relation or separation the mode of baptism was not in dispute, which would certainly have been involved if the same difference as to *mode* had existed as to *subject*. According to the tract: "'To Sion's Virgins," the mode of baptism in the Lathrop church was unquestionably *sprinkling*.

In the year 1638 there was another secession of the same character from the Jacob church, but based solely upon the judgment of Mr. Eaton, which joined Mr. Spilsbury, and who was evidently, at this time, pastor of the 1633 secession which had probably become entirely Anabaptist and which is known as the first Particular Baptist Church. Crosby errs (Vol. III., p. 42) in calling this 1638 secession a separate church, since it joined Mr. Spilsbury, who was then pastor of the 1633 secession. There were six persons in this last secession who, "being of the same judgment with Sam Eaton," were "convinced that Baptism was not for infants, but for professed believers;" and this is the first intimation, so far as the Records show, that infant baptism was a ground of separation. These were all Anabaptists, and the presumption is that the 1633 secession had in 1638 become entirely Anabaptist under Spilsbury's pastorate. It may however have been a mixed church, since Spilsbury was an open communionist and a pulpit affiliationist.

In 1639 Crosby says: "Another Congregation of *Baptists* was formed, whose place of meeting was in Crutched-Fryars; the chief promoters of which were Mr. *Green*, Mr. *Paul Hobson*, and Captain *Spencer ;*" but the Records say : "Mr. Green with Captain Spencer had begun a Congregation in Crutched-Friars, to whom Paul Hobson joyned who was *now* [1644] with *many* of that Church one of ye Seven"—having just mentioned the "Seven" in the preceding 1644 paragraph which, out of order, is followed by the 1639 paragraph. There is no evidence that this was an Anabaptist church, since only Paul Hobson "with *many* of that church," probably by separation, had become one of the Seven Particular Baptist Churches which, in 1644, issued the Confession of which Paul Hobson was one of the signers;

and so far as I have found, Green and Spencer were both Brownists and the associates of Barebone in Brownist conventicles and preaching, about the year 1641. (New Preachers, New; Brownist Conventicles, &c., p. 4.) Ivimey classes Green and Spencer with the Baptists; but so he does Barebone, with whom they associated and who himself was also a Brownist. Green, the "felt maker," is probably "Hatmaker" of the secession of 1633, mentioned in the Records; and Spencer was called the "horse-rubber" along with Barebone, who was called the "leather-seller."

According to Crosby this ends the origin of the Particular Baptist Churches prior to 1641—except the 1640 movement for the restoration of immersion which was introduced by these people. In 1644 the Particular Baptists numbered seven English and one French Church, all in London, of the same faith and order, according to the Jessey Church Records.

The old Jacob-Lathrop Church (Independent) according to these Records, founded in 1616, was not only the mother of many of the Independent but of the Particular Baptist Churches which took their rise in London. If there was an Anabaptist element "intermixed" with this old church at the time of the secession of 1633-1638, then from 1640 to 1645, under the pastorate of Mr. Jessey, it may be regarded as a Particular Baptist Church in transition—if not such before that date. It finally became Baptist in 1645, pastor and people; and, as already said, it was from this church that the mixed church and communion practice is traced through the English Particular Churches down to the present time. As originally the Anabaptists were "intermixed" and in communion with the Puritans, so the Puritans have thus remained with the Particular Baptists. Perhaps in embryo the Jacob-Lathrop Church was Baptist from 1633 onward—just as the Separatist Church of John Smyth was such on going to Holland; and in the providence of God these two churches were the twin mothers of the Baptist denominations —especially General and Particular—in England. Whatever may be true of individual Baptist elements in England between 1600 and 1641, the two original Baptist movements, 1611 and 1633, took formative shape in the churches of Smyth and Jessey, both of which became Baptist and gave birth to the English Baptist denomination which unitedly had 47 churches in 1644. Some of the Congregational Churches, after 1641, as the Broad-

Origin of the Particular Baptists.

mead, Bristol, and others, became Baptist; and if it is possible, which is historically unknown, that there were any of the old Lollard or Anabaptist elements or conventicles from the sixteenth century latent in England before or after 1641 which developed into Baptist Churches, they were absorbed by the general movement of 1640–41, at which date they adopted immersion along with the entire body, which together restored immersion at that time and completed the reformation.

The immersion movement of 1640–41 is a special feature of Particular Baptist origin, although it became the movement of both Baptist bodies about the same period along different lines of restoration; but as I shall give, in another chapter, a fuller history of that movement I shall here confine myself to the inquiry: Did the Particular Baptists sprinkle or immerse before 1641? The more than probable practice of the Helwy's Anabaptists, after the custom of the Mennonites, was affusion down to the time of Blunt's deputation to Holland in 1640; and we shall now discover that aspersion must have been the practice of the Particular Baptists, according to the custom of their Puritan ancestors, from 1633 to 1641. They had no other baptism than that of their infancy while "intermixed" with the Puritans; and it was not until their separation that they adopted believers' baptism evidently by the same mode. As intimated, there was no controversy with the Puritans about the mode before or after the separation; and according to "Sion's Virgins," 1644, the practice of the Puritans, especially the Jacob-Lathrop Church, was sprinkling. The Jessey Records show that of the secession of 1633, "Mr. Eaton with some others" received a "further baptism," or as Crosby puts it, a "new baptism." This baptism was after the undisputed mode of the Puritans; for if there had been a change of mode, as there was of subject under the same contention, then we should have heard that these Anabaptists adopted immersion in 1633, as Barclay (Inner Life, pp. 74, 75) thinks they did by mistake from not having seen the date, 1640–41, of the original Jessey Church Records, when Blunt was sent to Holland. If there had been any difference between the Puritans and Anabaptists as to the *mode*, we should have had some record of that fact, just as we have a record of their difference and separation based upon the *subject* of baptism in 1638. As between Smyth and the Brownists, so between Spilsbury and the Independents, the difference was well defined as to the subject, but not as to the mode of baptism; and although Anabaptism by any mode was the offense down to 1641, immersion never became the crime until after that date. Was it because it was taken for granted on account of its prevalence before that date? Exactly the reverse was true among those from whom the Anabaptists separated and with whom they were in controversy; and according to undisputed authority immersion in the English Church had become extinct by 1600 A. D., and was in "disuse" in England, according to Crosby, prior to the Blunt movement, 1640-41. It would be unaccountable that Smyth and Spilsbury should split with the Puritans on the mode of baptism, as on the subject, and neither of them, before 1641, should leave a single sentence of such controversy so voluminous about believers' as opposed to infant baptism in the literature of the period.

This is strong circumstantial evidence growing out of the facts of separation itself; but this evidence is amply confirmed by the direct testimony of the Records of the Particular Baptist Movement of a little later date and by the testimony of Hutchinson, Crosby and other writers of the time. The immersion agitation among the Baptists, 1640-41, indicates that not only the General, but the Particular Baptists did not practice immersion until that date. It originated in the question of a "proper administrator," which resulted in the discussion and adoption of a *proper mode* of baptism at that time; and although the movement has been ascribed to the first Particular Baptist Church of England, it seems to have originated, according to the Jessey Church Records, in a joint inquiry between some of the members of both the Spilsbury and the Jessey churches—one an Anabaptist church and the other an Anabaptist church in transition. Perhaps the agitation had been going on for several years; and if so, it had continued on down to 1640 through 1638, and it may be from 1633, when believers' baptism was likely introduced without a baptized administrator. Possibly the Blunt party were affected by the succession views of their Pedobaptist ancestors and in conflict with the anti-succession principles of the Anabaptists, foremost among whom was Spilsbury, who said: "Baptizednesse is not essential to the administrator of baptisme." At all events the agitation which began about a "proper administrator" developed into the discovery of the proper mode of baptism.

According to the so-called Kiffin Manuscript, or the Jessey Church Records, the immersion movement came to a head in

1640, apparently led by Richard Blunt with Mark Lucar, Thomas Shepard and others of the "forenamed" of Spilsbury's church on the one side and Samuel Blacklock with others of Jessey's church on the other, who became "convinced," after much conference and prayer, that dipping was baptism and could only be enjoyed by sending to Holland for its administration. The conclusion was based (1) upon Rom. 6:4; Col. 2:12; and (2) upon the affirmation of the Manuscript: "*None having then so practiced in England to professed believers;*" and Richard Blunt was deputed to the Netherlands, where he received immersion from John Batten, of the Collegiants, and who upon his return baptized Blacklock, the two baptizing the rest that "were so minded" to the number of 53 persons, whose names are given in the document, January 9, 1641. Hutchinson confirms this Manuscript account of sending to Holland for a "proper administrator"; and Crosby substantially employs the Manuscript in his version of precisely the same facts. He paraphrases the main sentence: "None then having so practiced in England to professed believers," so as to read thus:

"They could not be satisfied about *any* administrator [proper or irregular] in England to *begin* this practice; because though some in this nation rejected baptism of infants [Anabaptists], yet they had not as they knew of *revived* the ancient custom of immersion." (Vol. I., pp. 101, 102.)

Just before this, on page 97, Crosby affirms that "immersion had for some time been *disused,*" in England; and when his paraphrase and this affirmation are put together he perfectly agrees with the Records in the main sentence and expresses his opinion, in so many words, that immersion down to 1640 had not been "*revived*" by the Anabaptists of England and that they were, therefore, practicing sprinkling and pouring. If immersion had been "disused" in England prior to Blunt's deputation to Holland in 1640, and if there were some known in England as Anabaptists who "rejected the baptism of infants," but who were not known to have "revived" the "disused" ordinance, then so far as known they were in the *continuance* of sprinkling or pouring and had never *begun* immersion, which is the logic of the case. In other words, according to Crosby, *they were known to be sprinkling or pouring, but they were not known to have "revived" the "disused" custom of immersion;* and hence the declaration of the Jessey

Records: "*None having then* [up to that time, 1640] *so practiced in England to professed believers.*"

But could the fact have been known, if they had "revived" it? For, historically, it is implied that they had not *continued* it, nor *begun* it, since its "disuse" in England. Surely, if they had begun or continued it, Blunt and his party would have known it; for Crosby's logic is that the Anabaptists could not have been practicing immersion without *reviving* or *beginning* it anew. It was not a question of *continuance*, but *revival*; and it is certain that if Spilsbury and his church, to which Blunt, Lucar, Shepard and the rest of the "forenamed" belonged, had begun or continued immersion from 1633, they would have known it. Some of the party, if such had been the case, had probably been immersed; but this, in the light of the Records, is a *reductio ad absurdum* since Blunt and his party, in 1640, reached the conclusion that dipping only, according to the Scriptures, was baptism; that up to that time it had not been practiced in England to professed believers; and that to enjoy it they must go to Holland for it. Hence the conclusion is that the Particular Baptists had not "revived" or continued immersion, and were therefore sprinkling, after the custom of the Puritans. Among the number baptized by Blunt and Blacklock were such men as Lucar, Shepard, Gunne, Kilcop, and latterly, perhaps, Kiffin, three of whom were signers of the Confession of 1644; and such men as these would have subsequently corrected the statements of the Jessey Church Records if they had been false. The writings of both Kiffin and Kilcop confirm the main sentence of the so-called Kiffin MS.

But could Blunt and his party have known if the General Baptists had "revived" immersion before 1640; for Crosby and the Records both imply that they had not begun its practice with their origin, and of course had not continued it down to 1640. They were among the Anabaptists of England, of whom it was not "known" that they had "revived" in order to "*begin*" the ancient but "disused" custom of immersion; and hence were known to be sprinkling or pouring for baptism. They were in London and the country and in correspondence with each other and with the Mennonites; and if some of them had begun or restored the ordinance all of them would have known it; or if some of them had "revived" it, all of them likely had done so. The fact, in London, could not have well escaped Blunt and his party, who lived there; and if it had escaped them, it could not have

ORIGIN OF THE PARTICULAR BAPTISTS. 63

eluded the surveillance of their enemies for thirty years, from 1611 to 1641. Crosby, with all the records before him in 1738-40, declared that immersion had been "disused" in England prior to Blunt's deputation to Holland; and in his interpretation of the Jessey Church Records he affirms that it was historically unknown if the Anabaptists of England had "revived" the "disused" ordinance down to that time, which was 1640. It was known that as Anabaptists they were practicing baptism by affusion, so long as they had not "revived" or begun immersion; and without any record of revival, the inference is that they continued their affusion down to 1640. This is Crosby's logic and it is thoroughly sustained by the Jessey Records and by the silence of any history to the contrary. Not a single instance of believers' immersion has been pointed to as occurring among the Anabaptists of England prior to 1641; and with the fact of its "disuse" historically set up, this is presumptive evidence that such a custom among Baptists did not exist until 1641. It is useless to argue the question *ab ignorantia*, if the question is historically settled as to the practice of the General and Particular Baptists as denominations. There might have been sporadic cases of immersion in practice as in utterance; but this in no way affects the question at issue. As a denomination of people the English Anabaptists, if Crosby and the Jessey Records are true—yea, if all the Baptist writers who touch the subject in the seventeenth century are true—did not practice immersion between 1611 and 1641; and inferentially they practiced sprinkling and pouring as a fact well known, if it was not known that they had *"revived"* immersion.

It has been affirmed that there were three Baptist churches, Hill Cliffe, Eythorne and Bocking, which dipped before 1641, and three individuals, William Kiffin, Hanserd Knollys and John Canne, with Paul Hobson thrown in for "good measure," who were dipped before that date. As already shown, the antiquity of these three churches, as *Baptist*, is purely traditional. Even if they had a continuance from the early Lollards, or Anabaptists, and anciently practiced immersion, that practice had long been "disused" before 1641. There is not the slightest evidence that they were in the practice of immersion prior to 1641, when the English Baptists *"revived"* it; and if the so-called Kiffin Manuscript, or Hutchinson, Crosby, Spilsbury, Tombes, Lawrence, Barber, Kilcop and other writers are authority, it is clear, if these churches belonged to the "English Baptists" of

1640-41, that, like the rest of them, they were practicing affusion down to that date.

As to the three individuals cited there is not a shred of history in proof that they were immersed before that date. William Kiffin, as we shall see in another chapter, under the caption of his own name, evidently never became a Baptist until 1641, according to his own showing (Sober Discourse, p. 1) and other citations which I shall give. Knollys, though an Anabaptist in principle from 1636, was, as already seen, a member of the Dover, N. H., Church [Puritan] in 1640; and after his return to England he was evidently a member of the Jessey Church, in which, in 1643, according to the Jessey Records, he was in a controversy about the baptism of his child. He could not have been immersed until after 1641; and it was not until 1645 that he appears as a Baptist pastor in London. Rev. Charles Stovel, who published the biography of John Canne, says:

"When introduced to us in the Broadmead Records at Easter after 1640, that is, April 25, 1641, he appears to have been received as a man well known, &c."

It was at this date that he appears as a "baptized man," April 25, 1641, three months and a half after immersion had been introduced by Blunt at Southwark, where Canne was well acquainted, and where he was probably immersed. (A Quest. in Bapt. Hist., p. 77.) The inference that Paul Hobson was immersed before 1641, because he joined a supposed Anabaptist church in 1639, and because Crosby erroneously calls it "Baptist," is in the light of history, a gross logical *non sequitur*.

The only remaining question under this head arises: Which was the first immersion church in England? As we have seen, the Particular Baptists, some of them, took the initiative in the restoration of immersion; and, as we shall see, the whole Baptist community, General and Particular, joined in the reformation about the year 1640-41. Crosby (Vol. III., p. 41) quotes Neal (Hist. of the Puritans, Vol. II., p. 400) as saying that Mr. Jessey "laid the foundation of the first Baptist congregation that he had met with in England;" but Crosby characterizes Neal's statement as a "strange representation" in view of the Kiffin MS. before him, showing that there were three Baptist churches, 1633, 1638, 1639, in England "before that of Mr. Jessey's," which never became Baptist until 1645. Neal seems to have

ORIGIN OF THE PARTICULAR BAPTISTS. 65

very carelessly read or remembered the Kiffin manuscript, which Crosby lent him, and which fixes the first Baptist secession from the Puritans in 1633, of which Spilsbury is supposed to have been the pastor. Neal (Vol. III., p. 173, Hist. Puritans) makes this first secession in 1638, and places Mr. Jessey as pastor; and hence his further mistake in saying that Jessey "laid the foundation of the first Baptist congregation in England." Jessey became pastor of the Jacob-Lathrop Church in 1637; and the second Baptist secession from this old church in 1638 went also to Mr. Spilsbury's church—a secession which Crosby seems to err in making a separate church, if Spilsbury was pastor of the 1633 secession.

Not only does Neal blunder in ascribing the first Baptist organization in England to the year 1638, under the pastoral care of Jessey, but he blunders worse than ever when he says (Vol. III., pp. 173, 174) that Mr. Blunt was sent by this Jessey church of 1638 to the Dutch Baptists of Amsterdam, *in* 1644, for a proper administrator of immersion, and upon his "return he baptized Mr. Blacklock, a teacher, and Mr. Blacklock dipped the rest of the society, to the number of fifty-three," in that year (1644). He seems to have been wholly at sea with reference to dates as well as with regard to the original organizations and pastors of Baptist churches prior to the year 1640–41, the date at which the so-called Kiffin Manuscript fixes the deputation of Blunt to Holland and the baptism of the fifty-three persons Neal found in the MS. The year 1644 was the date of the adoption of the Confession of Faith by the Baptists in which they first defined baptism as dipping; and it is utterly impossible to suppose that Blunt was sent to Holland for immersion in that year upon the plea of the Kiffin Manuscript that "none had then so practiced in England to professed believers." Neal even goes so far as to chronologically connect the Blunt movement and Featley's statement that, in 1644, the Baptists had "rebaptised one hundred men and women" in the rivulets and some arms of the Thames, all of which goes to show his criminal indifference as to the date and connection of facts, and the facts themselves, in dealing with Baptist history—as well charged by Crosby.

But what became of this first immersed congregation is a question of importance only in determining to what church it belonged. In the manuscript it is spoken of as "two companies," evidently from the two churches (Spilsbury's and Jessey's) which "mett" and did "intend to meet after this;" and the indication is that they entered into an uncovenanted but formal agreement by which they "proceeded together," not only in setting apart one respectively to baptize each company, which was solemnly performed by Blunt and Blacklock, but that they were afterwards a common body to which "many being added" they "increased much." This was probably the church of Blunt with whom were associated Emmes and Wrighters, in 1646, and which Edwards in his Gangræna (Pt. III., p. 112) calls "one of the first and prime churches of the Anabaptists now in these latter times." He got his information concerning this from "a woman who sometime was a Member of a Church of the Anabaptists," June fifth, 1646. She says that "the church broke into pieces, and some went one way, some another, divers fell off to no Church at all." (Ibid, 113.) Wrighters, according to Edwards (Gangraena, Pt. I., pp. 113, 114), became a Seeker; and what became of Emmes I am not informed. In what year, prior to 1646, this Blunt Church broke up is not stated, nor is its location given; but if it were "the two companies" baptized by Blunt and Blacklock, 1641, then it became extinct before 1646, and the regular baptism theory based upon sending to Holland for a proper administrator died among the English Baptists. About 1676 Bampfield sought in London to find the original administrator of immersion; but while he discovered several of the irregular methods by which immersion had been restored in England, he gives no mention of the Blunt method of going to Holland for its regular administration, which tends to substantiate the Edwards account and to lead to the conclusion that his movement, rejected by the great body of the English Baptists as "needless," was an insignificant affair which went to pieces and was soon forgotten. It was quite common at the time Edwards wrote for Anabaptists to seek another dipping, or what they called in some of the literature of the time a "fourth baptism;" and some of them abandoned their dipping altogether and turned Seekers under the teaching and influence of the Familists. Hence it is not strange that the Blunt movement under such influence, and under the general ban of the Baptists, should have broken up and been forgotten. The controversial writings of the period make very slight intimation of the movement, if they refer to it at all; and it is certain that neither the General nor Particular Baptists, subsequent to 1641, ever adopted or defended it.

It has been usual to ascribe this first immersion movement to the first Particular Baptist Church in England, as Evans does; and if the immersed body returned with Blunt, Shepard, Marke Lucar, and others who were once or already members of Spilsbury's Church, to that church, then the movement was absorbed and as such lost in that church, so that the large secession from Jessey's Church, 1641, went then to the first Particular Church, which, though anti-successionist in the main, became immersionist by the Spilsbury method about the same time—possibly, as Dr. Newman suggests, in 1640. At all events, this regular movement of Blunt seems to have been lost sight of in the great anti-succession movement of the great body of the English Baptists, as we shall see in the more fully detailed account of the movement in a subsequent chapter. It is evident, at least, that very few, if any, of the English Baptists, General or Particular, ever adopted the Blunt method, or took their baptism from him or his people, in the restoration of immersion as elaborately detailed by Crosby, who declares that "the largest number and the more judicious of the English Baptists" repudiated this method and adopted the anti-succession or irregular method of restoration.

This concludes the origin of the Particular Baptists of England included between the years 1633 and 1641. A full account of the restoration of immersion in England at the latter date will occasion some repetition of a few items under this head; but that event deserves a more specific and extended treatment since Crosby dignifies it as a Baptist "reformation" or "beginning."

ENGLISH BAPTIST REFORMATION.
(FROM 1609 TO 1641 A. D.)

CHAPTER VI.
DISUSE OF IMMERSION IN ENGLAND.

In his Preface to Vol. I., Crosby traces the history of the Antipedobaptists from Luther's time (sixteenth century) backward to primitive Christianity—confining his research almost exclusively to our Continental brethren from p. xviii. onward. His purpose was to refute the charge of Pedobaptists and Catholics that Baptists had their origin with the fanatics of Munster. In the body of Vol. I. Crosby begins what he claims as English Baptist history with John Wyckliffe, 1371; and through the Lollards, Wyckliffeites and foreign Anabaptists of the fifteenth and sixteenth centuries, he traces this irregular evangelical line as a kind of Baptist succession without reference to the mode of baptism or church organization and with reference simply to the practice of believers' baptism as opposed to infant baptism and to their devotion to certain other Baptist principles and peculiarities. He traces no organization among the Anabaptists of England till 1611-1633, and he does not refer to immersion as a mode of believers' baptism until in "later times" it was restored by the English Baptists about 1640-41.

In his Preface to the Second Volume he is reminded that he has not treated of English history from the first to the fourteenth century; and with a new turn to his thoughts he goes back to the first century in England, and traces immersion from 100 A. D. to 1600 A. D., when he says it became *"disused."* He refers to the introduction of immersion in the world by John the Baptist; and without tracing its history through other countries he comes directly to England. On page ii. of his Preface to Vol. II. he says:

"The great prophet, John, had an immediate commission from heaven before he entered upon the actual administration of his office. And as the English Baptists adhere [now] chiefly to this principle, that John the

Baptist was, by divine command, the first commissioned to preach the gospel, and baptize by immersion, those that received it; and that this practice has been ever since maintained and continued in the world to the present day [1738-40]; and it may not be improper to consider *the state of religion in this kingdom;* it being agreed, on all hands, that the plantation of the gospel here was very early, even in the *Apostles* days."

With this introduction, Crosby enters upon an enquiry as to the early planting of Christianity in Great Britain, and he shows that probably, for the first 300 years, adult immersion was the only form of baptism known to the ancient British Christians. For that period of time those who so practiced, he thinks, were Baptists—although Evans thinks it only probable. In his Brief Reply to John Lewis's Brief History of the Rise and Progress of Anabaptism in England, &c. (1738, pp. 41, 42), Crosby refers to this point in the Preface of his second volume then going to press, on which he says:

"I shall endeavor to show, that Christians in the Island were *English Baptists*, and that they continued so for 300 years; and that, when, by a general Massacre of the Monks of *Bangor*, the subject of Baptism was changed, yet the *Mode* continued about 1200 Years afterward. But I shall lay no great Stress upon these Things. For if it did appear, that the Practice of the *English* Baptists was but Yesterday; yet if it be found consentaneous with the Word of God revealed in the Bible, all *Customs*, Decrees of Councils, Articles of Churches, &c., would be to me of no effect."

Granting that Crosby is right as to the first Christians in Britain being "English Baptists," he here forbids their succession and admits their continuance for only 300 years from the first century; and this, so far as Baptists were concerned, is all that his Preface to the second volume was intended to show. From this period down to 1189 A. D.—especially from 603 A. D.—according to Crosby and Evans, no trace of the Baptist element is discoverable in England at all; and so far as immersion is concerned, Crosby only traces it after the first three hundred years—not through Baptists, who ended with that period—but through the Romish and Episcopal Churches, as an infant rite, down to 1600 A. D., and there he declares it was "disused" and changed to "sprinkling." Not only does he deny the succession of Baptists from the first 300 years, but he breaks the succession of immersion at 1600, even as a perverted infant rite. Of course, immersion under some form had "continued" somewhere "in the world" from John the Baptist till 1738-40, and at that time was practiced by the "English Baptists;" but in England neither Baptists nor immersion had had an unbroken succession after the first 300 years of the Christian era.

But let us see what the Preface says. From pages xiv.-xviii. of his Preface, Vol. II., he shows, by the authority of such writers as Fox, Rapin, Fuller and others, that the Saxon invasion, 469 A. D., drove the British Christians into Wales, after destroying their churches and most of their people, and that in 596 A. D., Austin's invasion and subsequent massacre either completed their annihilation or subjected them to the Church of Rome. About the year 600 A. D., Crosby thinks that infant baptism was introduced by Austin, although it is almost certain that it existed long before among the ancient British Christians, and on page xxxiii., Preface, he says again:

"The *subject* of baptism being now changed in England and that by a Romish emissary . . . . . Yet the *mode* of baptism *continued about one thousand years longer;* and baptism was performed by dipping those who were baptized [whether infants or adults] into the water."

Crosby goes on then to show that adult immersion along with infant immersion continued in the Romish Church in England until the adult population had been converted to Christianity—so-called; but as the centuries rolled on, adult immersion gradually decreased, and infant immersion took its place; the font taking the place of the baptistery and the river.

On page xliii. of this Preface, Crosby says again : "Though the baptism of infants seems now (1016 A. D.) to be pretty well established in this realm; yet the practice of immersion continued many years longer;" and he points out subsequently that there were "persons not wanting to oppose infant baptism"—alluding to certain Waldenses from France, Germany and Holland, who, he says, "had their frequent recourse and residence in the kingdom." This is Crosby's first mention of Anabaptism in England since the conflict of Austin with the Welch Christians, 603 A. D., a space of over four hundred years, a fact which Evans and later authorities do not mention. In the year 1158 A. D. about "thirty" other Waldenses came over to England who were supposed to reject infant baptism; and this is

DISUSE OF IMMERSION IN ENGLAND.

Crosby's second mention of Anti-pedobaptism in England. The people of the date at which Evans asserts that history claims the first revolt to Rome in England. Crosby mentions other Anabaptists in England in the reign of Henry II., 1182 A. D., and in the time of Henry III., 1235 A. D., also in 1315 A. D., when he notices the introduction of the Lollards, which brings him down to the time of Wyckliffe, 1371 A. D., and where he begins Baptist history, so-called, in his first volume, as already mentioned.

On page xlvi., Preface, Crosby further observes:

"Of Wyckliffe, his opinion, and his followers who were called Lollards, I have given are account in chap. i. of the first volume. I shall now only further observe, That the practice of immersion, or dipping in baptism, continued in the church [of England] untill the reign of King James I., or about the year 1600."

He quotes on page xlvii., Preface, Sir John Floyer, an English churchman, who says:

"And I do here appeal to you, as persons well versed in ancient history, and cannons, and ceremonies of the Church of England; and therefore are sufficient witnesses of the matter of fact which I design to prove, viz., That immersion continued in the Church of England till about the year 1600. And from thence I shall infer, that if God and the church thought that practice innocent for 1600 years, it must be accounted an unreasonable nicety in this present age, to scruple either immersion or cold bathing as a dangerous practice."

On page lii. Crosby says again: "Though the practice of immersion was now *generally disused in England*, yet there were some who were unwilling to part with this laudable and ancient practice;" and he cites Sir John Floyer again, who speaks of several persons who dipped their infants about 1640 (p. liii). On the same page he speaks of the Welch who had "more lately left off immersion." Henry Denne (A Contention for Truth, p. 40), 1658, like Sir John Floyer, says: "Dipping of infants was not only commanded by the Church of England, but also generally practiced in the Church of England till the year 1600; yea in some places it was practiced until the year 1641 until the fashion altered." There was an occasional exception, here and there a sporadic practice of infant dipping by the

English Church people; and now and then there was an exceptional defence of the ancient practice of infant immersion as by John Wesley, Sir John Floyer, Master Rogers, George Downame, and others; but in 1600 A. D. infant dipping had expired as an ordinance in the Church of England—still allowed as at the present time, but not practiced.

On page liv. (Preface, Vol. II.) Crosby concludes as follows:

"Thus I have traced the practice of the *British Churches* in point of baptism till sprinkling took place. And to me it seems evident beyond contradiction, that about three hundred years after the first plantation of the gospel in Britain, no other baptism was used but that of adult persons, by immersion, or dipping the body of the person, upon the profession of his faith; and that after the *subject* was changed, and infant baptism introduced by a massacre of almost all that refused to comply with the change; yet the *mode* of baptism by immersion continued about twelve hundred years"—

that is down to 1600 A. D. from the first century inclusive. Jeffrey Watts (Scribe, Pharisee, &c., London, 1656) says:

"The Church of England hath been now a long time, time out of mind, *mind of any man living*, in firm *possession* of baptism, and practice of it by sprinkling, or pouring on of water upon the face and forehead."

Watts was a learned English clergyman, rector of Much Leighs, and knew what he was saying; and his testimony is proof that no man living in 1656 could remember when immersion was practiced in England until the Baptists restored it.

Crosby does not show just when adult immersion, practiced along with infant immersion, ceased in the "British Churches;" but it ended when the font took the place of the baptistery and the river, and when, as Bishop Burnet puts it, "'The whole world in that age [the Reformation] had been baptized in infancy." (Hist. Ref., Vol. II., part ii., p. 113.) There was perhaps no such thing as adult immersion in the Church of England at the beginning of the sixteenth century; and infant immersion had begun to be substituted by affusion at that date. In 1528 Tyndale seemed to complain because the people manifested a preference for immersion over affusion as a mode of infant baptism; and in 1570, the Catechism of Noel, which was adopted as sole authority in the Church of England, at that time, prescribed sprinkling as indifferent with immersion in the baptism of infants. (Latin Collection, A. Howell, p. 207, Parker Publication Society.) The Puritans universally sprinkled from the start; and the Presbyterians who, in 1643, rejected immersion even as the alternate form of baptism, had long since abandoned dipping. At the beginning of the Seventeenth century sprinkling or pouring, with but little exception, was the universal mode of baptism of all parties both on the Continent and in England; and in England there is no mention of adult immersion at the hands of anybody until the Baptists restored it in 1640-41. There were, as we have seen, some exceptional cases of infant immersion up to 1640-41 and perhaps afterward; but no authority seems to cite a single exception of adult immersion at the hands of any religious body—not even by a legitimate inference.

In Vol. I., pp. 95-107, Crosby, as we shall see in the next chapter, details the restoration of immersion in England by the "English Baptists," and he prefaces the movement by the facts revealed in his Preface to Vol. II., pp. ii.-liv., namely, that "immersion," in England, "had been for sometime disused" (p. 97); and this whole section in Vol. I. is in exact accord with the Preface of Vol. II., which traces immersion in England only through the "British Churches" down to the year 1600, when it ended. He never mentions immersion by Baptists after the British Christians of the first 300 years in England until about 1640-41. So far as Crosby or any other historian can show, there is a hiatus of 1241 years in English history in which there is not an allusion to Baptist immersion; and the Jessey Church Records and Crosby's Preface to Vol. II. are in absolute accord as to the "disuse" of immersion before 1640-41 and its restoration by the English Baptists at that time. Crosby's Vol. I., pp. 95-107, and his Vol. II., Preface, pp. i.-liv., are thoroughly consistent with each other. Immersion had continued "in the world," in some form, somewhere, from John the Baptist's to Crosby's time, and was then in practice by the English Baptists, 1738-40; but in England it was "disused" in any form by 1600, with but slight exception, as an infant rite, anywhere, even in the English Church. As an adult rite and as the practice of Baptists the succession of immersion is broken by a hiatus of 1241 years until it was restored by the English Baptists in 1640-41. The Poland Anabaptists restored immersion in 1574. The Collegiants of Holland restored it in 1620. The Collegiants may have received the ordinance from the Poles, and the Poles from the Swiss Anabaptists and the Swiss from the Waldenses, and these last from those who continued it from the apostles; but immersion as an adult act seems to have been lost in England long before the close of the sixteenth century under the prevailing mode of sprinkling or pouring, and was only recovered by the Baptists in 1640–41.

Now, if we take the account of Crosby, the first Baptist historian, we are irresistably driven to the foregoing conclusion, namely, that the Anabaptists of the Sixteenth and first forty years of the Seventeenth century did not immerse in England. It cannot be assumed in his account that he took immersion for granted among the Anabaptists of this period, and therefore did not trace its succession in England through them. On the contrary, he distinctly claims the British Christians of the first 300 years as Baptists, and asserts that they practiced immersion. He then loses these first Baptists in the massacre or usurpation of the Romish Church, and he traces Baptist elements no further in England for centuries. When he finds them again, especially in the 16th century, as foreign elements, or when he traces the origin of the English Baptist Churches to 1611–1633, he says not a word about the immersion of the Baptists until they revived it at a later date; and yet he goes on carefully to trace the succession of Romish and Episcopal immersion from 600 to 1600 A. D., when it ended in sprinkling. Before the Baptist revival of immersion Crosby positively asserts that it "had been for sometime disused"—that is, from 1600 A. D. to the time of its revival; and he thus clearly implies not only that immersion was in disuse among the Pedobaptists, but also among the Baptists. Therefore Baptists and Baptist immersion from the first centuries had no unbroken succession in England; and when the foreign Anabaptists came into England in the 16th century, and when the English Anabaptists organized their churches in 1611–1633, they did not, according to Crosby, practice immersion. If they had so practiced he would have mentioned the fact in tracing the history of immersion in England for the first 1600 years through the Romish and Episcopal Churches.

Nothing could be more absurd than to suppose that Crosby, the first Baptist historian, would have traced a succession of immersion for 1600 years through a Pedobaptist line, and left such a succession out of the Baptist line, if it had existed. He does not even trace it through the intervening gap of forty years from 1600 to 1640, during which period he gives the origin of the first English Baptist Churches; and surely for that period he would have mentioned the fact if immersion had been the practice of the Baptists. On the contrary, he says, in his version of the Jessey Church Records, that it was not known if they had "*revived* the ancient custom of immersion" down to the date of the manuscript, which was 1640–41. As a Baptist historian it would have been his pride and glory, to say nothing of his duty, to trace the history of immersion even through this reformatory beginning of the English Baptists. He was an earnest defender of the ordinance—he made a relentless fight against infant baptism and sprinkling—he was a thorough Baptist; and it would be unaccountable with the material before him, and after such a voluminous record of Baptist and related history, that he should trace the line of baptismal succession in England, and never find it except in the Romish and Episcopal Churches after the first three centuries, if there was the slightest discovery of such a succession among Baptists before 1640–41. His history of the English Baptists is a most unpardonable blunder, if the Anabaptists from 1535 to 1641—or from 1611 to 1641—practiced immersion; and if they did so practice he has recorded the most palpable mistake in Baptist history, namely, that between 1600 and 1641 immersion was in disuse in England, and that the Baptists restored it about the latter date. Such a blunder cannot be predicated of such a Baptist as Crosby. His Preface to Vol. II. was written for the express purpose of tracing the history of immersion in England; and he did all that could be done for Baptists in showing their practice for the first 300 years, and their return to the lost practice in 1640–41.

But naturally it will be asked: Why does Crosby call these Anabaptists "Baptists," if immersion was lost in England and they restored it at a later date? How can a people be called Baptists by a Baptist historian when they did not practice immersion? I can only say that it was the custom among writers of his day to so call all the Anabaptist sects who practiced believers' baptism and rejected infant baptism, whatever the mode. Robinson (Hist. Baptism, 1790, p. 547) says:

"The Dutch *Baptists* reject infant baptism, and administer the ordinance only to such as profess faith and repentance; but they baptize by *pouring.*"

Evans (1862) calls the English Anabaptists by the name "Baptists" at the very time he is conceding the more than probability that they practiced Mennonite affusion. Crosby called everybody "Baptists," from the Lollards and Wyckliffeites down, whom he regarded as holding Baptist principles, practicing believers' baptism and opposing infant baptism; and the very people who restored immersion, 1640–41—and before they restored it—he called "English Baptists" who adopted different methods to accomplish what he calls their "beginning," or "reformation," in baptism. Strictly speaking, those Anabaptists were not Baptists until they adopted immersion; but in other particulars of doctrine and practice they were Baptists—and so called for this reason. Crosby, speaking of the origin of the "English Baptists" (Vol. I., p. xviii., P.), says:

"They are generally condemned (1738–40) as a *new sect*, whose *opinion and practice* with relation to baptism was not known in the Christian Church till about 200 years ago"—(1549).

He is here and onward speaking of their "opinion and practice" regarding believers' baptism, with no reference to mode before 1640–41; for he never pretends to show that the practice of immersion was adopted by the "English Baptists" until that date. He nevertheless calls them "English Baptists" for 200 years back; and so we are accustomed to speak of far more unbaptistic sects before them—such as Montanists, Novatians, Donatists, Paulicians, and the like, who would not now be fellowshiped, ecclesiastically speaking, in any regular Baptist church in America.

According, then, to Crosby, our first Baptist historian, who is thoroughly sustained by all modern research in Baptist history, there was no unbroken succession of Baptists or dipping in England down to 1640–41. There was an occasional defense and practice of infant dipping (and still is) among the English Church people after the year 1600; but at that time sprinkling or pouring became general, if not universal, among English Churchmen, Presbyterians and Puritans. What was true of these was true of the Anabaptists from 1538 to 1641 in England; and if among them there were any exceptional or sporadic cases of believers' immersion, the fact is historically unknown. It is impossible to suppose the case otherwise, else, as already seen, Crosby, who traces the only line of immersion in England for the first 1600 years, would not have ignored a single instance of immersion among his Baptist brethren, nor would he have otherwise recorded the fact that after the lapse of 1241 years they restored immersion at a "later date." To be sure, he only implies that the Anabaptists from 1611 to 1641 were pouring or sprinkling for baptism; but he clearly takes the fact for granted when he only traces immersion through the British churches down to 1600, and then records its restoration by the English Baptists after its *disuse*. He perhaps did not desire to emphasize the fact as a matter of Baptist history, but he certainly implies the fact that the Baptists were affusionists before 1640-41 by showing, at that date, that they restored the "disused" ordinance, which they could not have been practicing.

To sum up, Baptist succession, according to Crosby, was lost in England after the first 300 years of Christianity in the Island. The first Baptists were lost by extermination or usurpation, but immersion continued through the Romish Church to 1535, with the subject changed from the adult to the infant; and from 1535 to 1600 this infant immersion continued through the Episcopal Church and was lost—having gradually changed to sprinkling. Crosby faintly discovers a trace of Anti-pedobaptist elements in England through the 13th, 14th and 15th centuries; he discovers the line "more clearly" through the Dutch Anabaptists who came into England during the 16th century; he finally traces the origin of the English Baptists to their organizations, 1611, 1633; but he makes no claim for them of any sort of organic or baptismal succession from prior Anabaptist sects or elements. On the contrary, he demonstrates that they were Separatists from the Brownists or Congregationalists, among whom, as Crosby asserts, the Anabaptists were elementally "intermixed;" and then he shows that at a later date—after their organization—they adopted immersion. Crosby, with all the English Baptist writers I have read, repudiates the doctrine of *visible* succession, in any form, among Baptists. Denominationally he did not regard the Baptists as a "new sect." He claimed the Anabaptist sects as Baptist people before his day. Like other Baptist writers of his time, and before him, he traced the pedigree of Baptist people and principles back to the New Testament Churches; but with all other Baptist writers of that period, he regarded any succession of the visible order of those churches as having been repeatedly broken. No doubt he would agree with Barclay (Inner Life, pp. 11, 12) that "the rise of the Anabaptists took place long prior to the foundation of the Church of England"—that "small hidden societies" holding Anabaptist "opinions" existed on the Continent "from the times of the Apostles"—that in the sense of the "direct transmission of divine truth and the true nature of spiritual religion," Baptist Churches have "a lineage or succession more ancient than the Roman Church;" but he takes the same position with Barclay that "in England, although traces are found in history of the existence of the *opinions* of the Anabaptists from the earliest times, it is doubtful whether any churches or societies of purely English Baptists have a distinct consecutive existence prior to 1611." Crosby knows of no such "consecutive existence;" and in the origin of the English Baptist churches which he repeatedly represents as having had a "beginning," and as having set up a "reformation" of their own, he distinctly repudiates their visible succession, organically or baptismally, from preceding Anabaptists. He distinctly shows that they organized 1611–1633 upon the principle of believers' baptism, and that afterwards they revived immersion; and if there were any Anabaptist churches or societies which existed in England prior to 1611, they were historically unknown to Crosby and the Baptist writers of the 17th century. Even if they had existed, Crosby traces no succession of immersion through them; and he shows that at a given date the English Baptists, without distinction, "revived the ancient practice of immersion."

ENGLISH BAPTIST REFORMATION.

(FROM 1609 TO 1641 A. D.)

CHAPTER VII.
RESTORATION OF IMMERSION IN ENGLAND.

As Crosby is the only Baptist historian who has undertaken to trace the history of immersion in England and to show the point at which it became "disused," in the year 1600, so he is the only one who details the facts and the methods of its restoration at a later date by the "English Baptists," 1640-41. This section of English Baptist history has already been anticipated; but Crosby makes it so elaborate, plain and important that it needs a special and larger treatment. It has been avoided, or else perverted, by most of our Baptist historians; but since Crosby had the candor to acknowledge and incorporate it in his History of the English Baptists (Vol. I., pp. 95-107)—employing twelve pages for the purpose—it is but the part of the unpartisan and honest reader to give it a candid investigation and a fair place in the annals of our denomination. It has been sought to show that in this section of his history he is merely detailing the movement of a handful of Pedobaptists who, upon the abolition of the High Commission Court of England, got to reading their Bibles, discovered that immersion was Scriptural baptism, adopted it, and thus in a proper sense restored it in 1641; but if there is anything clear in this part of Crosby's history, it is that he details one of the most important and extraordinary movements of Baptist annals. It was, in his own language, a Baptist "beginning," "reformation," in baptism; and he shows us the starting point at which modern, English-speaking, Baptists strictly became such according to the external mark—*immersion*—by which we are distinguished. But for the irrational and unscriptural tradition of "succession"—a Romish dogma which the great body of early English Baptists, from Helwys to Spilsbury, and all the rest, repudiated—we should find no difficulty in understanding and accepting Crosby's account of the restoration of immersion by the English Baptists; and to the end of a right understanding of facts in the case, I humbly dedicate this effort, in the interests of true Baptist history and to the honor of our denomination, which is built upon the word of God, and not upon traditional fictions.

This section in Crosby's history is apparently a digression in which he pauses to meet an objection, chiefly urged by Dr. Wall, that the Baptists had no "proper administrator" of immersion, since it had been disused, and since they had received it as restored by John Smyth, who had baptized himself in Holland (Vol. I., p. 95). In order to meet this objection, and to repudiate the succession of Smyth's baptism to the English Baptists, Crosby shows that the Baptists restored immersion in England, according to the Hutchinson Account, the so-called Kiffin Manuscript and the writings of such men as Spilsbury, Tombes, Lawrence, and others, at a given time, distinct from the time of Smyth and his followers. This date is fixed by the Kiffin Manuscript, which Crosby uses as valid historical testimony, and which sets 1633, 1638, 1639, 1640 and 1641 as the respective periods in which the first Particular Baptist Churches were formed and in which the baptismal restoration movement took place. Crosby does not retain the date 1641 in his, for substance, version of the Kiffin Manuscript, but he does retain all the other dates, including 1640, in his reference to what he calls the Kiffin Manuscript; and he minutely details all the facts which belong to the 1641 date, so that it is unequivocally implied in Crosby's account of the restoration movement. The facts, as he relates them (Vol. I., pp. 96–107), are as follows:

" 'T is certain (p. 96) that when some of the English Protestants ["English Baptists," p. 97] were for reviving the antient practice of immersion, they had several difficulties thrown in their way about a proper administrator, to begin that method of baptizing.

"Those who rejected the baptism of infants, at the beginning of the reformation in England [1535], had the same objection made against them; as Bishop Burnet observes:

" 'One thing,' says he, 'was observed, that the whole world in that age, having been baptized in their infancy, if that baptism was nothing, then there was none truly baptized in being, but were all in a state of nature. Now it did not seem reasonable, that men who were not baptized themselves, should go and baptize others; and therefore the *first heads* of that

Restoration of Immersion in England.

sect, not being rightly baptized themselves, seemed not to act with authority when they went to baptize others.'

"In like manner," says Crosby (p. 97), "did they now argue against reviving the practice of *immersion*, which had for sometime been *disused:* If immersion be the essential form of the ordinance, then there is none truly baptized; and can an unbaptized person be a proper administrator; or can a man be supposed to give that to another, which he has not first received himself?"

This is the Pedobaptist argument which began upon the agitation of the revival of immersion by the Baptists—before, or when they "*were for reviving* the ancient practice"—and the argument in 1640–41 was precisely the same in principle at the beginning of the Puritan Revolution that it was at the beginning of the Episcopal Reformation in 1535. The Anabaptists who adopted believers' baptism, most likely by affusion, in 1535, and rejected infant baptism, according to Bishop Burnet, nullified the baptism of the "whole world," which had been received in infancy, and when the Anabaptists, who had no other baptism themselves, to begin with, introduced believers' baptism without any previous or proper administrator. Just so now in 1640–41, the Pedobaptist argument is the same with reference to the *mode* of baptism. If these Baptists, who had already adopted believers' baptism by affusion which nullified all baptism received in infancy, now adopt immersion as the essential *form* of baptism, then they argue that "there is none truly baptized" as to *mode;* and like their ancient progenitors who had no proper administrator to begin believers' baptism by any mode, so these Baptists had no proper administrator to begin the practice of immersion. This Pedobaptist position is an argument which unanswerably proves that this agitation for the restoration of immersion was a Baptist movement, to begin with, whenever it was.

"This difficulty," continues Crosby, " did not a little *perplex* the English Baptists [p. 97, margin]; and they were divided in their opinion how to act in the matter, so as not to be guilty of any *disorder* or *self-contradiction.* Some indeed were of opinion that the first administrator should baptize himself, and then proceed to baptize others. Others were for sending to those foreign Protestants that *had used immersion for some time*, that so they might receive it from them. And others again thought it necessary to baptism that the administrator be himself baptized, at least in an extraordinary case; but that whoever saw such a *reformation* necessary, might from the *authority of Scripture* lawfully *begin* it."

Nothing is clearer here than that, according to Crosby, this was a *Baptist* movement. None but Baptists, already in the practice of believers' baptism and proposing to change from affusion to immersion, could have been "divided" and "perplexed" so as to avoid "disorder" or "self-contradiction" in the change. They were in a difficulty about a previous or proper administrator; and as they had the true theory of church organization based upon regenerate church membership and believers' baptism, they still wanted to be consistent with Scripture, not only in adopting the right mode of baptism, but in having a proper administrator. All this would never have occurred to Pedobaptists desiring to adopt immersion. The very fact that the division of opinion is expressed by the suggestion of the three modes proposed for the restoration of immersion, shows it to have been a Baptist movement. 1. There was the old self-baptism theory of some of the old Helwys Baptists who never changed from Smyth's idea even when he abandoned it. 2. There was the Puritan idea of regular baptism suggested by some of the Particular Baptists who caught their view from the Puritans. 3. There was the Spilsbury idea of some who took the position that when immersion was lost, some one had a right under the Scriptures to begin it without a baptized administrator —like John the Baptist. There is no possible chance to ascribe this perplexity and division of opinion—characterized by the several shades of well-known Baptist sentiment—to Pedobaptists trying to meet a Pedobaptist argument, which is an absurdity. More than this, a *restoration* of immersion could not be predicated of Pedobaptists, at all, if the Baptists were at the same time practicing immersion all around them.

Crosby continues (p. 97) to say of the first, or self-baptism, method proposed: "I do not find any Englishman among the first restorers of immersion in this latter age accused of baptizing himself, but only the said John Smyth; and there is ground to question that also." On pages 97–99, Crosby proceeds to answer the charges of Ainsworth, Jessop and others that Smyth baptized himself. He did not have Smyth's writings; but he argues from their quotation of Smyth (Character of the Beast, pp. 58, 59) the probability that he did not baptize himself. Unfortunately for so candid a historian as Crosby is, he mutilates and garbles the quotation—that is, if he had it entire—and his argument is wholly fallacious. However, he summarily drops the subject and thus (p. 99) concludes :

> " But enough of this. If he were guilty of what they charge him with 'tis no blemish upon the English Baptists; who neither approved of any such method, *nor did they receive their baptism from him.*"

If this be true they did not receive their immersion from Helwys, Morton or their church, who were baptized by Smyth, and who "joined with him," Crosby says, in that " reformation of baptism," whatever it was, which took place in Holland, 1609. Crosby evidently believed the "tradition" that Smyth was immersed, though not satisfied about his self-baptism; but he emphatically repudiates his baptism as never having succeeded to the " English Baptists." Hence, he could not have believed that immersion from this source was ever brought to England; or if he did he must have believed it was lost in the " some time " which preceded its restoration, which he positively ascribes to the "English Baptists." Otherwise his opinion would be contradictory of his restoration account, which is impossible. The true reason, however, which makes his restoration account consistent with the facts in the case, is that Smyth was affused and never immersed, and this is the baptism which Helwys and his church brought to England.

After summarily dismissing the self-baptism method as never having been adopted by the "English Baptists," whether from Smyth or any one else, and which absolutely precludes the idea of receiving it from Helwys, Morton or any of Smyth's followers, who had never *begun* or *revived* immersion before 1640–41, Crosby proceeds (p. 100) to say :

> " The *two other methods* I mentioned, were *both taken* by the *Baptists*, at their *revival of immersion* in England ; as I find it *acknowledged* and *justified* in their *writings.*"

This settles the question in a single paragraph. It was a " Baptist" movement by " two other methods " than the Smyth method or succession of self-baptism; and it took place in " England," not in Holland. Nor was it a matter of "tradition," but drawn from the writings of English Baptists, who both *acknowledged* and *justified* the movement based upon the "*two methods*" of restoration. It was a well-known movement about which there was, at a given time, a sharp and prolonged controversy; and Crosby gleaned from it his clear and accurate account and handed it down to us from such writers as Hutchinson, Kiffin, Spilsbury, Tombes and Lawrence. It was a movement of "ENGLISH BAPTISTS," as a *body*, without distinction of General or Particular, or of section or locality; and no sort of sophistry or casuistry can here frame an argument which can ascribe such a movement to a handful of Pedobaptists, or characterize it as an insignificant or obscure affair confined to a few. Nor was it just an impulse of liberty, in the year 1641, "when the Baptists came out of their holes to publish their views" which, because unknown before the "Year of Jubilee," were considered "*new!*" This was to some extent true; but the half has never been told. In that year the Baptists made a new departure. They had a new "beginning," instituted a "reformation," in which, "*at their revival of immersion in England*," they created a new era—"acknowledged and justified" by their writers at the time and afterwards. But let us now examine the "two methods" by which the English Baptists wrought this important revolution.

1. *The regular baptism method.* Crosby says (p. 100):

"The former of these [methods] was, to send over to the foreign Anabaptists, who descended from the antient Waldenses in France or Germany that so one or more receiving baptism from them, might become proper administrators of it to others. Some thought this the best way and *acted accordingly*, as appears from Mr. Hutchinson's account in the epistle of his treatise of the Covenant and Baptism."

On pages 100, 101, Crosby quotes this Hutchinson account in full and in confirmation of the restoration of immersion by this first method of sending to Holland for a "proper administrator." Hutchinson says:

"The great objection was, the want of a proper administrator; which, as I have heard, says he, was removed, by sending certain messengers to Holland whence they were supplied."

On pages 101, 102, Crosby cites the 1640–41 section of the so-called Kiffin Manuscript in confirmation of the adoption of this "*former method*" of restoring immersion by the "*Baptists*" of England. "This [Hutchinson's Account] agrees," says he, "with an account given of the matter in an antient manuscript, said to be written by Mr. William Kiffin, who lived in those times, and who was a *leader* among those of *that persuasion*"— that is, perhaps of the regular baptism theory of those who sent to Holland for a "proper administrator" of immersion. This manuscript, as Crosby quotes it, details the facts which led these Baptists seeking regular baptism to the conviction that baptism should be administered by dipping in resemblance of burial and resurrection (Rom. 6:4; Col. 2:12), and to send Richard Blunt to the Netherlands, where he received immersion from John Batte[n] [of the Collegiants and successor to the Brothers Van der Codde, according to Barclay], and who upon his return baptized Samuel Blacklock, a minister, these two in turn baptizing "the rest of the company, whose names are in the manuscript, to the number of fifty-three."

"So," says Crosby, "those who followed this scheme, did not derive their baptism from the aforesaid *Smyth*, or his *congregation* at Amsterdam, it being [from] an antient congregation of foreign Baptists in the Low Countries to whom they sent."

This is another repudiation of the baptism of Smyth and of his "*congregation*," as never having succeeded to the "English Baptists;" and it is an unqualified statement of the fact, according to the authority of Hutchinson and the Jessey Church Records that it was the *first* or "former method" by which the "English Baptists," as such, restored immersion in England— and that, too, in the year 1641, which is the date of the event as recorded in the manuscript from which Crosby substantially but explicitly quotes. This is the *first* or "FORMER METHOD;" but this is only a small part and only the beginning of the movement. Further and bigger,

2. *The Anti-succession Method.* On page 103, Crosby continues to record what he calls the "*last* method of *restoring* true baptism" by the "*greatest number* of the *English Baptists*, and the *more judicious ;*" and which he declares also did not succeed from Smyth. He says: "But the greatest number of the English Baptists, and the more judicious, looked upon all this [the sending of Blunt to Holland for a proper administrator of im-

mersion] as *needless trouble,* and what proceeded from the old Popish Doctrine of right to administer the sacraments by an uninterrupted *succession,* which neither the Church of Rome, nor the Church of England, much less the modern dissenters, could prove to be with them. They [the largest number of the English Baptists, and the more judicious] *affirmed* therefore and *practiced accordingly,* that after a *general corruption* of baptism, an *unbaptized* person might *warrantably* baptize, and so *begin* a *reformation.*" This was the anti-succession or "LAST METHOD" of restoring immersion by the "largest" and "more judicious" of the "English Baptist" body who *"affirmed"* this theory not only in opposition to the Smyth method of self-baptism, but against the Blunt method of succession, as the great body of Baptists considered it, and who *"practiced accordingly"* upon the adoption of their method upon or after the sending of Blunt to Holland.

In confirmation of this "last method" of restoring immersion, Crosby (pp. 103, 104) quotes Spilsbury, who took the position "that where there is a beginning, some one must be first;" and he assumed that "baptizednesse is not essential to the administrator" of baptism thus *begun.* "Now," says Crosby, "it is not possible that this man [whom Wall charged with going to Smyth, in Holland, for baptism] should go over sea to find an administrator of baptism, or receive it from the hands of one who baptized himself." Thus both the "former" and the "last" methods of restoring immersion are made to have no connection with Smyth or his congregation.

On pages 104, 105, Crosby quotes Tombes, also, in confirmation of this "last method" of restoration. He says: "The learned Mr. Tombes does very excellently defend this *last method of restoring true baptism"*—keeping up, in the order of time, the precedence of what they called and stigmatized as the succession method of restoring immersion before that of the anti-succession method which followed upon or after the agitation of the first.

On pages 105, 106, Crosby quotes Lawrence in defense of this "last method," who takes the same position as Spilsbury and Tombes that *"after an universal corruption"* of baptism, and when "no *continuance of adult baptism can be proved,"* as was the case at that time, the ordinance could be restored by an unbaptized administrator, as was "John the Baptist." Crosby speaks of Lawrence as "another learned Baptist, who has excellently defended the *true baptism*, and the manner of *reviving it* in these *later times*.

Crosby concludes his history of the restoration of immersion by the "English Baptists" (pp. 106, 107) as follows:

" 'Tho' these things were *published at different times*, I have put them together, to end the matter at once. It was a point *much disputed* for *some years*. The *Baptists* were not a little uneasy about it at first; and the *Pedobaptists* thought to render all the baptizings among them invalid, for want of a proper administrator to *begin* that practice: But by the excellent reasonings of these and other learned men, we see their [the Baptists'] *beginning* was well defended, *upon the same principles on which all other Protestants built their reformation*."

To the point at issue, this final passage, like all the rest that Crosby says on the subject, speaks for itself; but I wish to draw, in conclusion, the following argument from Crosby's premises, which I think is unanswerable:

1. There was a "general" or "universal corruption" of baptism. "Immersion had for some time been disused." "No continuance of adult baptism could be proved;" and the English Baptists revived immersion at a period called then *"later times."*

2. The "English Baptists," in these "later times," had a *"beginning"* which is called a *"reformation"* established "upon the same principles on which all other Protestants built their reformation"—that is by self-originated introduction—"beginning" in *principle* with John Smyth and ending in *practice* in 1640–41.

3. According to Crosby, the earliest organizations of Baptists in England were respectively 1611, 1633; and he details the restoration of immersion by these "English Baptists," in England, without distinction as a body at a given time, without any division as to date, at a later period.

4. The Baptists of England, according to this first historian, who stands uncontradicted, could not have had any organic continuance before 1611, 1633, in England; and whether organized or unorganized, they could not have had a continuance of immersion from the first century if they had an immersion "beginning," or "reformation," in the "later times" to which Crosby refers. Crosby wholly proves that the Baptists of England have no organic succession before 1611, 1633; and no baptismal (im-

mersion) succession before a "later" date, this side of their organization.

5. The question remains: What is the date within the period of the "later times" when the "English Baptists" restored immersion, or had a baptismal *"beginning,"* or *"reformation,"* as "other Protestants" did and upon the "same principles?" The only answer which can be given, according to the history of the time, is 1640–41. Crosby left out the 1641 date, and hence Ivimey, who follows him, says that the date of this event is uncertain; but the Jessey Church Records, or the Kiffin Manuscript, which is Crosby's authority for the facts of that date, supplies that date beyond all question.

6. Hence, Crosby's Preface, Vol. II., perfectly agrees with this section of Vol. I. (pp. 95–107). In the former he shows that immersion which continued in the "British Churches" only from the 1st to the end of the 16th century and was "disused," even as an infant rite; and in the latter he shows that after its disuse in general for forty-one years—and when "the continuance of adult immersion could not be proved," or was "universally corrupted"—it was restored by the "English Baptists," that is, in 1640–41, prior to which it "had for some time been disused"—so "long disused," according to the Bampfield Document, "that there was no one to be found who had been so baptized."

7. The restoration of immersion in England, 1640–41, was, therefore, a Baptist movement—a Baptist "beginning" or "reformation"—and not a Pedobaptist movement; and the most absurd proposition recently stated is that such a movement could have been properly a restoration of immersion at the hands of Pedobaptists, while the Baptists all around them were practicing immersion!

Ivimey (Vol. I., pp. 139, 140), Hist. English Baptists, says of this movement:

" It must be admitted that there is some obscurity respecting the manner in which the ancient immersion of adults, which appears to have been discontinued, was restored, when, after the long night of anti-Christian apostacy, persons were at first baptized on a profession of faith. The very circumstance, however, of their being called *Anabaptists* as early as the period of the Reformation proves that they did, in the opinion of the Pedobaptists, *re*baptise, which is not likely they would do, by pouring or sprinkling, immersion being incontrovertibly the universal practice of the Church of England at that time."

Ivimey is at sea with reference to the time of this restoration of immersion, which did not take place with the Anabaptists at the beginning of the Reformation of the English Church, 1535, but at the beginning of the Puritan Revolution, 1641. More than this, the very thing he takes to be unlikely is more than likely, namely, that the Anabaptists at the time of the Reformation did pour or sprinkle for baptism; and it is not "incontrovertibly" true that the English Church, even before the close of the Reformation period, universally immersed.

Again Ivimey (p. 144), after giving Crosby's history of the restoration of immersion by the English Baptists, says:

"It may perhaps be thought that this statement is incompatible with the history of the Baptists already given. What occasion, it may be objected, was there to send out of the kingdom a person to be baptized by immersion, if there were at the same time so many persons in it who had been baptized in the same manner? Might not one of them have been the administrator?"

Yes, verily, if any of them had been immersed; but the Jessey Records and the Bampfield Document show that there were none such, and for this very reason Blunt was sent to Holland for the ordinance for the benefit of those who sought regular baptism; whereupon the anti-successionists originated an administrator of their own, and likewise began immersion without sending to Holland for it. Ivimey tries to answer the objection, which he raises for the sake of argument, that at the time Blunt went to Holland it would have been difficult to find an immersed minister by reason of persecution which had driven "almost all the Baptists out of the Kingdom," which is denied by Evans; but then (p. 145) he adopts the probability that if such a minister could have been found by those who sent Blunt to Holland, they would have been so affected by the Popish doctrine of succession that they would not have accepted immersion from such a minister unless he had had it by succession himself—all of which Evans also shows as more than improbable, since the General Baptists who preceded the organization of the first Particular Baptist Church and Blunt's deputation to Holland were affusionists and not immersionists. (Evans, Vol. II., pp. 52, 53, 79.)

Of course, Ivimey did not have these facts before him when he wrote in 1811; nor did he have the original Jessey Church Records before him, as Crosby had, which gave the date of the restoration of immersion as 1640–41. Hence he says: "It is not known at what precise period this happened." (p. 145, Vol. I.)

Dr. Armitage had the identical so-called Kiffin Manuscript before him (1887); but, like all the other Baptist historians who have dealt evasively with the restoration movement of the English Baptists, he regards the attempt to show that *none* of the English Baptists practiced immersion prior to 1641 as "feeble and strained." He cites the testimony of Leonard Busher, 1614, with regard to the definition of baptism as being immersion, and also Dr. Featley's tract, "The Dippers Dipt," as proving that immersion was practiced by some of the Baptists before 1641; but even he concedes that some of them practiced affusion before that date, and that John Smyth's self-baptism was affusion, though he is not certain of the fact. (Hist. Baptists, pp. 439, 440.) The case of Leonard Busher furnishes the only argument that presents a difficulty in the way of the present thesis; but in the light of so much strong testimony which favors the view that the English Anabaptists did not immerse before 1641, it must be conceded that Leonard Busher must have stood alone in his view, and was but a shining star that flashed across the black sky to light up the way to the great movement of Blunt, 1640–41, who came to the same conclusion that Busher did in 1614, twenty-six years before, and who put in practice among his brethren what Busher could not or did not do. There is no other conclusion to which we can come, with the light now shed before us by the great balance of testimony presented by Hutchinson, Kiffin, Spilsbury, Tombes, Lawrence, Barber, Collins, Crosby, Barclay, Muller, Scheffer, Newman, Whitsitt, Vedder, Dexter and others; but of the Kiffin Manuscript or Jessey Records, which are in dispute by some, we shall treat as evidence in the next chapter.

ENGLISH BAPTIST REFORMATION.

(FROM 1609 to 1641 A. D.)

CHAPTER VIII.
THE SO-CALLED KIFFIN MANUSCRIPT.

The Kiffin Manuscript, so-called, is identical with that part of the Jessey Records which include the origin of the Particular Baptist Churches, the restoration of immersion and a list of the signers of the Confession of 1644. In the collection of 1712 it is marked "Number 2;" and it is but part and parcel of the Jessey Church Records from 1604 to 1645. Crosby quotes the 1633, 1638 parts of the Jessey Records and calls it the Kiffin Manuscript; and if the 1633, 1638 parts ascribed by Crosby to the Kiffin Manuscript are the Jessey Records, the 1639, 1640, 1641 parts so ascribed by him are also the Jessey Records, or an abstract from them. Possibly the document, after Kiffin's death, was found by Adams, his colleague, among his papers and so received by Crosby as his manuscript from the collector; but it is evident that Kiffin was not the original author of it by reason of its identity with the Jessey Records.

Upon this document Crosby partly founds his history of the restoration of immersion by the English Baptists, so far as the first or "former method" is concerned. He uses the Hutchinson Account before this manuscript as the basis of his history, but he gets the details out of the document. In fact, Crosby is wholly indebted to the Jessey Church Records for the origin of the first Particular Baptist Church founded in 1633-38; and it is in view of Crosby's use of this document as a whole that I wish to examine it. It has been charged that he used the 1640-41 part indirectly as if to discredit it; but if so, he discredits the whole of it. It has also been charged that the original document as discovered and copied by Rev. Geo. Gould, of London, and recently used by Dr. Whitsitt, is a forgery; that Crosby never saw it, but only saw some such document, the substance of which he gives in history, and hence this particular manuscript is a forgery of "recent date," not more than forty years old.

Now I wish to show that this manuscript, in its original form, ascribed to Kiffin by Gould, who found it among the "Ex. MSS. of Mr. Jessey," was before Crosby when he wrote his History of the Baptists; and I wish to say that if this document is a forgery then all the other documents discovered and copied by Gould are forgeries, since they are all found together. Among them is the Bampfield Document, No. 18, which I have verified by the work of the author; and I am satisfied that I have found confirmation sufficient in the writings of Jessey to identify him as the author of this manuscript, or, at least, cognizant of the facts it records. I shall here give a comparative collation of what are designated as the Jessey Records, the Kiffin Manuscript and Crosby's version for substance of these two documents which are identically the same, with minor exception, under their respective dates.

1633.

1. THE JESSEY RECORDS. "1633. There having been much discussing, these denying Truth of ye Parish Churches & ye Church become now *so large* yt it might be prejudicial, these following desired *dismission* that they might become an Entire Church & further ye Communion of those Churches in Order amongst themselves, wch at last was granted to them* & performed *Sept.* 12, 1633, viz: Henry Parker & Wife, Widd Fearne. . . . Hatmaker, Marke Luker, Mr Wilson Mary Wilson Thos Allen Jo: Milburn. To these joined Rich. Blunt, Thos Hubert, Rich: Tredwell & his wife Kath: John Trimber, Wm Jennings & Sam Eaton, Mary Greenway, Mr Eaton *with some others* receiving a *further baptism.*

"Others joyned to them."

2. THE KIFFIN MANUSCRIPT. "1633. Sundry of ye Church whereof *Mr Jacob* and *Mr John Lathrop* had been pastors, being dissatisfyed with ye Churches owning of English Parishes, to be true Churches desired *dismission* & joyned together among themselves, as Mr Henry Parker, Mr Tho Shepard, Mr. Sam Eaton, Marke Luker, and others, with whom joyned Mr. Wm Kiffin." †

---

*As already shown, this was an Independent secession with a few Anabaptists in its membership. It may be regarded at the time of the secession as a mixed church of Anabaptists and Independents, whatever it afterwards came to be.

†This Record errs in placing Kiffin with the secession of 1633.

3. CROSBY'S VERSION FOR SUBSTANCE. (Vol. I., p. 148.) [1633.] "There was a Congregation of Protestant Dissenters of the Independant Persuasion in London, gathered in the year 1616, whereof *Mr Henry Jacob* was the first pastor; and after him succeeded *Mr John Lathrop*, who was their minister at this time. In this society several persons, finding that the congregation kept not to their first principles of separation, and being also convinced that baptism was not to be administered to infants, but such only as professed faith in Christ, desired that they might be *dismissed* from that communion, and allowed to form a distinct congregation, in such order as was most agreeable to their own sentiment.

The church considering that they were now *grown very numerous*, and so more than could in these times of persecution conveniently meet together, and believing also that these persons acted from a principle of conscience, and not obstinacy, agreed to allow them the liberty they desired, and that they should be constituted a distinct church; which was performed the *12th of Sept.*, 1633. And so they believed that *baptism* was not rightly administered to *infants*, as they looked upon the baptism they had received in that age as invalid: whereupon most or all of them received a *new baptism*.* Their minister was Mr. John Spilsbury.† What number they were is uncertain, because in the numbering of the names of about twenty men and women, it is added *with others*."

1638.

1. THE JESSEY RECORDS. "1638. These also being of the *same judgment* with Sam Eaton and desiring to depart and not be censured, our interest in them was remitted with prayer made in their behalfe June 18th 1638. They having first forsaken us & joyned with *Mr Spilsbury*, viz Mr Peter Ferrer Hen Pen Tho: Wilson Wm Batty Mrs Allen (died 1639) Mrs Norwood.

2. THE KIFFIN MANUSCRIPT. "1638. Mr Thomas Wilson, Mr Pen & 3 more being *convinced that Baptism was not for infants, but professed Believers*, joyned with Mr. *Jo Spilsbury*, ye Churches favor being desired therein."

3. CROSBY'S VERSION FOR SUBSTANCE. (Vol. I., p. 149.) [1638]: "In the year 1638, Mr. William Kiffin,‡ Mr. *Thomas Wilson*, and others, being of the *same judgment*, were upon their request, dismissed to the said *Mr. Spilsbury's* congregation."

---

*The Records of 1633 say: "Mr. Eaton with some others receiving a further baptism."

†The Records of 1633 make no mention of Mr. Spilsbury.

‡Kiffin is not mentioned in the 1638 Records.

1639.

1. THE KIFFIN MANUSCRIPT. "1639. Mr. Green with Captn Spencer had begun a Congregation in Crutched-Fryars, to whom Paul Hobson joyned who was now with many of that Church one of ye Seven."

2. CROSBY'S ALMOST LITERAL VERSION. (Vol. I., p. 149.) [1639.] "In the year 1639, another Congregation of Baptists* was found, whose place of meeting was in Crutched-Fryars; the chief promoters of which were Mr. Green, Mr. Paul Hobson, and Captain Spencer."

1640–1641.

1. THE KIFFIN MANUSCRIPT. "1640. 3rd Mo.: *The Church became two by mutual consent just half being with Mr. P. Barebone, & ye other halfe with Mr. H. Jessey.* Mr. Richard Blunt with him being convinced of Baptism yt also it ought to be by dipping in ye Body into ye Water, resembling Burial & rising again. 2 Col. 2:12. Rom. 6:4 had sober conference about it in ye Church, & then with some of the forenamed who also ware so convinced. And after Prayer & Conferance about their so enjoying it, *none having then so practiced it in England to Professed Believers* & hearing that some in ye Netherlands had so practiced they agreed and sent over Mr. Rich. Blunt (who understood Dutch) with letters of Commendation, and who was kindly accepted there, and returned with letters from them Jo: Batte a Teacher there and from that Church to such as sent him.

"1641. They proceed therein, viz Those Persons that ware persuaded Baptism should be by dipping ye Body had met in two Companies, and did intend so to meet after this, all these agreed to proceed alike togeather And then Manifesting (not by any formal Words a Covenant) wch word was scrupled by some of them, but by mutual desires and agreement each testified:

"Those two Companyss did set apart one to Baptize the rest; so it was solemnly performed by them.

"Mr. Blunt Baptized Mr. Blacklock yt was a Teacher amongst them & Mr. Blunt being baptized, he & Mr. Blacklock Baptized ye rest of their friends that ware so minded, & many being added to them they increased much.

"The names of all 11 Mo. Janu: begin

1. Richard Blunt	Sam Blacklock	Tho. Shephard)
2. Greg Fishburn	Doro. Fishburn	his wife)
3. John Cadwell	Eliz. Cadwell	Mary Millison)

---

* The word "Baptists" is not in the original records and is added by Crosby.

4. Sam Eames	Tho. Munden	
5. Thos. Kilcop	William Willieby	
6. Robert Locker	Mary Lock	
7. John Braunson	John Bull	
8. Rich. Ellis	Mary Langride	
9. Wm Creak	Mary Haman	
10. Robert Carr	Sarah Williams	
11. Martin Mainprise	Joane)	
	)Dunckle	
	Anne)	
12. Henry Woolmare	Eliz. Woolmore	
15. Henry Creak	Judeth Manning	
16. Mark Lukar	Mable Lukar	
17. Henry Darker	Abigal Bowden	
13. Robert King	Sarah Norman	
14. Thomas Waters	Isabel Woolmore	
Ellis Jessop	Mary Kreak	
	Susanna King	
	41 in all	
11th month	11 January 9 added	
understood		
as appears	John Cattope	George Wenham
above: &	Nicholas Martin	Thomas Davenant
this was	Allie Stanford	Rich. Colgrave
Jan 9th	Nath Matthon	Eliz. Hutchinson
	Mary Birch	John Croson
		Sybilla Lees
		John Woolmore
	Thus 53 in all	

2. CROSBY'S VERSION FOR SUBSTANCE, INCLUDING LITERAL QUOTATIONS. [1640] (Vol. III., p. 41.) *"For in the year* 1640 *this church became two* by *mutual consent; just half, says the manuscript, being with Mr. P. Barebone,* and *the other half with Mr. Henry Jessey."* "This" [manuscript], says Crosby (Vol. I., p. 101), " relates, that several sober and pious persons belonging to the congregations of the dissenters about London were *convinced* that believers were the only proper subjects of baptism, and that it *ought to be administered by immersion,* or dipping the whole body in *water, in remembrance of a burial and resurrection,* according to 2 *Colos. ii.*'12 and

Rom. vi.:4. That they often *met together to pray and confer* about this matter, and *consult* what methods they should take to *enjoy* this ordinance in its primitive purity: *That they could not be satisfied about any administrator in England to begin this practice; because tho' some in this nation rejected the baptism of infants, yet they had not as they knew of* REVIVED *the ancient custom of immersion:* But hearing that some in the *Netherlands* practiced it, they *agreed* to send over one *Mr. Richard Blount*, who *understood the Dutch Language:* That he went accordingly, carrying *letters of recommendation* with him, and was *kindly received* by the church there, and Mr. *John Batte*, their *teacher:* That upon his return he baptized *Mr. Samuel Blacklock*, a minister, and *these two baptized the rest of their company*, whose names appear in the manuscript, to the number of *fifty-three.*"

The italics mark the almost literal quotations of Crosby from the original Kiffin Manuscript, showing that the document was then and there in existence as we now have it.

Now it is clear that the original MS., as ascribed to Jessey (1633, 1638), and that ascribed to Kiffin (1633, 1638, 1639, 1640, 1641), were before Crosby when he wrote his history. He took his account of the origin of the first Particular Baptist Church and the restoration of immersion directly from these documents, as a comparison of his account with these original records will show.

1. As a rule Crosby took the liberty to quote substantially, and, as he saw fit, to make corrections (which were mostly blunders) by addition, substraction, or explication. He used the Jessey Records and the Kiffin Manuscript as the same document in his version of the secession of 1633; and in his marginal note (Vol. I., p. 149) he refers the Kiffin MS. to the "Records of that church," which were doubtless the Jessey MSS. On page 41 (Vol. III.) he brackets the exact words of the Kiffin MS. (1633), "[with whom joined Mr. William Kiffin]" as if to correct the mistake, since Kiffin never joined the 1633 secession, nor any church at that time; and Crosby himself, by mistake, puts Kiffin with Spilsbury in 1638, contrary to the later accounts of Ivimey and Orme, who place him with Jessey at that date. In the 1639 account Crosby follows the Kiffin MS. almost literally, except in adding the word "Baptist," which was another blunder. In the 1640–41 section of the Kiffin MS., so-called, Crosby combines the separate accounts of the two dates, which almost literally correspond with the document. He omits the date, 1641, but incorporates the date 1640; and most of his

THE SO-CALLED KIFFIN MANUSCRIPT. 97

transcript, after the 1640 quotation, is a somewhat literal detail of the precise facts as related in the MS. There is absolutely no essential difference between Crosby's indirect and the direct statement of the document as to the matters of fact in the whole section included under the 1640 and 1641 dates.

2. But the fact that the original documents, as we now have them, were in Crosby's hands is more manifest by the literal and direct quotations of sentences, phrases and words found in his transcript. In Vol. III., p. 41, he quotes the very words from the original manuscript: "For in the year 1640, this Church became two by mutual consent; just half, says the *manuscript*, being with Mr. P. Barebone, and the other half with Mr. Henry Jessey"; and on the same page (41) he quotes verbatim the bracketed clause, 1633 "[with whom joined William Kiffin]," referring the clause to the "*same* manuscript." Over on page 42 (Vol. III.) Crosby continues to refer to this "*same* manuscript" as including the 1638 and 1639 paragraphs, as in Vol. I., p. 149, written by William Kiffin; and this identifies the 1633, 1638, 1639, 1640, 1641 paragraphs of the original MS., ascribed to Kiffin, as all belonging to one and the same manuscript, according to Vol. III., pp. 41, 42.

In the remainder of the 1640–41 paragraphs of this MS. cited (Vol. I., pp. 102, 103) Crosby closely follows Blunt's *conviction* with others ("several sober and pious persons") that baptism ought to be by dipping, according to Rom. 6:4; Col. 2:12. He mentions their frequent prayer and conference about how they should "*enjoy*" the ordinance in its primitive purity. He paraphrases the main sentence: "*none having then so practiced it in England to professed believers*," so as to read: "they could not be satisfied about any administrator in England to *begin* this practice;" and he gives a reason which makes his paraphrase stronger than the original sentence: "Because tho' some [Anabaptists] in this nation rejected the baptism of infants, yet they had not as they knew of, *revived* the antient custom of immersion," which, he says, "had for sometime been *disused*." He then details the sending of Richard Blunt to the Netherlands, because he understood Dutch and because some in the Netherlands had *for some time* used immersion; and he particularizes his letters of introduction, his kind reception by John Batte and the church, Blunt's return, his baptism of Samuel Blacklock, a minister [teacher], and closes with the fact that Blunt and Blacklock baptized the "rest of the company" to the number of "fifty-three," whose names were "in the manuscript," just as we now have them, showing that he quoted directly from the document; and the strange part of it is that he did not put down the date, "11 Mo. Janu., 1641," for it was before his eyes! What a blunder! Crosby's use here of the 1640 and the 1641 paragraphs of the MS. is identified by his literal quotation of the first sentence of the 1640 paragraph (Vol. III., p. 41); and this identification with the other identification of the 1640 paragraph with the 1633, 1638 and 1639 paragraphs as belonging to the "same manuscript" (Vol. III., pp. 41, 42), shows that the 1641 paragraph is simply a part of the original document as a whole and as one and the same MS. (1633, 1638, 1639, 1640, 1641), though mentioned by Crosby in separate sections and in different volumes.

Crosby leaves out nothing material to the 1641 paragraph except the date, 1641; but since he elsewhere uses the 1640 date, at which the Blunt movement began and which was consummated upon his return, the omission of 1641 is not essential because he minutely details all the facts which follow 1640 and identify 1641. He is given to the neglect of dates in many details of his history; but here, fortunately, his detail of facts according to the order of the MS. establishes the date, 1641, at which, by the first method, the Baptists of England restored immersion. If Crosby omitted the date, 1641, he did not omit the facts of 1641; and if the facts of this paragraph of the MS. are valid history as he uses it, then the date 1641 is a valid fact in history—confirmed by Hutchinson and by the larger body of Baptists who at the same time Crosby says regarded Blunt's deputation to Holland as "needless trouble." The Bampfield Document is another confirmation of the same fact, the caption of which reads thus: "An Account of ye methods taken by ye Baptists to obtain a proper Administration of Baptism by Immersion when that practice had been so long disused, yt there was no one who had so been baptized to be found." How strikingly does the main sentence of the Kiffin MS., "None having then so practiced it in England to professed believers," correspond with the like declaration of the Bampfield Document!

The expression: "Said to be written by William Kiffin" (Crosby, I., p. 101,) does not indicate Crosby's discredit of the authenticity whatever he may have thought of the authorship of the MS. He uses this part of it as valid history confirmed by Hutchinson and others, just as he so regards elsewhere the other parts of the document; and in Vol. I., p. 148, where he quotes the 1633, 1638, 1639 parts he speaks of the citation as an "account collected from a manuscript of Mr. William Kiffin," just as here he speaks of this (1640–41) paragraph as "an account given of the matter in an ancient manuscript said to be written by Mr. William Kiffin." The manuscript referred to is the "same"; and so he calls it the "same manuscript" in his literal references to the 1633 and 1640 paragraphs (Vol. III., p. 41) and to the 1638 and 1639 paragraphs on page 42 of the same volume. He means the same when he speaks of the "manuscript of William Kiffin," that he does when he speaks of the "ancient manuscript said to be written by William Kiffin." When he cites any of the paragraphs, he represents them as found in this *same* manuscript"; and he does not cite the 1640–41 section as a manuscript by itself—"another manuscript said to be written by William Kiffin"—but as found in the *same* "ancient manuscript," elsewhere identified as such. Discredit one part and you discredit the whole MS.

It is objected that Crosby quotes the 1640–41 paragraphs without quotation points—indirectly—and therefore implies his doubt or caution as to its validity; but he frequently so quotes authentic documents, as in Vol. IV., pp. 169, 178, 181, 188, 197, 254, and in forty other places. He cites this section as fully and accurately as he does any other part of the MS., and emphasizes and confirms it as history. More than this, he signalizes its authenticity by the fact that Kiffin, " said to be " its author, "lived in those times [1640–41] and was a leader among those of that persuasion;" and he thus identifies Kiffin, the alleged author of the document, both with the date and the movement of the MS. He specifies that whether Kiffin was the author of it or not, he was connected with its movement and times; and Crosby shows that he has not the slightest doubt of its historical validity. He makes not a single qualification of its authenticity and confirms it by contemporaneous authority. The 1641 date of the manuscript is thoroughly confirmed by Barebone, in 1643, who dates Baptist dipping back " two or three yeares " to its beginning in England. The same is true of Edwards, who in 1646 includes among many other heresies Baptist " dipping " as having originated in England within the " four years past." So of Watts, in 1656, who dates the beginning of Baptist dippers in England " about 13 or 14 yeare agoe."

Ivimey, Evans and Gould agree with Crosby in the trustworthiness of this manuscript. Dexter is cited as "giving up the manuscript," but this is untrue. He suggests that its genuineness might be open to question and suspicious for its vagueness but for Kiffin's connection with it, and for the reason that Wilson, Calamy, Brook and Neal know nothing of Blunt and Blacklock outside of the MS.; but he cites Edwards as discovering one Blount (1646) at the head of a prominent Anabaptist Church, refers to Barclay (Inner Life, p. 75) as having discovered John Batten, who probably administered immersion to Blunt, and regards Hutchinson as confirming Blunt's deputation to Holland for a "proper administrator" of baptism. Prof. Rauschenbusch, in a book entitled Geschiedenis der Rhynsburgische Vergardering, also discovers *Jan Batte*, who was from the beginning a prominent teacher in the Rhynsburger Congregation, and he has no doubt of his having baptized Blunt. (17th ch. Hist. Baptists, Baptist.) Hutchinson's account has been denied as showing that the deputation to Holland involved the revival of dipping; but Crosby uses Hutchinson in confirmation of the MS. for that very purpose; and Hutchinson himself in his Treatise, pp. 2-4, Epistle to the Reader, begins the paragraph quoted by Crosby, thus: "Besides it [persecution] has a considerable tendency to advancement of divine grace, if we consider the *way* and *manner* of *Reviving* this costly truth"—that is, *baptism* for the "proper administrator" of which by immersion Blunt, 1640, was deputed to Holland. The "reviving" of this ordinance is the very thing about which, in this paragraph, Hutchinson was writing.

Another strong confirmation of this Manuscript and its date, by contemporaneous authority, is by John Taylor (A Swarme of Sectaries, &c., 1641, London), who connects Spilsbury and Eaton with the "new found Separation"—who represents Spilsbury, "of late," as rising up to "rebaptize" Eaton in "Anabaptist fashion"—and who pictures Eaton as baptizing an "impure dame" at the bankside of some stream. This was in 1641; and it is distinctly stated in the Manuscript that Eaton was in the 1633 Secession from the Lathrop Church and clearly implied that he was with Spilsbury in 1638. In 1633 "Eaton with some others received a further baptism," that is, Anabaptist aspersion; but now "of late," in 1641, he is rebaptized again by Spilsbury in "Anabaptist fashion," which was now immersion, and which

Eaton proceeded immediately to practice upon an "impure dame." This record also confirms Crosby's account of restoring immersion by the "last method," that is, by an unbaptized administrator which Spilsbury advocated and which he here introduced in 1641—at the same time that the "first method" by Blunt was introduced, by regular administration from Holland. These facts are perfectly consistent with and thoroughly confirmatory of the account given in the so-called Kiffin Manuscript, or the Jessey Records.

A final confirmation of the Kiffin Manuscript or Jessey Records is found in the life and writings of Henry Jessey himself. In a work entitled, The Life and Death of Mr. Henry Jessey, London, 1671, written by E. W., I find on page 9 the following with regard to the division of the Jessey Church, 1640:

"Upon the 18th day of the third Month called May, 1640, they divided themselves equally, and became two Congregations, the one whereof continued with Mr. *Jessey*, the other joyned themselves to Mr. *Praise God Barebone*, each of the churches renewing their Covenant and choosing distinct officers of their own from among themselves."

On page 83 the author says:

"In 1644. He held several debates with the Leaders of Several Congregations, Concerning Pedo Baptisme, for he questioned whether it could Be proved from Scripture that any others had right to that Ordinance of the Sacrament, but such as can give account of their Faith in Christ, and their answers not seeming to him Satisfactory; He was (about *Midsummer*) the year [1645] following baptized by Mr. Knowles, though his own Congregation at that time was most of them for Infant Baptisme."

This part of Jessey's history is substantially found in the so-called Kiffin Manuscript, or Jessey Church Records. The author does not mention the Blunt movement found in the same connection; but as he was writing simply the life of Jessey, who did not join with Blunt in his movement, except in conviction and council, only that part of the history which immediately related to Jessey and Barebone is recorded.

In Jessey's own book (A Storehouse of Provision, &c., London, 1650), on page 15, where he is discussing baptism as a lost ordinance and the right to restore it, according to the Scriptures, he says: "Say not in thine heart, Who shall goe into Heaven, or to sea, or beyond the Sea for it? but the word is nigh thee (Rom. 10). So we need not goe for administrators to other Countries, nor stay [wait] for them: but looke to the word." On page 80, speaking of some believers who had been "slack," and some who had "longed" to "enjoy" the ordinance after its introduction, he says: "Such Considerations as these I have had, But yet, because I would do nothing *rashly*; I would not do that which I should renounce againe. I desired Conference with some Christians differing therein in opinion from me; about what is requisite to the restoring of ordinances, if lost; Especially what is Essentiall in a Baptizer? Thus I did forbeare and inquired above a yeares space."

Now in all this it seems clear that Jessey alludes to the Blunt idea of "going beyond the sea"—"to other countries"—for a "proper administrator" of baptism, which Jessey regarded as "needless." His difficulty was with the method of "restoring" immersion as involved in the essential qualifications of a "Baptizer," or "proper administrator"; and though convinced, after the agitation of 1640-41, that immersion was Scriptural, he delayed baptism for several years—finally accepting the Spilsbury theory of restoring the ordinance instead of the Blunt theory of going "over sea" for it. All this is in accord with the Kiffin Manuscript or Jessey Records and the history of the case; and some of Jessey's expressions—such as the ordinance being "lost" and going "beyond the sea" for "administrators"—those who longed to "enjoy" the ordinance and did not "tarry" for it as he did—what is "requisite to the restoring" of the ordinance, "especially what is essential in a Baptizer," or "proper administrator" —corresponds with the substance of the Manuscript and to some extent its phraseology. His delay "above a yeares space," that is, from 1644 to 1645, after "Conference" with some who differed from him about the burning question of Pedo-baptism, and his subsequent immersion in 1645, is distinctly referred to in "No. 4," of the Jessey Records, which mention the "Conferences" in the Jessey church "about infant baptism by which Mr. Jessey and the greatest part of the Congregation were proselyted to the opinion of the Antipedobaptists." So does the history of Jessey, by E. W., involve this same event and confirm this No. 4 section of the Jessey Records as stated in the caption of the Collector, as he also confirms the 1640 division of the church between

Jessey and Barebone. Now, if Jessey himself and his biographer confirm the No. 4 section of the Jessey Records in their detail of the substance of the so-called Kiffin Manuscript—and partly in the use of its phraseology—they also confirm the document itself. Jessey unquestionably confirms the thesis of restoring immersion, about 1640-41, by both methods, as detailed by Crosby; and this for ever silences the charge that the Kiffin Manuscript or the Jessey Records are a forgery. Jessey was one of the chief actors in the drama of 1640–1645.

For a full account of "Document No. 4," as found in the Jessey Church Records, I refer the reader to Crosby (Vol. I., pp. 310, 311). He thoroughly confirms, as far as Jessey is concerned, both the Kiffin document, "No. 2," and the document "No. 4." In the Kiffin Document Blunt is represented as being "convinced with him," that is with Jessey last named in the connection of the sentence in which the fact is mentioned, that "baptism ought to be by dipping," according to Col. 3:12 and Rom. 6:4; and Crosby shows that by repeated secessions from Jessey's Church to the Baptists, especially the large secession in 1641, Jessey was led to investigate the subject and became convinced that immersion was baptism. In 1642 Jessey proclaimed not only his conviction, but that "for the future" he would practice immersion; and so from that time on he dipped the children. Crosby then refers to the Conferences of 1644 in which infant baptism became the question in controversy—already begun in the church in 1643—and to the fact that when Jessey was convinced that Pedobaptism was wrong he concluded he ought himself to be immersed and was dipped in June, 1645, by Hanserd Knollys, who, with his wife, had been so convinced and baptized a year before, when, after the controversy about baptizing his own child had resulted in another secession from the Jessey Church, he and his wife withdrew, according to the No. 4 document. Here this document is thoroughly confirmed by Crosby, who clearly uses it, names and all, so far as Jessey is concerned. See Appendix: Document No. 4.

ENGLISH BAPTIST REFORMATION.
(FROM 1609 TO 1641, A. D.)

CHAPTER IX.
OBJECTIONS TO THE KIFFIN MANUSCRIPT.

Every effort has been made to discredit this document. It has been assailed as an "anonymous paper," a "flying leaf," without "a place of deposit" and without "attestation"—as ambiguous and contradictory—and yet those who have made this criticism have sought to use the document, at the same time, as evidence favoring another thesis. The most violent opposers of the 1641 thesis seeing that this criticism could not stand, have adopted the theory of "forgery;" and the world of literature has been ransacked in search of proof to establish this theory. I think I have, beyond the shadow of a doubt, established the authenticity and validity of this document, in the light of history, but I will here notice some of the objections made to prove it a "forgery" or a "fraud."

John Lewis, 1738 and onward, is represented as repudiating the Kiffin Manuscript and ridiculing Crosby for using it; but beyond his hypothetical conjectures and unsustained assertions, he gives no contemporary or other data by which to invalidate the credibility of the document. Baptist history preceding and following 1640–41, according to contemporary authorities, thoroughly confirm the manuscript.

Armitage, Cathcart, Burrage, Newman and others have been quoted as casting a shadow upon the genuineness and value of this manuscript. Armitage simply says that the "authorship of the document is only guessed at;" Cathcart says that "this transaction of Blunt *may* have happened" but that he would not "bear heavily upon it;" Burrage says that the "testimony of the Jessey Records may be genuine, but the genuineness has not been established;" Newman speaks of the obscurity of some of the statements of the Kiffin Manuscript (in his History of the Baptist Churches of the United States); but not one of these

Objections to the Kiffin Manuscript. 105

authors denies the genuineness of these documents, much less do they call them a "forgery." More recently, Dr. Newman, after a thorough examination of these documents, says of the Jessey Records: "The document in my opinion, bears every mark of genuineness." (Review of the Question, p. 186.) Including the Kiffin MS., he says again:

"These documents are all thoroughly consistent with each other and with what is otherwise known of the history of the time in general and of the Congregational and Baptist history in particular." [Ibid, p. 194.]

He says again:

"The value of these documents is in no way dependent on the correctness of the supposition that they were written by Henry Jessey and William Kiffin, respectively. . . . . . Some of Crosby's quotations are not found in either of these documents in precisely the form in which he has given them. This may be due to the fact that he dealt freely with these documents, extracting and abstracting as suited his purpose; or he may have had before him a different recension of the same materials." (Ibid, 196.)

Dr. Newman is a most thorough and competent investigator; and no doubt the other authorities cited would be of the same opinion with the same investigation.

It is objected that the Kiffin MS. is a forgery, since Kiffin to whom the manuscript is ascribed is found among the signers of the 1644 Confession, while Blunt and Blacklock, the leading characters in the document, do not appear in the list. True, but the manuscript is well authenticated by a list of the 53 persons baptized by Blunt and Blacklock, from among whom are Shepard [Skipard], Munden and Kilcop, who are in that group of signers; and for aught we know Kiffin, who became a Baptist in 1641, "who lived in those times and was a leader among those of that persuasion," was later in the year baptized by Blunt or Blacklock. Mark Lucar was a prominent name not found among the signers, yet in the list of 53 found in the MS.; but this does not argue that the document was a forgery. It is most likely that Blunt's church went to pieces before 1644, and that may have been the reason why his name was not affixed to the confession. In this connection it is boasted that Drs. Angus, Clifford and other recent English Baptist historians do not mention the names of Blunt and Blacklock; but they have done a thing far more incredible in giving credence to the Epworth-Crowle fraud, and in trying to build Baptist history upon traditions and fictions which have no historical foundation. Dr. Clifford (The English Baptists, p. 19), however, refers to the Kiffin account of the origin of the first Particular Baptist Church, which can be taken only from the so-called Kiffin MS.; and if he can take one section of the document, he can take the whole.

It is objected again that in 1640 the Jessey Church was not an "ancient congregation;" that at that date "many of ye Independent & Baptist Churches" had not "taken their rise" from it; that the title "Baptist Churches" was not then in use; that the word "antipedobaptism" was a later usage, &c.: therefore the Jessey Records are a forgery! As well shown by Dr. Newman, the Collector of 1710–12, and not the manuscript writer, was responsible for the title and heading of these Records, and therefore the objection falls to the ground.

It has been objected also that "there is nothing in the Kiffin MS. to prove that there were not other Baptists in England who had nothing to do with this transaction; and Crosby (Vol. I., p. 103) is cited in proof of the fact that there were such Baptists, as follows:

"But the greatest number of the English Baptists looked upon all this as needless trouble [sending Blunt to Holland], and what proceeded from the old Popish Doctrine of right to administer the sacrament by an uninterrupted succession, &c."

The objector, however, did not explain that this "largest number of Baptists," according to Crosby, were only objecting to the succession "method" of Blunt in restoring immersion, at that very time, and the objector failed to continue Crosby's quotation as follows:

"They [this largest number of Baptists] *affirmed* therefore, and practiced *accordingly*, that after a *general corruption* of baptism, an unbaptized person might warrantably baptize and so *begin* a reformation."

Crosby calls the Blunt "method" of restoring immersion the *"former"* and the Spilsbury, or anti-succession, method adopted by "the greatest number of the English Baptists," the *"last* method;" and so the whole quotation when put together is a complete confirmation of the manuscript in citing a contemporaneous and connected event which followed the Blunt movement and which objected to it in express terms.

It has been urged that the voice of Kiffin himself is against the so-called Kiffin Manuscript and the interpretation maintained by this thesis. In 1645, among other queries, Poole propounded the following to Kiffin:

"By what Scripture warrant doe you take upon you to erect new framed Congregations, separated to the disturbance of the great Worke of Reformation *now in hand*."

Kiffin (Briefe Remonstrance, p. 6, 1645, London,) replies:

"It is well known to many and especially to ourselves, that our congregations as they now are, were erected and framed, according to the rule of Christ, before we heard of any Reformation, even at the time when Episcopacie was at the height of its vanishing glory."

The allusion here is to the Westminster Movement from 1643 to 1649, which was (1645) *"now in hand"* as a Presbyterial reformation of the English Church; and this is shown by Kiffin's retort upon Poole (p. 7) in which he says:

"You tell us of a great Worke of Reformation, wee should entreat you to show us wherein the greatnesse of it doth consist, for as yet we see no greatnesse, unless it be in the vast expense [by the Assembly] of Money and Time: for what greate thing is it to change *Episcopacie* into *Presbytery*, and a Book of *Common Prayer* into a Directory, &c."

Without any controversy here as to the *mode* of baptism, Kiffin simply affirms the organization of Baptist Churches, based upon the principles of independency and believers' baptism, according to the rule of Christ, before this Presbyterian Movement began; and he fixes the date particularly: "even at the time when Episcopacie was at the height of its *vanishing* glory," that is, at the time "of ye revival of Antipedobaptism towards ye latter end of ye Reign of King Charles ye First," as the Collector of the Jessey and other Records put it in his caption of the "Hutchinson account." This, according to Kiffin, puts the beginning of Baptist churches in the neighborhood of 1641; and although Josiah Ricraft, in reply to Kiffin (A Looking Glasse For Anabaptists, &c., pp. 6-8, 1645, London) doubtfully grants for the sake of argument that Kiffin's own church, *possibly*, may have been erected before he heard of this Reformation, it does not imply that his church was organized before 1641. Kiffin, as I shall show, became a Baptist in 1641; and it is also clearly probable that he never was pastor of a church before 1643. For a further discussion of the subject and for a complete refutation of the objection that Kiffin's own writings in any way militate against his so-called manuscript, I refer the reader to my Chapter X., entitled William Kiffin.

The criticism which makes the "collector" of 1710-12 the "forger" of the Jessey Records or the Kiffin Manuscript on account of his "spelling," or on account of the more modern phraseology of his "captions," or on account of the errors in the minor details of the documents, is extremely absurd. The collector affirms that these Records, including the Kiffin Manuscript, were received by him from Richard Adams, the colleague and survivor of William Kiffin; and while he says of his whole collection that some of his documents were "original papers," others were "faithful extracts." The transcript of the Jessey Records which he received from Richard Adams is called the "Ex-MSS. of Mr. Henry Jessey," and was evidently not the original or exact draught of church minutes; and it is possible that they had passed through more than one recension from the original. So far as the spelling was concerned, this was common to some manuscript writings down through the 17th century; and so far as the copying of the "collector" goes, as of the Hutchinson Account and the Bampfield Document—if he was the copyist—he is exceedingly "faithful" in his "extracts," with the simple difference in the spelling. His more modern phraseology in the caption and reference to Strypes Memorials (of Cranmer) properly belonged to 1710. His use of the word "antient" (1710) with reference to the Jacob Church (1616) is in keeping with Crosby and other writers of the time who speak of the early churches of the 17th century as "antient;" and his application of the name "Baptist" to the Anabaptist Churches prior to 1641 is in keeping with Crosby, Evans, Robinson and others. It is a vicious perversion to charge the collector with saying that "all the Baptist churches in London," or "the first Baptist churches in England," took their rise from the Jacob church. The caption of the Records only speaks of *"many* of ye Independent & Baptist Churches *in London"* which "took their *first* rise" from this "Antient Congregation of Dissenters"—all of which is true of the Spilsbury, Hobson, Jessey and other Particular Baptist Churches springing out of these. So of the Congregational Churches. This document does not include the General Baptist churches already existent in London and other parts of England since 1611. The statement that the Baptists, "intermixed" with the Independents, separated, 1633, and formed churches of their own, is not the statement of the Records or the Collector, but of Crosby; and there is no evidence of conflict between these Independents and Baptists, at that time, sharing, as they did, a common persecution at the hands of the Established Church.

The charge of forgery upon the collector of these Records, because of minor errors in giving the titles and dates of two of Jacob's books; in the time of his pastorate and the date of his visit to Virginia; in the fact of his return to England and death in London; in the interval between Jacob's and Lathrop's pastorates; in the arrests, trials and imprisonment of the members of the church in 1632, involving a few mistakes regarding individuals, names and places—all this is straining out a gnat and swallowing a camel in capricious and exaggerated criticism. The Jessey Church Records embrace the history of Jacob from 1604 to 1624 and of the church from 1616 to 1645; and they chronicle the main facts, from beginning to end, which no historian disputes. History has followed these Records, not the Records history; and there is no ground for the calumnious charge of forgery upon the collector who gives or copies them just as he received them from Adams. Even in the section criticized the Records give the same general facts as cited by the court and other records. Only a fact not material to the history of the church, is left out or misconceived: Jacob's death in London instead of Virginia, 1622 instead of 1624, an error, if true, of the Oxford historian, of Neal and others, all of whom, before and since the collector, must therefore be forgers! The slighter errors about a couple of names, individuals, or places of imprisonment, in no way affect the general fact of the arrest, trial and imprisonment of the members of the church in 1632; and yet the whole thing is a forgery, and the collector, without any conceivable reason, or assignable motive, is pronounced a forger! According to the critic, he was too ignorant and stupid to be a forger—and yet he was shrewdly appropriating history to his purpose! It does seem that a forger would get the substantial facts wrong and the minor details right—not *vice versa*.

The criticism that the 1633 secession from the Jacob Lathrop Church could not have occurred in that year, since all those named in the secession were in jail from 1632 to 1634, is without proof. Only about 30 of the church seem to have been arrested on this occasion in 1632, or remained in jail, and some of their fellow-sufferers were converted in prison and "added to the church" during that time. The secession of some 20 members from the church, 1633, were not necessarily in jail; and if some of them were they could have been "added to the church." This was as true of Sam Eaton as others if he was in jail from 1632 to 1634. It is alleged that he was again in jail from 1636 to 1639 and died in the latter year; and it is charged that the Jessey Church Records make him join Spilsbury and receive "another baptism" in 1638. This is false, since the Records show that another small secession from the Lathrop Church, in 1638, "*being of the same opinion with Sam Eaton*," joined Spilsbury, then pastor of the 1633 secession, to which Eaton, already rebaptized in 1633, belonged. If Eaton died in 1639 then there is a contradiction between the court records and John Taylor, who in 1641 represents Spilsbury as "of late" rising up to rebaptize Eaton by immersion and Eaton himself practicing the same ordinance. This could not have been the rebaptism of 1633, when, with some others, he received "another baptism"—especially if he was in jail; nor could he at that time and under such conditions have been so practicing. Spilsbury was not in the 1633 secession; and if he had been he could not have, in those days, immersed Eaton or others in an English jail. It was not then the "Anabaptist fashion"—even if it had been facilitated or allowed in jail. In view of Taylor's historical testimony in 1641, there must be some mistake about Eaton's death in 1639. He speaks of a "late" matter, and could not have been satirizing a dead man whom he joins with Spilsbury in terms which indicate a very recent event and which classify both as belonging to the "*new-found separation*," that is, Baptist separation.

Evidently Taylor and the Jessey Church Records agree in associating Eaton with Spilsbury and both with the Baptist movement of 1641; and if Taylor was not guilty of mistaken identity Eaton was alive at that time. In the frequent arrests of so many "heretiques" and in their trials and imprisonment it is just possible that the court records were careless and sometimes mistaken about names; and it seems quite possible, too, that John Taylor, a bitter enemy of the "sectaries," should be right in his confirmation of the Jessey Church Records by his relation and classification of Spilsbury and Eaton in the immersion movement of 1641. Grant, however, that Eaton died in 1639 and that Spilsbury neither immersed him, nor that he immersed others. Then it is a case of mistaken identity as to Eaton, or else Taylor falsifies the facts. We have no reason to suppose Taylor false in fact; and we must conclude that in 1641 Spilsbury, of the "new-found separation," rose up "of late" and rebaptized somebody by immersion and set him to baptizing others—whom Taylor confounds with Eaton. Whether false in fact or mistaken in person Taylor properly designates the "new-found separation" and indicates the Baptist immersion movement, 1641, in perfect accord with the Jessey Church Records—Spilsbury, at least, being a prominent and initial factor in that movement according to the history of the time.

The court records wholly separate Eaton from the Anabaptist movement from 1633 to 1641 and associate him with the Lathrop people down to the day of his alleged death. The Jessey Church Records are charged with an utter perversion of his history in relating him to the secession of 1633 or to Spilsbury in 1638. This is the criticism offered in view of this supposed fact, according to which he could not have been an Anabaptist receiving "another baptism," nor have had any connection with the Anabaptist movement whatever; but the joint testimony of Taylor with the Jessey Church Records shows that there must be a mistake in such a conclusion. Even, however, if we leave Eaton wholly out of the case, it in no way affects the general and substantial record of facts contained in the Jessey documents. Crosby does not find it necessary to use Eaton in his account.

The objection that the secession of 1633 was not caused by "dissatisfaction" with the "Parish Churches" is based upon ignorance of the facts. In the Confession of the Jacob Church, 1616 (Hanbury's Memorials, Vol. I., p. 297), the church never declined, in some particulars, to withdraw fully from the "Parish Churches." They still recognized "the truth of the Parish Churches" in preaching and communion; and this led some of them to have their children baptized in the "Parish Churches," which was regarded by others as not keeping their "first estate."

The Covenant of 1630 was a compromise measure which still did not satisfy some who objected to the "truth of the Parish Churches;" and on this account they withdrew, 1633, that they might have communion with those Independent churches which were "in order" and did not "communicate" with the "Parish Churches." A part of this 1633 secession were Anabaptists, which seems finally to have led it to Baptist position, or at least into mixed church membership and communion, under Spilsbury, who was pastor in 1638. The fact of this "dissatisfaction" with the "Parish Churches," as a cause of separation in 1633, is the basis of Particular Baptist Church "beginning" in England; and no fact established by the Jessey Church Records is a better confirmation of their truthfulness.

The objection that these Records are a "forgery" because of the use of the apostrophic "'s" is so microscopically absurd that it scarcely needs to be noticed. Williston Walker's work (Creeds and Platforms of Congregationalism, pp. 90, 155, &c., New York, 1893) gives instances of its use from 1617 to 1647.

It has never been denied that some minor errors have crept into these Records; but the history of the time shows that the main facts are correctly stated. There can be no doubt about the 1633, 1638, 1639 secessions; the 1640 division of Jessey's Church; the 1640-41 movement for immersion; the 1643 and 1644 "Conferences;" the 1644 list of signers to the Confession; the final transition of the Jessey Church to the Baptists in 1645. These Records are not all exact minutes of the church as kept by a regular secretary, but they are made up of fragments and recollections by Jessey and others as gathered in after years—so indicated by reference to past and present events at the time of writing down the facts in the Records. The minor discrepancies between these and other records regarding dates may often arise from the difference between the Puritans and others in the chronologies and calendars of that period—Old Style and New Style. Errors in exact dates, names and places may be accounted for upon the ground that every minor fact was not regularly or accurately chronicled, or not precisely recalled by those in after years who sought to gather up the facts of Baptist history which before the close of the 17th century became a matter of interest to the Baptists. Again errors in detail may be accounted for by transcription and transmission. The collector of 1710-12 gave us these Jessey Church Records from 1604 to 1645 just as he received or copied them from the venerable Richard Adams; and if he gave them their captions or orthography, he never changed their form or substance. He was unquestionably a Baptist receiving these Records from a Baptist and for the purpose of Baptist history. Whether it was Benjamin Stinton who collected materials for a Baptist history, and who died in 1718, I know not. Crosby puts Stinton's "introduction" in the Preface of his first volume, and doubtless had Stinton's collection; and in Crosby's collection we find the Jessey Church Records, including the Kiffin Manuscript, which he "lent" to Neal, and all of which he used in his history of the Baptists as perfectly reliable testimony.

These Records are said to be "anonymous," but not more so than the Epistle to the Hebrews; and the Epistle to the Hebrews fits no more closely to the Gospel than these Records to the Congregational and Baptist history of the time. The Bible reveals interpolations and variations, ellipses and anachronisms, but only infidels reject it on that account; and there would be much of the Bible and history destroyed if the principles of criticism applied to the Jessey Church Records were applied to them.

Even if these Records were a forgery, the Blunt movement a myth and the date, 1641, not distinctly stated, the immersion "revival" about that time, is demonstrated in the controversial literature of the period. The Blunt movement, which the Jessey Church Records describe, and which Crosby says the great Baptist body, at the same time, repudiated as "needless trouble" in view of their own "method of revival," was in itself a small affair and went to nothing. The great contemporaneous movement of the "greatest number" of the "English Baptists" is *the* fact revealed in the literature of the period; and the chief value of these Records lies in fixing the date and showing the agitation which resulted in the change of the Anabaptists of 1641 to immersion—confirmed especially by Hutchinson (1676). These Records, however, are neither a forgery nor a fiction; and they will never down before the silly and captious criticism of those who claim no theory to advance, yet go stalking these Records through the literature of the 17th century to discover, if possible, the vain hope of discrediting their testimony in favor of the unprovable and impossible doctrine of *visible* Baptist Church Succession. But these Records stand, like Gibraltar, invulnerable to criticism; and, in conclusion, their confirmation may be thus summarized:

1. John Taylor, 1641, connects Spilsbury and Eaton according to their association in the Jessey Church Records, and shows their introduction of immersion in 1641.

2. R. B., 1642, affirms that until *lately* "there were no baptized persons (immersionists) in the world."

3. Spilsbury, 1642, characterized "dipping" as the "old," but "*new found*, way."

4. Barebone, 1643, gives the age of the "totall dippers" of England as "two or three yeares old, or some such short time."

5. Cornwell, 1645, claims that the Baptists under the "discovery" and "commandment" of Christ had *resumed* "dipping."

6. Henry Denne, 1645, calls the delivery of the doctrine of baptism by the church a "*new born babe.*"

7. Edwards, 1646, puts the origin of "dipping" among the English Baptists within the "four years past."

8. Jessey, 1650, confirms the substance of the Kiffin Manuscript, in its 1640–41 paragraphs by an evident reference to Blunt "going over the sea" for baptism; and he also confirms the "No. 4" document of the Jessey Records.

9. Kaye, 1653, asks and answers the question: "How comes it to pass that this doctrine of baptism [dipping] hath not been before revealed?"

10. Watts, 1656, points back "13 or 14 yeare agoe" as the date at which the English Baptists began to immerse.

11. The biographer of Jessey, 1671, distinctly mentions the 1640 division of Jessey's Church and the facts embraced in the "No. 4" document, both contained in the Jessey Church Records.

12. Hutchinson, 1676, directly points out the deputation to Holland for a "proper administrator" in "reviving" the "truth" of immersion first received from Holland.

13. The Bampfield Document, 1681, and the Kiffin Manuscript agree in the statement that immersion in England had been "disused" and that up to the time of its revival by the Baptists there "were none" who had so practiced to be found—the date 1641 being fixed by the Kiffin Manuscript.

14. All the other writers of the 17th century, who touch the subject, imply the recent introduction of immersion by the Baptists of England, about the year 1641.

15. Crosby, 1738, declares that before its restoration by the Baptists of England, "immersion had for some time been disused"; and he evidently adopted the statements of both the Kiffin and the Bampfield documents and implied the 1641 date of the former, according to the facts.

16. Ivimey, 1811, though not certain of the date, and disposed to dodge the issue, confirms the 1641 restoration, according to the Jessey Church Records.

17. Geo. Gould, 1860, (Open Communion) recognizes the Kiffin MS. and Jessey Records as we now have them as valid documents.

18. Evans, 1864, clearly agrees with Crosby and Ivimey in the credibility of these documents and the fact of restoring immersion by the Baptists, 1640–41.

19. Barclay, 1871, and Rauschenbusch, 1899, fully indentify John Batte as the "teacher" who immersed Blunt.

20. Dr. A. H. Newman, 1897, a competent and thorough—a *scholarly*—investigator, declares that the Jessey Records (including the Kiffin MS.) "bear every mark of genuineness" and "are thoroughly consistent with each other."

For further answers to objections to the Jessey Records and Kiffin MS., see Appendix at the close of this work.

Such a confirmation of the Jessey Church Records ought to suffice against the captious objections which seem to be on the still hunt for criticism instead of true history; and I claim that this discussion, from beginning to end, is consistent with the history of the case. The writers cited, with the exception of the Baptist historian, Crosby, and those following down to the present time, all belong to the 17th century; and these last base their conclusions upon the 17th century documents. The Jessey Church Records are, beyond question, an old 17th century document, perfectly consistent with and thoroughly confirmed by the 17th century history here cited.

ENGLISH BAPTIST REFORMATION.

(FROM 1609 TO 1641 A. D.)

CHAPTER X.

WILLIAM KIFFIN.

On account of being the alleged author of the so-called Kiffin Manuscript and of his reputed connection with the Blunt movement for the restoration of immersion, 1640-41—and because it has been confidently asserted that he was an immersionist before 1641, and that his writings contradict the thesis of the restoration of immersion at that date—I have thought it proper to devote this chapter to William Kiffin. Crosby says (Vol. I., p. 101), in the use of the Kiffin Manuscript, that he "lived in those times, and was a leader among those of that persuasion"—those, I suppose, to whom the document refers, i. e., Blunt and others who originated the regular baptism and administrator-theory of restoration. Kiffin gives no account of himself becoming a Baptist; but from his own and the writings of others we may infer how, why and when he became such—the inference being clear that he reached Baptist conclusion at the time Blunt and his party restored immersion in 1641, and that he was of the Particular, close-communion, if not regular "persuasion."

It is said in the 1633 date of the document ascribed to Kiffin that he went out with the first secession from the Jacob Lathrop Church, but this is an unaccountable error which crept into the records and which indicates that Kiffin was not the author of them. Crosby, in his version of the records, places Kiffin, 1638, with Spilsbury—another mistake, in which Ivimey at first followed Crosby, and so of others repeatedly since that time. According to Kiffin himself (Ivimey, Vol. II., p. 297; Orme's Life of Kiffin, p. 14), he joined, in 1638, when 22 years of age, an Independent congregation not Spilsbury's as the sequel shows. Orme (*ibid*, p. 115, Note XXI.) says of Mr. Jessey: "He was pastor of the Independent Church of which Kiffin was a member, and changed his sentiments some time after Kiffin left it." This settles the fact that Kiffin, who was born 1616, and who joined the Jessey Church when 22 years of age, that is, in 1638, was not in the secession of 1633, nor was a member of Spilbury's Church in 1638.

The probability is that Kiffin became a Baptist and was immersed in 1641. Gould is the first who logically draws this inference (Close Communion, pp. cxxvii., cxxviii., cxxix.) from Kiffin's "Sober Discourse of Right to Church Communion," p. 1, London, 1681, in which he says:

"I used all endeavors . . . that I might be directed in a right way to worship; and after some time concluded that the safest way was to follow the footsteps of the flock, namely, that order laid down by Christ and his apostles, and practiced by the primitive Christians in their times, which I found to be that, after conversion, they were baptized, and added to the church, and continued in the Apostles' doctrine, fellowship, breaking of bread and prayer, according to which I thought myself conformable, and have continued in the profession of the same *for these forty years.*"

Forty years subtracted from 1681, the year in which he wrote his Sober Discourse, leaves 1641, the year in which he became a Baptist. The year 1641 is the date which the Jessey Church Records assign to the immersion of the fifty-three members of the Jessey and Spilsbury churches by Blunt and Blacklock—the year in which, according to Crosby (Vol. I., p. 310), "a much greater number" than before withdrew from the Jessey Church of which Kiffin must have then been a member; and although his name does not appear in the fifty-three baptized up to Jan. 9, 1641, he must have been baptized soon after that date in the same year, as the number continued to be "added to" and "increased much." At all events Kiffin with some others appears, Oct. 17, 1642, in a controversy with Dr. Featley at Southwark, in which he is seen to be a full-fledged Baptist. By his own showing in 1681, when 40 years a Baptist, his immersion must have taken place in 1641, when 25 years of age.

Ivimey represents Kiffin as leaving the Jessey Church in 1638 and joining Spilsbury, and soon after separating from Spilsbury and his people on the occasion of a dispute about "the propriety of suffering ministers to preach among them who had not been baptized by immersion." Mr. Kiffin, says he, "was at the head of those who opposed this principle, and an amicable secession took place, it is *supposed* soon after 1640, when the church, which still assembles in Devonshire Square, was founded, and he became their pastor." (Ivimey, Vol. II., p. 297.) Ivimey's account of this matter was evidently drawn from Crosby (Vol. III., pp. 3, 4), in which he speaks of "Mr. William Kiffin, minister to a Baptist congregation in Devonshire Square, London." He says:

" He was first of an Independant congregation, and called to the ministry among them; was one of those who were concerned in the conferences held in the congregation of Mr. Henry Jessey; by which Mr. Jessey and the greatest part of the congregation became proselyted to the opinion of the Baptists. He joined himself to the church of Mr. John Spilsbury; but a difference arising about permitting persons to preach amongst them, that had not been baptized by *immersion*, they parted by consent, yet kept a good correspondence."

It will be seen here that Crosby gives no dates, and while he represents Kiffin as being pastor of the Devonshire Square Baptist Church, in London, he says nothing about the time when Kiffin became pastor, nor does he intimate that Kiffin founded it at any date. More than this, the incident of separation by Kiffin from Spilsbury's church, on account of pulpit affiliation with *unimmersed* preachers, takes place, according to Crosby, after the mention of certain Conferences in the congregation of Mr. Jessey, in which Kiffin was "one of those who were convinced," and by which the greater part of Mr. Jessey's congregation with himself were "proselyted to the opinion of the Baptists." Now the "Conferences" mentioned by Crosby, and which were held in Mr. Jessey's Church, occurred early in 1644, according to an old MS., supposed to have been written by Mr. Jessey himself (Gould, Open Communion, p. cxxx.; Review of the Question, Newman, p. 193.) (See also Jessey Records.) Preceding these Conferences, or among them, was the controversy in the Jessey Church, 1643, concerning the baptism of Hanserd Knollys' child, in which Kiffin was "one of those concerned." (Gould, Open Communion, p. cxxix.) Orme, as already quoted, says that Kiffin was a member of Mr. Jessey's Church, and that Jessey "changed his sentiment sometime after Kiffin left it;" and it is agreed on all hands that Kiffin joined Spilsbury for a short time after leaving Jessey. If according to Crosby's notice of this fact he joined Spilsbury after the above Conferences, in which he was one of those concerned, then he left Jessey late in 1643 or early in 1644, and not in 1638, as Ivimey first stated the matter. Gould says:

"It is worthy of remark that Crosby does not give us any account of the duration of Kiffin's membership in this [Spilsbury's] church; and his words are clearly compatible with a very brief connection. I am led to the conclusion that such was the case. The 'Confession of Faith . . . Printed in the yeare of our Lord, 1644' [and published Oct. 16] was signed by Kiffin and Patience as the representatives of one of the seven Congregations in London, which agreed in that Confession. Between the months of May and October, therefore, in the year 1644, Kiffin had ceased to be a member of Mr. Jessey's church, had also connected himself with and had then withdrawn from Mr. Spilsbury's Church, and thereupon in conjunction with Mr. Patience, had organized a new Congregation." (Gould, Open Communion, p. cxxxi.)

It is noteworthy also that Ivimey, at a later date, changed his view of this subject. He says (Life of Kiffin, p. 17):

"About the year 1653, he [Kiffin] left Mr. Spilsbury, and became the pastor of a Baptist Church, which for many years met in Fisher's Folly, now Devonshire Square."

On this passage Gould says:

"This is the *latest form* in which Mr. Ivimey has stated his conclusions as to the date of the formation of this Church. In 1814, when he published Vol. II. of his History of the English Baptists, he '*supposed*' that it [the Devonshire Square Church] was founded 'soon after 1640' (p. 297). Of course his supposition was incorrect, as Kiffin was not a Baptist at that date. The loss of the original Church Book of this congregation forbids the hope of unravelling its early history." (Open Communion, p. cxxxi.)

Gould further observes:

"If this statement is to be understood as meaning that Kiffin, for the first time, organized a Baptist Congregation, it is certainly incorrect, as the Confession of 1644 proves: if it means that in 1653 Kiffin organized a new Congregation, I think it may be true, because it would reconcile statements as to his history which, otherwise, are difficult to harmonize; but if it asserts that the church thus formed did, from that time forward, meet in Devonshire Square, Ivimey is, as usual, not to be relied upon."

In the Lambeth Records (DCXXXIX., fo. 219 b.) Gould discovers in the "return made to Archbishop Sheldon, by the Bishop of London, in 1669, of the Conventicles in the Diocese of London," that there is no mention of Fisher's Folly, or Devonshire Square; and that the only entry in the "return" in relation to Kiffin is that he was "preacher" or "teacher" in "Finsbury's Court over against the Artillery Ground in Morefield"—or Bunhill Field. (Open Communion, p. cxxxii.)

If according to Ivimey's latest view, Kiffin was not pastor of Devonshire Square Baptist Church in 1644, nor founded it in 1640 as he "supposed" at first, he may be still mistaken as to 1653. Taking the facts of history as we find them, it is probable that Kiffin left Jessey late in 1643; had a short connection with Spilsbury early in 1644; united with Patient (whose name is joined with Kiffin's among the signers of the Confession as from the same church) in another organization later in 1644; and that afterwards, in 1653, or after 1669, he became pastor of Devonshire Square Baptist Church. The early records of the church having been lost, Kiffin's early connection with that church is largely traditional. At all events he did not leave Spilsbury in 1638, nor formed the Devonshire Square Baptist Church, "near 1640," as Ivimey first "supposed;" and it is clear that his contention with Spilsbury about pulpit affiliation with the unimmersed happened, if it ever occurred at all, after 1641. No such question was ever sprung among Baptists in England before 1641, so far as one can judge from the history of the times; and it may be only traditional that it happened after 1641— although it was possible with a man of Kiffin's views on pulpit affiliation and close communion at a later date. He was the "patriarch of Strict Communion Baptists," as Gould nobly styles him; but just when he became such cannot be definitely ascertained. He must have reached that position after 1643, for it seems impossible to separate him from the Jessey Church, though a Baptist, before that date. In 1643, according to Orme's Life of Kiffin (p. 22), after a return from Holland, Kiffin retired from his lucrative business, for a time, and devoted himself to the "study of God's word," being "greatly pressed," he says, "by the people with whom I was a *member* to continue with them"— evidently meaning the Jessey people with whom he had been associated since 1638. He was not a pastor at this time of any church, but only a "member," though doubtless he had been exercising his gifts as a preacher and a disputant before this. According to Crosby (Vol. III., pp. 3, 4) he had been called to the ministry by the Independent Congregation to which he belonged before becoming a Baptist; and no doubt, on becoming a Baptist he continued in the work of the ministry without cessation of his office.

These facts of history clearly put to silence the assumption which has been so vigorously pressed, that Kiffin was immersed before 1641—the proof of which depended upon his separation from Spilsbury, 1638, on account of the latter's pulpit affiliation with the unimmersed. The fact of such separation, without the date, was recorded by Crosby and chronologically misplaced by Ivimey; but we have seen that Ivimey and Orme correct this mistake at a later date, and that, as Kiffin's Sober Discourse shows, he could not have been a Baptist before 1641. Like the rest of the Baptists of his time, he regarded adult immersion as having been lost in the great apostasy, and restored by the Baptists; and in his argument for close communion based upon precedent baptism (Sober Discourse, p. 16) he says:

"For if it be once admitted that it [baptism] is not necessary to Church Communion, every Man of Sence will infer, That our Contention for it were frivolous, our *Separation* Schismatical, &c."

Again he says (*ibid*, p. 58):

"And if the first churches might not be constituted without this Ordinance of Baptism, neither may those that succeed them, because the same reason that made Baptism necessary then, makes it also necessary to us. For Gospel Order settled by Apostolicall Authority & Direction, as this was, hath not lost any of its native worth and efficacy, or obliging Vertue, by any *Disuse* or *Discontinuance* occasioned by any, but ought to be the same to us *now*, as it was to them in the *beginning* of such order, &c."

In his answer to Poole's querie: "By what warrant from the Word of God do you separate from our congregations, where the Word and Sacraments are purely dispensed?" Kiffin replies (Briefe Remonstrance, p. 6) that the Word and Sacraments were not purely dispensed among their congregations, and when they should be, he says:

"We (I hope) shall joyne with you in the same Congregation and Fellowship, and nothing shall separate us but death, but till then we shall continue our separation from you, according to the light we have received."

In reply to the charge of disturbing the " Reformation now in hand," he says (*ibid*, p. 7):

"I know not what you meane by this charge, unless it be to discover your prejudice against us, in *Reforming ourselves* before you"—

that is, before the Presbyterian movement, 1643-49, was finished.

In reply to Poole's charge that he received from their congregations "silly seduced servants, children or people," Kiffin replies (*ibid*, p. 10):

"We answer, it is well known to you, we receive none as members with us, but such as have been members of your church at least sixteen, twenty or thirty years."

In reply to the charge of Schism (*ibid*, p. 13) Kiffin says:

"Now for our part, we desire all and every one of these amongst you to be true and therefore do *separate* from you; so then when you have made satisfaction for *your* notorious schisme, and return as dutiful sonnes to their Mother, or else have cast off all your filthy Rubbish of her abominations, which are found among you, we will *return* to you, or show our just grounds to the contrary."

Thus Kiffin acknowledges that he and his church were Separatists from the Pedobaptist reformers; and he promises to *"return"* when they relinquish the filthy abominations of their separation from Episcopacy or Romanism. The truth is that the whole body of the Baptists of the 17th century were practically Separatists. In 1641 and at the time Kiffin wrote his Briefe Remonstrance they were nothing but Separatists from the Puritans and other Reformers—organically, to begin with, and by individual additions in their continuance and growth, as Kiffin acknowledges. There was not a Baptist preacher at that date, so far as I have learned, who was an original Anabaptist; and there were but few if any such during the 17th century. Smyth, Helwys, Morton, Spilsbury, Hobson, Kiffin, Knollys, Barber, Kilcop, Ritor, R. B., Jessey, Tombes, Lamb, Oates, Collins and most if not all the rest down to 1692 were sprinkled in infancy; and this is a significant fact in proof of the entire Separatist origin of the English Baptists between 1611 and 1641—and for some time afterward.

Daniel King, 1649, wrote a book entitled, "A Way to Sion," in which he shows that, notwithstanding the succession of faith and of true believers, the visible church, ministry and ordinances of Christ had been lost in the apostasy of Rome; that believers had the right to recover the ordinances of Christ at any time when moved to obedience; and that the true church, ministry and ordinances of Christ had been recovered by the Baptists. The Epistle Dedicatory to that book was written by Thomas Patient, John Spilsbury, *William Kiffin* and John Pearson, whose names are signed to the document and who most vigorously endorse and commend the book to the Baptists and the world. He occupies the same position as shown in "Wall's Infant Baptism from Heaven," 1692 (p. 22), in which Kiffin takes the current Baptist view of his century, namely, "that the Apostles did not Baptize as Apostles, but as Common-gifted Disciples," upon which ground they repudiated the doctrine of succession, and claimed the right to restore the church, ministry and ordinances by unbaptized administrators raised up to teach and therefore baptize. Wall arose to reply to Kiffin with the current Pedobaptist argument of that century, based upon succession, namely, "That the Commission, Matt. 28:20, was given to men in office"—when Kiffin, Keach and others left the room!

From all these quotations it is clear that Kiffin, though he may have been immersed, 1641, by Blunt or Blacklock, yet like Kilcop and others then baptized, he disclaimed succession and did not regard the regular baptism from Holland as in the line of succession. He held that baptism had been *"disused"* or *"discontinued"* under the Romish Apostasy and that it had been restored by the Baptists; he regarded the Baptists as Separatists and Reformers upon a higher plane than the Puritans; he claims that all the membership of his church, down to 1645, had been received from the churches from which the Baptists had separated; he pledges that when the schism from Rome had cut off the abominations of its Mother, the Baptists would *"return"* to the other Reformers; he endorses King's "Way to Sion," which is the strongest vindication of the Baptist right to restore baptism and which admits the fact that the Baptists had recovered Christ's church, ministry and ordinances; and he preached the current Baptist doctrine of the necessity of an unbaptized administrator in order to begin the Baptist reformation. All efforts to prove that Kiffin was a Baptist before 1641, or that his writings deny the statements of the so-called Kiffin Manuscript, is a failure; and so of any other Baptists in England—as claimed of Knollys, Canne, Hobson, or Vavasor Powell—the latter of whom was an Independent preacher in Wales and England from 1640 to 1655, and who, according to Thurloe (Dictionary of National Biography, Vol. XLVI., p. 250, British Museum), was, January 1, 1655, "lately baptized and several others of his party." Kiffin has no hesitation in claiming that the churches of some of the Baptists were erected and framed, organized, as they were in 1645, according to the rule of Christ before the Presbyterian Reformation *"then* in hand"—when "Episcopacie was at the height of its vanishing glory"—but he nowhere claims that immersion was in practice before 1641. Believers' baptism, the basis of Anabaptist organization, had existed from 1611 to 1641; but every implication from Kiffin's writings is that he agreed with the Baptists of his day, that immersion had been recently restored by the Baptists of England.

One difficulty is to account for Kiffin's connection with Jessey down to 1643, when he probably withdrew to Spilsbury on account of the controversy originating out of the baptism of Hanserd Knollys' child, and when sixteen others withdrew, at that time, from the Jessey Church. It is probable, as already suggested, that Kiffin's stricter views of communion and pulpit affiliation were never developed until after this separation and his union with Spilbury, whenever that was, and it is probable therefore that although an immersed Baptist, he felt no scruples in remaining from 1641 to 1643 with Jessey. This had been the custom of Baptists in principle before the secession of 1633 and 1638; and during this transition state from 1640 to 1645 it may have been the custom of Baptists in practice. Even when Kiffin broke with Spilsbury's church, it is said that they "kept good correspondence;" and perhaps this fraternal liberality, even at that time, explains why Kiffin, before he grew into stricter views, remained with Jessey down to 1643. Crosby seems to regard Jessey's church as a Baptist Church in transition when (Vol. III., p. 41) in his reply to Neal's statement he says: "Thus it appears there were three Baptist churches in England which Mr. Neal met with before *that* of Mr. Jessey's," that is, in 1638. There is also much early correspondence, such as found in the records of the Hexham Church, which shows the intimate fraternal regard held for the Jessey Church; and hence, after all, it may not be strange that Kiffin and perhaps many others of the immersed Baptists remained with Jessey sometime before he and his entire church were fully proselytized to Baptist opinion and practice.

The only difficulty which now remains is the identification of Kiffin with the ancient manuscript ascribed to him. That document is a part of the Jessey Church Records, and in the collection of 1712 is found with the "Ex-MSS. of Mr. Henry Jessey," and apparently a part of those Jessey documents which embrace the history of Mr. Jacob and his church from 1604 to 1645. On the basis of these records from 1633 to 1641, together with such writers as Hutchinson, Spilsbury, Tombes, Lawrence and others, Crosby's whole account of the origin of the Particular Baptist Churches, and the restoration of immersion by the Blunt Baptists rests. Dr. A. H. Newman (Review of the Question, p. 185) says:

"On the basis of these [documents] the present writer, years ago, reached the conclusion that immersion was introduced among English Baptists in 1641, in entire independence, so far as I can remember, of the considerations upon which Drs. Dexter and Whitsitt at first placed main reliance. It appears that neither of these writers, 1880–81, when this alleged discovery was independently made, was familiar with the quotations from these Records made by Rev. George Gould in his Open Communion of the Baptists of Norwich published in 1860."

It is not a question, therefore, with scholarship, as to the genuineness and value of these doctrines as corroborated by the history of the times, but as to their authorship. I think there can be no doubt of Jessey's authorship of these records; and it is probable that Kiffin had them, and turned them over to Richard Adams, his co-pastor who survived him, and who turned them over to the collector of these and other documents, probably Benjamin Stinton, who left them to Crosby. Either this or else he had a copy of these documents, or of that part of them which related directly to the origin of the first Particular Baptist Churches and the restoration of immersion by Blunt and others; and, having been found among his papers by Adams, was ascribed to Kiffin.

As already seen, Kiffin and Jessey, from 1638 to 1643, were associated in the same church, and both had some connection with the immersion movement of 1640-41. According to Crosby, Kiffin "lived in *those times* and was a leader among those of *that persuasion*," and it was in this connection that Crosby seems to ascribe to him the document called the "Kiffin Manuscript," or that part of the Jessey Church Records which relate to the events which occurred between 1633 and 1641. Kiffin, however, never mentions this document—nor does he allude to his baptism, although he implies the year 1641 as the date at which he became a Baptist. Jessey comes nearer alluding to this document in his work, Storehouse of Provisions, &c., 1656 (p. 80), when speaking of those who had hesitated to enjoy immersion, he says: "Such Considerations as these I had, But yet, because I would do nothing *rashly;* I would not do that which I would renounce againe; I desired Conference with some Christians differing therein in opinion from me; about what is requisite to the restoring of ordinances, if lost; Especially what is Essentiall in a Baptizer. Thus I did forbeare and inquired above a yeares space." The use of the word "Conference" found in the MS., the reference to the "restoring" of the lost ordinance, and the question of an "essentiall Baptizer"—a "proper administrator"—all savor of the Blunt movement and the so-called Kiffin Manuscript, or the 1640-41 part of it; and whether or not Jessey or Kiffin is the author of it, this passage is a strong confirmation of the truth of the document. Kiffin became a convert to immersion in 1641; and although Jessey became convinced of its scripturalness, he delayed it after his conviction for several years. It is somewhat natural for Crosby, by reason of Kiffin's connection with this movement—of his having "lived in those times" and of being of that "persuasion"—to have inclined to the view, apparently, that Kiffin was the author of the document; but Jessey's language in the above quoted paragraph would indicate that he was the author of the document.

Jessey like Kiffin, however, never mentions these records in his writings. Many of the Baptist writers of that day, unlike Jessey, Kiffin, Hutchinson, Tombes, Spilsbury, Lawrence, Barber, King and many others, do not allude to the restoration of baptism—the great movement of 1641; but it must be remembered that the Baptists of that day were more concerned about their principles than their history. The great question among them was that of believers' baptism rather than the mode—whether or not they were Scriptural instead of being traditional; and the gradually developed pride of denominational antiquity had not then begun to look back to see how old it was. Except as they were driven by controversy to touch upon their origin, or history, or their recent introduction of immersion, the Baptists said nothing of consequence on those subjects; but they were zealously engaged in defending their position from the Scriptures as the basis of their organization and practice and as opposed to infant baptism and other innovations of the Pedobaptist churches. When called upon to answer, they had no hesitation in denouncing succession as a "mark of the beast;" and they boasted of their separation and reformation as based upon this restoration of the true church, ministry and baptism of Christ. They called it "new," or rather a return to the "old;" and they thanked God that he had discovered or revealed the old truth and the right way to them in those "later times." Hence we hear of but little from Kiffin on these lines except his retort upon Poole that Baptist organization had preceded the reformation, 1645, *"then in hand"*— that Baptists were Separatists of a higher order, basing their constitution on believers' baptism—and that they were reformers upon this principle before the Puritan revolution—all of which was true from John Smyth's movement, 1609, to that date, irrespective of the mode of baptism.

ENGLISH BAPTIST REFORMATION.

(FROM 1609 TO 1641 A. D.)

CHAPTER XI.
THE BAMPFIELD DOCUMENT.

This document throws a flood of light upon the period of English Baptist history now under discussion. I have selected it as No. 18, from what is called: "A Repository of Divers Historical Matters relating to English Antipedobaptists, collected from original Papers or Faithful Extracts. Anno. 1712." These papers, among which are found the so-called Kiffin Manuscript or Jessey Records, were copied by Rev. George Gould, of London; and upon search for the original, I found Bampfield's book, entitled Shem Acher, or the Historical Declaration of his Life, London, 1681, pp. 38, which contains the extract found in the collection. Document, No. 18, reads as follows:

"*An Account* (1) *of ye Methods taken by ye Baptists to obtain a proper Administrator of Baptism by Immersion,* (2) *when that practice had been so long disused, yt there was no one who had been so baptized to be found.* with the Opinion of Henry Lawrence, Lord President, on ye Case.

"Mr. Francis Bampfield, in ye Historical Declaration of his Life, tells us (pp. 15, 16, 17). That after he had been convinced, yt ye True Baptism was by Immersion, & had resolved to be so baptized him selfe, he was a long time in doubt about a fit administrator of it. Whereupon he set himself to enquire diligently after ye *first Administrator* of Baptism by Immersion, (3) *since ye revival of yt practice* in *these latter times,* wt account he obtained of this matter he gives in the following words. Namely. That being in London and making Enquiry there, his dissatisfaction grew on; for upon search being made concerning either a *first,* or *after* Administrator of this Ordinance; He was informed either by, (4) *printed Records,* or by *Credible Witnesses,* That ye Administrator was

"Either a Selfe (5) Baptizer: But he *knew no such Administrator* to his Satisfaction; for if ye Historian have not wronged some of ye first so baptized in Holland, wch is too usual; (Ainsworth's Defense of Scrip. p. 3;

Clifton's Christn Plea, p. 181, 182; Mr. Jessop's Discovery of Errors of ye Anabaptists, p. 65). One John Smith, a member of Henry Hainsworth's Church there, being excommunicated for some scandalous offense, is reported to be one of ye first, who baptized him selfe first, afterwards baptized others: and this Story brought no good report of such an Administrator.

"Or two men (6) according to their Principle in their judgment altogether (a) unbaptized before, did Baptize one another at ye first, & afterwards did baptize others; & so ware many of ye Baptizings in London, originally reported to be in one, if not two instances, when also no exterordinary call from God thereunto, yt ever he heard of yet, is pretended or pleaded.

"Or else, a private Baptized Brother, (b) no lawfully called Minister of Christ, nor rightly ordained officer in a true Church, did baptize others; & so he understands ware some of ye choicest and best Baptizings in ye esteem of Several baptized Ones in London; carried on by one who always refused to be any Minister or ordained Officer in ye Church. (c) He has been credibly informed by two yet alive in this City of London, who ware members of ye first Church of baptized Believers here, yt their first Administrator was one, who baptized him selfe, or else he and another baptized one another, & so gathered a Church; wch was so opposed in Publick and private yt they ware disputed out of their Church, State & Constitution, out of their call to office; that not being able to justifie their principle and practice by ye Word, they ware broken and scattered.*

"Or else such one or more, (d) whom such a company of Believers who had no lawfully called, rightly ordained Minister or Church officer amongst them before, Nor any such Minister or Ministers, Officer or Officers, to ordain or Commission, Such & Yet do choose or undertake to ordain by laying on of hands, they being all private Brethren, some private Brothers or Brethren into ye Ministerial Office, & to send him or them forth to preach & Baptize.

"Or else some such one (e) who however pretending to be called and sent forth by men, Yet is not gifted, graced and qualified according to ye requirements of Christ in his word for such an honorable office & weighty work.

---

*Bampfield was satisfied that this baptism was not right, and he offers arguments to prove that either self-baptism or that an unbaptized person baptizing another, must be sent of God, and that such an administrator must have evidence of an extraordinary call, as he himself claimed to have, and who doubtless baptized himself in the river at Saulisbury. See his work (Shem Acher, or Historical Declaration of his Life, 1681, p. 38).

"Or otherwise some such (f) who say they ware at first passing under this Ordinance under an unavoidable Necessity of doing somewhat this way beyond and besides ye ordinary stated Scripture Rule & way, wch they hope ye Lord did accept of, they giving to him ye best they had according to their then understanding. Thus farr Mr. Bamfield Henry Lawrance Esqre, in his Excellent Treatise intituled Of Baptism discourses in ye last Chapter of ye Minister of Baptism wherein he shows, etc."

This document here continues with the added testimony of Henry Lawrence, whose theory of the administrator of baptism according to Bampfield's observations, is the same as recorded by Crosby (Vol. I., pp. 105, 106), and referred to in this volume, p. 86. Bampfield became a Baptist in London about the year 1676, and his work here referred to in this document, is catalogued among his other writings by Crosby (Vol. I., p. 368), and published, 1681, under the title: "A Name, A New One; or A Historical Declaration of His Life." The caption, introduction and conclusion of the document were written by some one somewhere between 1681 and 1710, when the Collection of 1712 was perhaps being gathered by Richard Adams, a Baptist minister who lived to a great age and who was co-pastor with Kiffin, whom he survived. Who the author of this document was is not mentioned; but he was evidently acquainted with the writings of Bampfield, Lawrence, Ainsworth, Clifton, Jessop and others of his day. The caption, introduction and conclusion of the document are therefore anonymous; but the work of Bampfield, the 15th, 16th and 17th pages, which he literally quotes, is not anonymous, nor is his quotation from Lawrence anonymous. The historical value of it consists in its confirmation of Crosby's account of restoring immersion by the English Baptists in the year 1640–41, and also in confirming the main sentence in the Kiffin Manuscript: "None having then so practiced [immersion] in England to professed believers," upon which Crosby's account, as to the Blunt movement, is based.

The most peculiar case in the restoration movement was that of Bampfield. He conceived himself as the parallel of Paul in an extraordinary conversion and call to the ministry; and as Saul took the new name of Paul, so he took the new name of Shem Acher. He believed that the true church, its ministry and baptism had been lost, and when convinced of Baptist principles, about 1676, he was on the point of being dipped in the Thames. . For some reason he delayed the act, and concluded to hunt for a proper administrator of immersion in London. He had evidently reached the conviction of the Seekers, that if baptism were restored, it must be at the hands of one extraordinarily commissioned of God for the purpose. Such a baptizer he nowhere found among the restorers of immersion in England—whether self-baptized or baptized by unbaptized administrators; and he does not pretend to have so much as heard of a claim to baptism by succession from the days of the Apostles, or from any succeeding sect. Hence it needed that some one should "perfect baptism" in order to restore it, and in order to meet the objection of the Seekers and others that the Baptists had no proper administrator, or ministry, or church. Having an extraordinary conversion and call to the ministry, he claims that he had an extraordinary commission from God to "perfect baptism," and so with another he went to Saulisbury and there passed under the waters of baptism in the river of that place—evidently by self-baptism and then baptized the man with him. Thus he was prepared now to meet the objection of the Seekers and to set up anew the order of Christ—repudiating all the methods of restoring immersion by the Baptists upon the ground that they had no proper administrator by extraordinary commission from Christ, as he had, to reintroduce the lost ordinance in the latter age. (See Historical Declaration, &c., pp. 18, 19.) He evidently did not hear of the little Blunt movement and only confined his search among the larger body of Baptists, who had repudiated the Blunt "method." As we have seen, the Blunt movement had likely gone to pieces before 1646 and had faded out of Baptist regard, or else Bampfield found none of the Blunt persuasion. He evidently never saw the Jessey Records or the Kiffin Manuscript which Richard Adams collected together with the Bampfield and other documents of the time.

In order, however, to get at the value of the Bampfield Document as historical testimony in favor of the thesis set up by the Kiffin Manuscript and Crosby's Account of the revival of immersion by the Baptists of England, 1640–41, I shall here give an analysis of this paper, according to the figures which number the points considered most important.

(1) The matter of *"methods."* Crosby speaks repeatedly of the "methods" by which the "English Baptists" revived immersion, 1640–41, both in his own text and in his version of the

Kiffin Manuscript; and the expression *"ye Methods taken by ye Baptists to obtain a proper Administrator of Baptism by Immersion"* in the caption of this document is almost identical with Crosby (Vol. I., p. 100, when he says:

"The two other *methods* that I mentioned, were indeed both *taken by the Baptists*, at their *revival of immersion in England.*"

It appears almost certain that Crosby copied this language from the Bampfield Document based upon the authority of Bampfield himself.

(2) The main paragraph in the Kiffin Manuscript: *"None having then so practiced [immersion] in England to professed believers,"* has its parallel in the caption of this document, which reads: *"When that practice [immersion] had been so long disused, yt there was no one who had been so baptized to be found."* On page 97, Vol. I., Crosby uses a similar expression when he speaks of "reviving" the practice of immersion which had for sometime been *disused;* and the parallelism between the two phrases *"so long disused"* and *"had for some time been disused"* indicates that Crosby had this document before him. The likeness of the two sentences found respectively in this and the Kiffin MS. indicates that the writer of this caption was acquainted with the Kiffin document, whether Bampfield was or not; and this document is a complete corroboration of the Kiffin Manuscript with respect to its leading sentence: "None having then so practiced, &c." The similar sentence in this document is a little more explanatory in declaring that "there was no one who had been so baptized to be *found*," and this expression may have led Crosby to the still stronger version of the Kiffin MS. when he says:

"They had not *as they knew of*, REVIVED the antient custom of immersion." (Vol. I., p. 102.)

(3) *"Since ye revival of yt practice in these latter times."* This clause follows the caption, in the introduction of this document in which Bampfield is represented as enquiring diligently for the *"first* administrator of baptism by immersion"—when? *"Since* the *revival* of that practice *in these latter times"*—that is, since 1640-41. This expression is also found almost literally in Crosby (Vol. I., p. 105) in which he speaks of the defense of "the true baptism, and the *manner of reviving it* in *these latter times,"* by

Henry Lawrence, whose name also follows in the same connection in the introduction of this document. Here is documentary proof that there was a revival of immersion in England by the Baptists at a given time; and that *since the revival* of that practice Bampfield made a diligent search for the *"first* administrator." Crosby evidently had this document and drew from it almost *verbatim* the above expression; and this among other authorities such as Lawrence, Tombes, Spilsbury and other writers of the times, was the documentary evidence upon which he based his account of the revival of immersion in England by the "largest number and the more judicious of the English Baptists," at the same time that Blunt and his party restored it according to the Kiffin MS., 1640–41. The Kiffin Manuscript and the Bampfield Document are the respective documentary proofs of the "two methods," according to Crosby, by which the English Baptists revived immersion in England—both written *"since ye revival* of that practice *in these latter times."* Surely the charge of "forgery" against the Kiffin Manuscript disappears in the light of the Bampfield document. Not only so, but the characterization of it as an "anonymous document," a "private paper" without signature and without deposit," a "flying leaf," and the like loses its force when placed by the side of this document. The "fifty-three" names incorporated in the Kiffin Manuscript are denied as signatures to the paper; but this "embodied list" is in the nature of a historic attestation, and adds immeasurably to the authenticity of the manuscript from an incidental standpoint—especially so in the light of the Bampfield paper and other historic data employed by Crosby.

(4). "He was informed either by *Printed Records*, or by *Credible Witnesses*, That ye Administrator was, &c." This information is drawn, by the showing of this document that Bampfield made diligent search for the *"first* administrator," from reliable authority, and not from hearsay or second-hand sources; and this is an evidence of the careful and credible authority of this document based upon the testimony of Bampfield's book and other data which he had at hand.

(5). The first information obtained by Bampfield was that the first administrator was a "Selfe Baptizer," but "he Knew no such Administrator to his *Satisfaction;* although John Smyth was *"reputed"* to him as having been "one of ye first, who baptized himselfe first, afterwards baptized others"—"in *Holland"*—which he seems to regard as scandalized. He found no evidence, in his research, that there was any succession of Smyth's self-baptism to the English Baptists; and this is in perfect accord with Crosby (Vol. I., pp. 99, 100), in which he repudiates Smyth's baptism as never having succeeded to the English Baptists—another evidence that this document was before him, when he wrote his history of the Baptists. As we have seen, the immersion of John Smyth was merely a traditional report, at the time, in England and even in the day of Crosby, who was not in possession of Smyth's writings; and as we have seen, Smyth's self-baptism was doubtless affusion, and therefore immersion could not have succeeded from him or his followers to the English Baptists—all of which this document fully confirms, after Bampfield's careful search for the "first administrator of baptism by immersion" in England.

(6). Bampfield's observations covered a heterogeneous mass of "methods" by which, in an irregular way, immersion was revived among the English Baptists at the time of its restoration, according to Spilsbury's theory, that "baptisednesse is not essential to the administrator." This was the "last method," according to Crosby, as distinguished from the "former method" of regular baptism adopted by Blunt and his party. There seems to have been a sort of chaos in the grossness and irregularity of the first or original administration of the ordinance upon its introduction by these "Baptists;" and I will try here to give an analysis of these methods if it be possible to come at them.

(a). Two men altogether unbaptized, baptized each other at first, and afterwards baptized others, without any extraordinary call from God for the purpose. It was thus that many of the immersions in London originated, although at first reported to have occurred in one, if not in two instances. This method of originating a "proper administrator" was based upon the theory of Spilsbury, and the one commonly held as legitimate among the English Baptist writers on the subject. This was the principle of Smyth, who baptized himself first in order to baptize others who might transmit baptism through the church thus organized and begun; and this was the theory of Helwys, Morton, and the rest who first followed Smyth and then afterwards excluded him and his faction for renouncing his method of baptism and for seeking the "true church" through the Mennonites, as already existent.

(b). Next was the method of a private member of the church, not lawfully called or ordained as a minister, who having been baptized himself by some one perhaps according to the above method, "did baptize others." From this source of administration, in the "esteem of several of the baptized ones in London," Bampfield learned that there "were at the beginning some of the choicest and best baptizings." This method was based upon the theory of lay baptism, the ordinance not being dependent for its validity on succession, nor on any sort of official administration. This theory, I believe, is common to the Campbellites of our day. It is also advocated in the Confession of the Seven Churches of London, 1644–1646. It is apt to prevail in the early years of all churches before they get time to develop sacramentalism and hierarchism.

(c). Two persons who were living at the time Bampfield made his inquiry, and who were members of the "first Church of Baptized Believers," in London, told him that their first administrator "baptized himselfe, or else he and another baptized one another and so gathered a church." It is added, however, that this church "was so opposed in public and private that they were disputed out of their church state and constitution," and their ministry, I suppose, "out of their call to office; that not being able to justify their principle and practice by the Word [of God], they were broken and scattered." This statement is in perfect accord with Crosby (Vol. I., p. 97), who says that, in the perplexity of the Baptists, at the time they revived immersion, about what methods they should pursue in order not to be "guilty of any disorder or self-contradiction," there were "some, indeed, [who] were of opinion, that the first administrator should baptize himself, and then proceed to the baptizing of others;" and it looks as if Crosby drew his information from this document. As indicated by both Crosby and this document, the plan failed by this method; and although it was attempted by those who gathered the first church of baptized believers in London, at the time, they were "broken and scattered," "disputed out of their church state and constitution," and "out of their call to office," because "unable to justify their principle and practice according to the Word." The opposition not only came, doubtless, from Pedobaptists who taunted afterwards the Baptists with this method from John Smyth, but from the Baptists themselves, at that time, who adopted and perpetuated the "two other methods" recorded by Crosby. We cannot tell what church this first body of baptized believers was, unless it was the original Helwys Church itself which sought to apply Smyth's old self-baptism theory to immersion in 1641. The idea was not dead among them; but at that period, the Baptists had taken higher ground—one party demanding regular immersion, and the other being satisfied to restore it by an unbaptized administrator after the fashion of John the Baptist and according to the Scriptures as quoted for the purpose by Edward Barber and others of the period. With but the exception of the original church of Helwys, the Baptist body adopted restoration by the regular and anti-succession methods and repudiated the self-baptism method; and, according to the information of Bampfield, the old first church of baptized believers—or some such church—went to pieces upon the old theory evidently inherited from Smyth and his original followers.

(d). Another method at the time was adopted by a "company of believers," without an ordained ministry, who came together and with private hands laid upon one or more of their number, set them apart to the ministerial office, and "sent them forth to preach and to baptize"—that is before they were baptized themselves. This does not imply church organization or church authority, necessarily, in setting apart these private brethren to preach and baptize; but it approaches the idea of having some necessary recognition at the hands of God's people in order to preach and baptize, and is in the nature of church authority for such a purpose, which is an idea now largely prevalent among Baptists.

(e). Bampfield instances another method of reviving immersion at the time by a self-appointed pretender, claiming to be "called and sent forth by men"—yet "not gifted, graced and qualified according to the requirements of Christ in his word for such an honorable office and mighty work." This accounts, perhaps, for the irresponsible and disreputable administration of the ordinance from 1641 and onward charged by Lamb, Featley, Richardson, Edwards, Allen, Bakewell, Hall, Goodwin, Watts, Houghton, Baxter and others from 1643 to 1675. Evidently, according to the history of the times, the introduction of immersion, 1640–41, was attended by some gross irregularities by reason of the irregular methods adopted for its restoration; and it is probable for this reason, and on account of the charges of their enemies, that in 1644 the Particular Baptists put into the 40th article of their Confession on Baptism, the directions about clothing—the charge having been preferred, whether true or false, that some of the Baptists immersed their candidates in a naked or semi-nude condition. I suppose that charge applied to the General Baptists. The literature of the time shows that this custom was widespread. It was apparently the universal custom of early Christian ages.

(f). Finally Bampfield speaks of some who claimed irregularity in the administration of the ordinance by reason of some "unavoidable necessity," "beyond and beside the ordinary stated Scripture rule and way;" and they are represented as apologizing for circumstances or conditions in which they "hope the Lord did accept of [their irregularity], they giving to him the best they had according to their then understanding." It is difficult to understand here what is meant by "passing under this ordinance under an unavoidable necessity, &c.;" but it would appear that those who introduced immersion according to this method did so in some extraordinary case without intelligent conviction of duty contrary to what they afterward found to be the "ordinary stated Scripture rule and way"—for which they hoped divine acceptance, having done the best they knew according to their then light.

Historically the so-called Kiffin Manuscript details the Blunt movement and the Bampfield Document details the general methods of restoring baptism according to the anti-succession theory. These two documents supplement each other; and the two put together constitute the main documentary evidence of the two-fold movement. There are points in each which are common to both and which mutually establish their authenticity and validity as documents relating to the same great event and to the same particular date; and then there are points which, though not in themselves common, are corroborative of each other in referring to the same common event in which, along different lines, the English Baptists as a body revived immersion—confirmed by other writings of the time which also make these documents supplemental to each other. The Jessey Church Records and the Bampfield Document, as evidence of a common event, are Siamese Twins bound together by the common ligament of a substantially similar sentence: "None then having so practiced [immersion] in England to professed believers"—"That practice [immersion] had been so long disused [in England], that there was no one who had been so baptized to be found." These two sentences refer both these documents to the same event in general and to the same date in particular.

The question arises: To what date does the event described in the Bampfield Document refer? Unquestionably to the same date of the Kiffin Manuscript, 1640-41. Both documents refer to the "methods taken by the Baptists [of England] to obtain a proper administrator of baptism by immersion, *when* that practice had been so long disused, that there was no one who had been so baptized to be found"—"'none *then* [at and up to that time] having so practiced in England to professed believers;" and the "*when*" and the "*then*" of these two sentences respectively point to the same date, 1640-41, given only by the Kiffin Manuscript. These two sentences identify the two documents as common to the same event, and to the same date; and Crosby's phraseology seems so evidently copied in some particulars from the Bampfield Document that he identifies it with the same event to which he applies the Kiffin Manuscript, and therefore to the same date. The restoration of immersion by the Baptists of England, a fact common to both documents, did not, so far as the history of the English Baptists shows, occur but once; and 1640-41 is the only date given in any document. That event, according to any known history, did not occur in 1611, 1633, 1638, or 1639, at which dates the origin of Baptist churches is mentioned; and it is not until 1640-41, that such an event is detailed by any document. Hence if the Kiffin and the Bampfield documents point to the same event they point to the same date—although that date is not specifically mentioned in the latter document.

It has been urged that the Hutchinson Account and the Kiffin Manuscript based the deputation of Blunt to Holland simply upon the ground of "legitimacy," that is, in securing a "proper administrator," the irregular practice of immersion being already existent among the General Baptists of England; but the Bampfield Document is "an account of the methods taken by the Baptists to obtain a proper administrator of baptism by immersion, when that practice had been so long disused, that there was no one who had been so baptized to be found;" and the document goes into detail of the several *irregular* methods by which a "proper administrator" was obtained.

In concluding this chapter I wish to cite the authority of Prof. Henry C. Vedder in a note of April, 1897, in which he confirmed the position of the writer in the use of the Bampfield Document in his work entitled: A Review of the Question, pp. 232–234. He says:

"A week ago precisely I mailed to the *Christian Index* some comments on the Bampfield Document, in which I took exactly the ground of your main contention, namely: That Crosby and Evans distinctly favor the opinion that immersion was introduced in 1641, and that Dr. Whitsitt has rediscovered what was once the general opinion among Baptists. The tradition that English Baptists always immersed is really of late origin, and apparently of American origin, since no reputable English writer can be quoted in its favor before the beginning of the present controversy."

As already said, I have thoroughly examined Bampfield's Shem Acher and find the extract here copied correct. He regarded either method of restoring immersion correct, whether by self-baptism or at the hands of unbaptized administrators; but he claimed like the Seekers, that there must be an extraordinary commission for such restoration, that is, in order to "perfect baptism." That commission he himself claimed to have; and, under that claim, he evidently baptized himself about 1676—after having sought to find a satisfactory "first or after" administrator of immersion. He found a number of methods by which the Baptists had restored immersion in England; but with his view of perfecting the ordinance in its restoration, none of the methods were satisfactory and so baptized himself under an extraordinary claim. He shows however that all the methods of restoration which he found had originated by unbaptized administrators; and hence the conclusion of the Bampfield Document that those methods were of recent date.

ENGLISH BAPTIST REFORMATION.

(FROM 1609 TO 1641 A. D.)

CHAPTER XII.

CROSBY'S WITNESSES.

Crosby ranks John Smyth among the first "restorers of immersion in this latter age;" but, as we have seen, it is almost certain that Smyth was not an immersionist and that he baptized himself by affusion—a fact to which Crosby did not have access in the day he wrote. Crosby is nevertheless right in assuming that Smyth wrought a "reformation in baptism" and that Helwys and Morton "joined with him" in the movement, in Holland, in 1609. (Vol. I., pp. 97, 99.) Smyth is the author of the leading English Baptist idea of restoring the true church and right baptism, *when lost*, by "believers having Christ, the Word and the Spirit;" and that even two believers can join together for the purpose. He claimed that the true church and right baptism could not be found in Rome, nor in the English Church, nor among the Separatists whose succession could be traced only through infant baptism; and he regarded the Mennonite Anabaptists as too heretical to claim to be the true church and to possess right baptism. Both were lost in the long night of Romish apostasy, Protestant variation and Anabaptist heresy. Hence Smyth began anew with a self-originated church and baptism upon the principle, however, that the first administrator may baptize *himself* in order to begin. He differed only from the subsequent English view in the method of self-baptism; but otherwise Smyth laid the foundation of English Baptist position, when necessary to reform, of self-originated church and baptism by an *un*baptized administrator (but not *self*-baptized) after the manner of John the Baptist. That view utterly repudiated the doctrine of succession as a Popish fiction from 1609 to 1641 and onward from that day till this among English Baptists.

This was the view of Helwys, Morton and their followers who became the General Baptists of England; and was also generally the view of the Particular Baptists who were self-originated in 1633. Helwys against "The New Fryelers" (Mennonites), 1611, held the original position of Smyth on this subject—vigorously maintaining it, and opposing "succession;" and in the celebrated tract, "Persecution for Religion Judged and Condemned," 1615, the same theory formulated by Crosby, is clearly stated, "that after a general corruption of baptism, an unbaptised person might warrantably baptize, and so begin a reformation." (See pp. 164–169, Tracts on Liberty of Conscience, Hanserd Knollys' Society Publications). "Every believer," says Smyth (A Description, &c., p. 164) "hath Christ and his apostles, commanding him to covet to preach, 1 Cor. 14:1; and to call all to come, Rev. 22:17; and when they come to baptize them." Smyth abandoned his view and sought regularity through the Mennonites afterwards; but his English followers held the position which he had surrendered.

"If in Turkey or America" (Perkins on Galatians (1604), p, 35), "or elsewhere, the gospel should be received of men, by the counsel and persuasion of private persons, they shall not need to send into Europe for consecrated ministers, but they have power to choose their own ministers from within themselves; because where God gives the word he gives the power."

This was the early view of founding the church and baptism, lost, anew; and the view has never been abandoned among the conservative majority of Baptist people.

In 1614 Leonard Busher, without regard to the principle upon which Baptists had the right to reform the church and baptism anew, went further in defining baptism as immersion, a burial and a resurrection, according to Rom. 6:4; Collos. 2:12; but there is no evidence that the followers of Smyth and Helwys followed his definition in practice. The contrary probability is established that they followed Smyth's affusion, after the Mennonite custom; but Smyth, in his Confessions, uses precisely the same figure of burial and resurrection as symbolic of baptism which, nevertheless, he represents as a *"washing."* So of the Confession of 1611 which, while it implies the symbols of death and life, calls the ordinance a "washing with water," after the usual phraseology of Pedobaptist and other confessions of that day and since, which enjoin affusion or aspersion for baptism.

The argument at that time among Pedobaptists and Mennonites was that while *baptizo* meant "to dip," it also meant "to wash," as in Mark 7:4,8; and they had no hesitation in using the symbolism of immersion in connection with the definition, "washing with water" by affusion. This, as we have before said, was most probably the view of Smyth and his followers; and it can only be conceived that Leonard Busher took an advance step in his exclusive definition of baptism which did not obtain among Helwys and the rest of the Anabaptists of his day. It remained for 1641 to Blunt and his followers to put in practice what Busher had defined by the same Scriptures; and upon which the whole Baptist fraternity followed not in the reformation of the principle but in the form of believers' baptism. Smyth and his followers had established the principle of believers' baptism and the true church based upon the Baptist model, restored from the chaos of the Romish, Protestant and what he conceived the Anabaptist apostasy; but, in 1641, the English Baptists took a higher step of progress in the restoration of the "ancient practice" of baptism by immersion, as exclusive of all other modes of administering the ordinance.

This step, so far as it was confined to Blunt and his party, was a new departure from the Smyth idea, that is, by the method of a "proper administrator," already baptized; and hence it is called by Crosby the "former method" as distinguished from the "last method" in opposition to what the great body of English Baptists regarded as a "succession" method of restoring the ordinance. Aside from the Kiffin Manuscript, or Jessey Records, already treated, Crosby introduces, as a witness, Edward Hutchinson (A Treatise concerning the Covenant and Baptism, 1676, pp. 2–4; Crosby, Vol. I., pp. 100, 101) in confirmation of this document. I will quote here the first and last part of the passage in addition to Crosby's citation. Speaking of Pedobaptist opposition to Baptists in their effort to restore immersion Hutchinson says:

"And what our dissenting brethren have to answer upon that account (who instead of taking up, have laid stumblingblocks in the way of Reformation) will appear another day. Yet notwithstanding the strenuous opposition of those learned ones, The mighty God of Jacob hath taken you [Baptists] by the hand and said be strong.

"Besides it has a considerable tendency to advancement of divine grace, if we consider the way and manner of Reviving this costly truth. When the professors of these nations had been a long time wearied with the yoke of superstitious ceremonies, traditions of men, and corrupt mixtures in the worship and service of God: it pleased the Lord to break these yokes, and by a very strong impulse of the Spirit upon the hearts of the people, to convince them of the necessity of reformation. Divers pious and very gracious people having often sought the Lord by fasting and prayer, that he would show them the pattern of his home, the goings out and the comings in thereof, &c., resolved, by the grace of God, not to receive or practice any piece of positive worship, which had not precept or example from the word of God. Infant baptism, coming of course under consideration, after long search and many debates, it was found to have no footing in the Scriptures, the only rule and standard to try doctrines by; but on the contrary a mere innovation, yea, the profanation of an ordinance of God. And though it was purposed to be laid aside, yet what fears, tremblings, and temptations did attend them lest, they should be mistaken, considering how many learned and godly men were of an opposite persuasion? How gladly would they have had the rest of their brethren gone along with them! But when there was no hope, they concluded, that as a Christian's faith must not stand in the wisdom of men; and that every one must give an account of himself to God; and so resolved to practice according to their light. The great objection was the want of an administrator; which as I have heard, says he, was removed by sending certain messengers to Holland, whence they were supplied. So that this little cloud of witnesses [Baptists] hath the Lord by his grace so greatly increased, that it hath spread over our Horizon, though opposed and contradicted by men of all sorts."

Hutchinson clearly takes for granted that immersion was lost; and he speaks of "the *way* and *manner of reviving* this costly truth"—assuming that it was restored under the Blunt method of a "proper administrator" which was supplied by sending to Holland. This movement is evidently referred by him to the Particular element of Baptists which Crosby represents as being "intermixed" with the Puritans, and as separating, 1633 and onward, and "forming churches of those of their own persuasion." His description of the movement 1640-41 accords with the details of the Kiffin MS., or Jessey Records, when he speaks of their fasts, prayers, councils, debates and the like, preceding their final conviction against infant baptism and in favor of believers' baptism; their discussion about a "proper administrator"—probably extending from 1633 to 1640; and, finally, when immersion, as the proper and only mode of baptism, became the essential conviction of these Anabaptists, there being no such practice in England, their deputation of Blunt to Holland for a proper administrator of the proper ordinance. Hutchinson clearly confirms "the way and manner of reviving" immersion in the movement detailed by the Kiffin MS., or the Jessey Records.

With regard to the *"last method"* of restoring immersion—the anti-succession movement—Crosby employs three very strong witnesses. The first of these is John Spilsbury who wrote a Treatise Concerning the Lawful Subjects of Baptism, &c., 1652, in which (4) he shows how *"wanting church or ordinance are to be recovered;"* (5) the "Covenant, not Baptism, forms the Church;" (6) "There is no *succession* under the New Testament, but such as is spiritually by faith in the Word of God." In proof of the restoration of immersion by the "last method," and by the "greatest number of the English Baptists," Crosby cites Spilsbury's Treatise of Baptism (pp. 63, 65, 66), 1644, in which (Crosby, pp. 103, 104, Vol. I.), he says:

"Where there is a beginning, some one must be *first.*" "And because," says Spilsbury, "some make it such an error, and so far from any rule or example, for a man to baptize others, who is himself unbaptized, and so think thereby to shut up the ordinance of God in such a strait, that none can come to it, but thro' the authority of the Popedom of Rome; let the reader consider who baptized John the Baptist before he baptized others, if no man did, and then whether he did not baptize others, he himself being unbaptized. We are taught by this what to do on like occasions.

"Further, I fear men put more than is of right due to it that so prefer it above the church, and all other ordinances besides; for they can assume and erect a church, take in and cast out members, elect and ordain officers, and administer the Supper, and all anew, without any looking after succession, any further than the Scriptures: But as for baptism, they must have that successively from the Apostles, tho' it come thro' the hands of Pope *Joan.* What is the cause of this that men can do all from the Word but only baptism?"

This is in answer to the Pedobaptist position on succession at that period.

It is possible that Spilsbury's position regarding the administrator of baptism created scruples with some after the secession of 1633. He evidently baptized at first without being baptized himself upon the theory that "baptizednesse is not essential to the administrator;" and in the agitation for immersion, 1640-41, which in all probability followed upon the dissatisfaction, it is possible, as Dr. Newman thinks, that Spilsbury began immersion upon his theory in May or June, 1640, before Blunt's return. At all events, Crosby uses Spilsbury in proof of the second method of restoring immersion, 1640-41. He certainly did not begin immersion in 1633 or 1638, since Blunt, Jessey, Blacklock, Lucar, Kilcop, Shepard, Munden and others who were immersed in 1641, based their action upon the fact affirmed in the Jessey Church Records that "*none*," down to 1640, "had so practiced in England to professed believers."

In two of Spilsbury's works, "God's Ordinance, the Saints Privilege," London, 1646, and "A Treatise Concerning the Lawful Subjects of Baptisme," London, 1652 (probably 1642), he squarely takes for granted that the true church, ministry and ordinances of Christ had been lost under the apostasy of Rome and that they had been restored by the Baptists of England; and in Barebone's assault upon him (A Defense of the Lawfulnesse of Baptizing Infants, &c., London, 1644) he charges him with this assumption in unmistakable terms. From page 62 to 67 of his Treatise Concerning the Lawful Subjects of Baptisme, he shows (4), "If either Church, or Ordinance be wanting, where they are to be found, and how *recovered;* (5) "The Covenant, and not Baptism, forms the Church, and the manner how;" and (6) "There is no succession under the New Testament, but what is spiritually by faith and the Word of God"— precisely agreeing with Smyth, Helwys and Morton, except (5) that the Covenant, not Baptism, forms the Church. He teaches (pp. 62, 63) that in order to recover Christ's lost ordinances that believers convinced of the truth and the necessity of obedience —the Spirit speaking in them—are to go to the Scriptures for them; and having thus found them, they are to be enjoyed by those desiring them at the hands of those whom God raises up to preach the truth, though not themselves baptized. In answer to the objection: "*How can such receive others into the Gospel order, that were never in themselves?*" he answers: "Where there is a *beginning*, some must be first;" and on page 64 Spilsbury meets two other objections (1) of those who hold a personal succession, and (2) of those who maintain that baptism is the form of the church. Here follows Crosby's long quotation, to which I refer the reader; and following the words quoted by Crosby, Spilsbury adds:

"And for the continuation of the Church from Christ's words, 'The gates of hell shall not prevail against it, &c.,' I Confesse the same with this distinction; which Church is to be Considered either with respect to her instituted State, as lies in the Scripture, in the rules of the foundation, or in her Constitution, or constituted form in her visible order. Against the first hell gates shall never prevail, the foundation stands sure; but against the last it hath often prevailed, for the Church in her outward visible order, hath been often scattered through persecution, and the like, in which sense she is said to be prevailed against as Dan. 7, Rev. 12, Acts 8:1. Otherwise where was their Church [Puritan Reformers] before it came from under the defection.

"Again, That which once was in such a way of being, and Ceaseth for a time, and then comes to the same Estate again, is, and may be truly said, to have ever a continuance, as Matt. 22:31,32 with Luke 20:38. In which sense the Church may truly be said ever to continue, for though she be cast down at one time, yet God will raise her up at another, so that she shall never be prevailed against, as to be utterly destroyed"—

precisely the position of Smyth, Helwys, Morton, Barber, and all other Baptists before and after him in the Seventeenth century.

On page 66 Spilsbury concludes the above position by saying:

"But we are to know this, that truth depends not on Churches, nor any mortal creature, but onely upon the immortal *God*, who by his Word and Spirit reveals the same, and when and to whom he pleases. And for succession of truth, it comes now by the promise of *God*, and faith of his people, whom he as aforesaid, hath taken out of the world unto himself, in the fellowship of the *Gospel:* to whom the ordinances of Christ stand only by succession of faith, and not of persons; for the same power and authority the Apostles had in their time for direction in godlinesse, the Scriptures have now in the hand of Christ, as the head of the Church, which make up but one body. 1 Cor. 12:12,27; Ephes. 1:22,23; Eph. 4:15,16. So that what the Church and the Apostles together might do then, the same may the head and body, together with the Scriptures, do now, the Scriptures having the same authority in the *Church* now as the Apostles had then, the same Spirit being present now to reveal them, as then to write them, 1 Cor. 5:4,5; 2 Tim. 3:15,16."

Of course, by the words, "the church," as here employed, Spilsbury is only meaning the spiritual, and not the organized body of Christ, which with the Scriptures and the Spirit can now recover the ordinances when lost, just as they were set up under the apostles.

In his Epistle to the Reader, pp. 2,3, he denies the charge of rebaptization, or a new way of baptizing, as follows:

"And yet not holding any rebaptizing, for he that is once baptized with the Lord's true Baptism, he needs no more. Nor yet a new way of baptizing, as some to please themselves, so call it; but only that good old way, which John the Baptist, Christ and his Apostles walked in before us, and left the same as a Rule under command in the holy Scriptures for such as will be followers of them to walk by."

He then proceeds to show that the meaning of *Baptizo* is to "dip, wash, or plunge one into the water"—the "good old way"—

"Though some please to mock and deride, by calling it a new found way, and what they please. Indeed it is a new found truth, in opposition to an old-grown error; and so it is a new thing to such, as the Apostles Doctrine was to the Athenians, Act. 17:19. But this being no part of the following discourse, I shall leave it, &c."

Here Spilsbury denies that immersion is a *"new* way" of baptizing, but he does not deny that it was a *"*new *found* way." On the contrary, he says:

"Indeed, it *is* a new found truth, in opposition to an old-grown error;"

and he implies that it was not only a "new found truth" to the Baptists who had revived it, but that it was wholly a "new thing" to the Pedobaptists. So Hutchinson speaks of "the *way* and *manner* of *reviving* this costly *truth*" of adult immersion here spoken of by Spilsbury as *"recovered,"* and which, of course, was a "new found way"—a "new found truth"—to the Baptists who had restored it. Before the days of Blunt and Spilsbury, "believers' baptism," as restored by Smyth and his people, was spoken of as a "new baptism" without reference to mode, but principle; but after 1640-41 the "*way* of baptizing," that is, by immersion, was also called "*new;*" and although the Baptists denied that it was a new way or truth, they admitted that it was a "*new found* way," a "*new found* truth," that is, a "costly truth revived." It was in view of this admission, or rather of the facts in the case, that Praisegod Barebone, in his reply to Spilsbury (A Defense of the Lawfulnesse of Baptizing Infants, &c., London, 1644, p. 18), charges that Spilsbury had overthrown "the baptisme of believers' infants" and the "baptisme in defection of Antichrist"—and concludes by saying:

"So as like a workman indeed he hath overthrown the outward Christianity, and relation to Christ in that way, priviliges of grace, and saintship aud whatnot; all which are of much concernment every way, unto men; *and that of all persons in the world, only these few ; so of late baptized by totall dipping.*"

Spilsbury had himself admitted that believers' immersion was indeed a "new found truth;" and Barebone is perfectly right in speaking of the Baptists as "of late baptized by totall dipping."

In the whole of his reply to Spilsbury, Barebone argues that baptism under the defection of Antichrist had succeeded to the Reformed Churches, and had not been lost, and was Scriptural as an infant rite; that if lost as an adult rite, as claimed by the Baptists, it could not be restored except in the orderly way by extraordinary commission evidenced by miracle; and that Spilsbury having rejected his first baptism, and assumed a second, had separated himself from the true church, and renounced the true baptism which he had in infancy. He holds strenuously to the doctrine of succession to the reformed churches through the defection of Antichrist by means of infant baptism; and while Spilsbury admits such a succession as this to Pedobaptists, he repudiates it as a mark of the Beast, and affirms that the only succession known to Baptists is that of the Scriptures and the faith of true disciples. Upon this he bases his theory of recovery of the ordinances of Christ, the true church and its ministry. He holds precisely with Smyth except that he puts the church before baptism, just as Lawrence does, and makes the covenant instead of baptism the constitution of the church. Like Smyth and his followers he is charged with setting up a "*new* baptism" as applied to believers versus infants, and hence called rebaptism; but unlike Smyth and his followers he is charged with a "new *way* of baptizing," that is, by immersion; and as both declare that believers' baptism, irrespective of mode, is the old baptism, so Spilsbury and his followers declare immersion, though the old *way*, to be the *"new-found"* way.

In his work (God's Ordinance, the Saints' Privilege, London, 1646) Spilsbury, in the first part, meets the objection of the Seekers that the true church, ministry and ordinances of Christ—all the visible or outward forms of Christianity—had been lost under the reign of Antichrist, and that they could not be restored without extraordinary commission approved by miracle. He admits the fact that they had been lost, but that they could be recovered under the succession of the Scriptures and the faith of true believers to whom God should reveal the truth and the duty to obey. He meets all objections to the want of a proper administration of the ordinances, as he does in his "Treatise Concerning the Lawful Subjects of Baptism"; and his argument under this head is substantially the same in both of his works here quoted. The doctrine of Spilsbury is not succession, but reproduction. Romanism and Protestantism claimed succession upon the basis of infant baptism and their whole church state, inwardly and outwardly, depended upon this brittle thread of continuance; but Baptists, though preserved in the line of faith, depended upon the truth of the Scriptures for their perpetual reproduction in the recovery of their visible order and constitution—so often broken and destroyed. Wherever the Gospel has existed, even in the darkest ages of Popery, there have been true believers; and when God has willed to reveal the truth to his people and prompt their obedience by his Spirit they have restored the outward order of the Gospel. Their existence and continuance did not depend upon the succession of this outward order, as claimed for Rome and her daughters; and of the two doctrines, succession or restoration, the latter is the true evidence of God's sovereignty and power in the keeping and continuance of his visible institutions without generating the sacramental pride of his people. Reproduction—this is the original Baptist idea of succession to the external order of Gospel institutions; and this ideal is in perfect keeping with Baptist history according to Spilsbury, King, Blackwood, Smyth, Helwys, Cornwell and others, who admit the spiritual succession of God's people through all ages, but who deny a visible succession of churches, ministry or ordinances.

Spilsbury was the foremost Baptist writer of the 1641 period. He was scholarly and well informed. He became an Anabaptist after 1633 and was pastor of the first Particular Baptist Church in 1638. He was thoroughly conversant with the 1641 movement for the restoration of immersion, and was of the largest and most judicious body of the Baptists who maintained the revival of the ordinance by unbaptized administrators. Accordingly we find him in 1641 rising up to rebaptize Sam Eaton who had been rebaptized in 1633—then by aspersion, now by immersion; and this was probably the first immersion ever performed by Spilsbury. Hence the clear, clean cut utterances of Spilsbury in his writings against the Popish doctrine of succession; his candid admission that the visible order of Christ's churches, ministry and ordinances had been lost under the reign of anti-Christ; his plan for their recovery according to the Scriptures; his explanation that the gates of hell had often prevailed against the outward or constituted state of the church, though never against the inward or instituted state; his unequivocal confession that while immersion was the "good old way" and not a "new way" or a "new truth," yet it was a "new *found* truth" or a "new *found* way" in "opposition to an old grown error"—all this takes for granted the recent erection of Baptist churches in England upon the principle of believers' baptism and the still more recent introduction of immersion about 1640–41 at which time he seems to have been one of the first administrators. There is no difference between Spilsbury and Smyth except as to the question regarding baptismal mode. This never came up in Smyth's writings because he practiced the same mode that his opponents did; but after 1641 it was not only charged that Baptists practiced a "new baptism," that is, believers' as opposed to infant baptism, but that they practiced a "new way" of baptism, that is, immersion as opposed to sprinkling. Hence Spilsbury and the Baptist writers after 1641 had often to combat this point in controversy—a thing unknown before 1641, although sprinkling was universally in vogue in England from 1600 to 1641, even among the Anabaptists—so far as known.

Spilsbury is in perfect accord with Smyth, Helwys, Morton, Barber, King, Blackwood, Jessey and all the other Baptist writers of the period, so far as I know, upon the subject of Baptist succession. They all give the keynote to Baptist position on this question. Every one of them agrees that Matt. 16:18 refers to the invisible or spiritual body of Christ, and not to the visible or local churches of Christ; and they prove their position invariably (1) by the past history of God's people and (2) by the constant admission, either express or implied, that the English Baptists began by the erection of the church and baptism anew—that they were a separation or a reformation. They know nothing of any connection, organically or baptismally, with any prior sect, societies or churches preceding their origin, 1611-1633, and if any such connection had existed in the 17th century such men as Spilsbury, Tombes, King and the like would have known and acknowledged the fact. Hence the 17th century writers settle the question of Baptist succession. They utterly deny it except in the spiritual sense; and they repudiate it as a Popish or Pedobaptist fiction.

ENGLISH BAPTIST REFORMATION.

(FROM 1609 TO 1641 A. D.)

CHAPTER XIII.

CROSBY'S WITNESSES—CONTINUED.

Crosby (Vol. I., pp. 104, 105) cites "the learned Mr. Tombes who," says he, "does very excellently defend this *last method* of *restoring* true baptism." John Tombes (An Addition to the Apology For the Two Treatises Concerning Infant Baptism, 1652, London) in reply to Baillie's charge that he maintained the right of unbaptized persons to baptize others, did not hesitate to defend the proposition upon the ground that baptism had been lost and that the Baptists had restored the ordinance at the hands of unbaptized administrators, among whom, for a long time, he was himself such. As quoted by Crosby (pp. 10, 11, Section IV. of his Addition) he says, as follows:

"If *no continuance of adult baptism can be proved* and baptism by such persons is *wanting*, yet I conceive what many protestant writers do yield, when they are pressed by the Papists to shew the calling of their first reformers; that after an *universal corruption* the necessity of the thing doth justify the persons that reforme though wanting an ordinary regular calling, will justify in such a case both the lawfulnesse of a Minister's baptizing, that hath not been rightly baptized himself, and the sufficiency of that baptism to the person so baptized. And this very thing that in case where a baptized minister cannot be had, it is lawful for an unbaptized person to baptize, and his baptism is valid, is both the resolution of Aquinas and of Zanchius, and eminent protestant. *Quæritur an is possit baptizare eos, quos ad Christum convertit, cum ipse nunquam fuerit baptizatus baptismo aquæ? non dubito quin possit, & vicissim, ut ipse ab alio exillis a se conversis baptizetur. Ratio est: quia minister est verbi, a Christo extraordinem excitatus: eoque ut talis minister, protest cum Ecclesiolae consensu symistam constituere & ab eo ut baptizetur curare.* [It is asked whether a man may baptize those whom he has converted to Christ when he himself is unbaptized? I doubt not but that he may and withal provide that he himself be baptized by one of those converted by him. The reason is because he is a minister moved extraordinarily of Christ; and so as such a minister may, with the consent of that small church, appoint one of the communicants, and provide that he be baptized by him.] Whereby," says Mr. Tombes, "you may perceive that this is no new truth that an unbaptized person may in some case baptize another, and he baptize him, being baptized of him."

Baillie also charged Tombes with carelessness in not having been baptized himself, although preaching the gospel and perhaps baptizing others—nay, for many years debating and defending Baptist position with all his learned ability; and it was not until after 1652, under the pressure of Baillie's charge, that Tombes was himself immersed. (Ibid., p. 18, Sect. XIII.) It would seem among other reasons for his delay that at first he was not fully persuaded as to a proper "administrator;" but after having reached the above conclusion that an unbaptized person moved by Christ to preach and convert others was a proper administrator of baptism, it seems strange that he delayed observance of the rite so long as to himself. Tombes, like Jessey, Spilsbury and some others, was an open communionist, believing that the church was before baptism; and he went so far as to assume that an unbaptized person could partake of the Lord's Supper (An Apology, &c., London, 1646, pp. 53,54), as well as that an unbaptized person could administer baptism. From all this it is evident that Tombes rejected the theory of an unbroken succession of Christ's church, ministry or ordinances, or the theory that the validity of the church and its ministry depended upon baptismal succession. He takes for granted that adult immersion had been lost, and that its continuance could not be proved; and he planted himself upon the great Baptist position at that time which claimed the right to restore the church ministry and ordinances of Christ, being lost. He wrote his "Apology" in 1645, and his "Addition" to that apology in 1652. He was a very learned man and well acquainted with Baptist polity and history in the Kingdom—had been all about and among the Baptists of England and had been in constant controversy with the Pedobaptists, besides being in high position with the State—and yet, in 1652, he bases his theory of the right of an unbaptized person to baptize, upon the premise that adult immersion could not be proved as having had any continuance in England. Surely if there had been such a continuance—if there had been a Baptist or a Baptist church at that time having such a claim—such men as Tombes, Spilsbury, Lawrence, Kiffin, Barber, Hutchinson, Collins and the like would have found out the fact and have emphasized it. Tombes had no hesitation in retorting upon Pedobaptist controversialists—such as Cragge, Baxter, Marshall and others, who charged that Baptist immersion was a new thing in England—that infant baptism was an innovation and comparatively a new thing as then advocated. He regarded believers' baptism, adult immersion, as the "old way"—just as all the Baptists of his time claimed; but, like all the rest, he admitted that it had been lost under the reign of Antichrist, that its continuance could not be proved, and that it was a "new-found truth;" and upon this fact, like all the rest, he based his argument from the Scriptures of the right of true believers to restore it—and he is so quoted by Crosby, who wrote the first history of the English Baptists who revived the ancient practice of immersion.

In his work (Antipedobaptism, &c., London, 1652, p. 260) he writes an Introduction addressed to Lord General Cromwell, Chancellor of the University of Oxford, of which he was an alumnus; and, on page 2, says:

"It were too long to tell your Excellency what devices Satan hath used to hinder the *restoring* of the ordinance of Baptism, not only by those who are rigid asserters of Infant Baptism, but also of others, who of their own heads, without the least warrant from holy Scripture, do most presumptuously and dangerously evacuate, & many of them contemptuously deride the plain and holy institution of the Lord Jesus. The most eminent opposition to the work of *restoring* the right use of water-baptism necessary to an orderly forming of Christian Churches, hath been by those learned men, who maintain still by their arguings and colorable pretenses the corrupt innovation of Infant baptism."

Here is an example of Tombes' stigma of "innovation" upon infant baptism while at the same time he vindicates the *restoring* of believers' immersion—that is, the going back to the "old," but "new found," way which, though restored, was not an innovation as was infant baptism which he says to Baxter (Praecursor, London, 1652, p. 94), originated in the "third age," and that "the conceit of peculiar privilege to infants of believers is a *late innovation*."

In his Praecursor (pp. 48, 49) he replies to Baxter, who charges him with being a "Sect-Master," where he says:

"Nor have I baptized (save one nearly related to me) but where I was chosen a preacher; where I conceived myself bound to baptize (by Christ's Rule, Mat. 28:19) those disciples to whom I preached"—

that is, during the period he was himself unbaptized—and thus we see Tombes' agreement with Spilsbury and others who claimed that, in restoring immersion, an unbaptized administrator could baptize those to whom he preached according to Christ, Matt. 28:19, the usual Scripture proof to which all the Baptists of that day referred for their right to restore Christ's lost ordinance. Further on (p. 49) he refers to Mr. Jessey's determination (Storehouse of Provision, &c., London, 1650, p. 101) to practice open communion in order to procure more favor towards immersion as a restored ordinance, and gives the same reason for the same practice as advocated by himself, namely, "because men are so possessed with the *restoring* of baptism, as if it were an error, schisme, a practice accursed of God, that conscientious timorous men do of themselves shew us, and others furiously oppose us." In his Catechism (London, 1659, pp. 1-3), Tombes says:

"For a more facile understanding of the Truth than by reading larger *Tracts* is this *Compendium*, in a manner of Catechism composed and published at this time . . . Which I have thought necessary to be done, because of the importance of *restoring right baptism*"—

that is, believers' immersion.

It is clear that Tombes takes for granted that immersion was lost in England before its restoration in 1640-41—that he regarded it as having been restored after a "universal corruption," and when "no continuance of adult baptism could be proved," and if there was a man in England who knew what he was talking about and could have proved such a continuance if it had existed, it was the great Dr. John Tombes whom Crosby selects as a witness to the "*last method* of restoring *true baptism*." He lived in Bewdly, Oxford, Bristol and London—held controversies at Rosse, Abergavenny, Hereford and other places—traveled all over England—from 1641 to 1676 wrote extensively— and if any Baptist author of the 17th century could or should have known whether or not adult immersion was practiced in England before 1641, it was the learned Dr. Tombes.

The last great witness cited as such by Crosby was Henry Lawrence, who is also cited by the Bampfield Document in proof of the fact that the English Baptists *restored* "baptism by immersion when that practice had been so long disused that there was no one who had been so baptized to be found." He is certainly a good witness twice cited for the purpose now in hand. Crosby (Vol. I., pp. 105, 106) quotes him as "another learned Baptist, who has excellently defended the *true baptism* and the *manner* of *reviving* it in these *later times.*" Lawrence (Of Baptism, &c., Rotterdam, 1646, p. 407) says:

"It cannot be reasonably objected, that he that baptizeth should necessarily be himself a baptized person, for though ordinarily it will be so, yet it is not necessary to the ordinance, no more than it is simply necessary to a church state, that the members be baptized, for not the personal baptism of him that administers, but the due commission he hath for baptizing, is alone considerable to make him a true minister of baptism; and here that expression holds not, one cannot give what he hath not, as a man cannot teach me that wants knowledge himself, because no man gives his own baptism, but conveys as a public person that which is given us by Christ. A poor man that hath nothing of his own, may give me gold, that is, the money of another man, by virtue of being sent for that purpose; so if any man can show his commission, the writing and seal of him that sent him, it is enough here, else what would become of the great Baptizer, John the Baptist, who had a fair commission to baptize, but was not himself baptized that we read of, or if he should be, which cannot be affirmed, yet the first Baptizer whoever he was, must in the time of his first administration be unbaptized."

Lawrence differed from Smyth and the Anabaptists generally upon the point that baptism constituted the church. On the contrary he assumes that the church comes first and that the ministry or the ordinances are made or administered by the church. His definition of a church is this: "An assembly of saints, knit together to a fellowship with Christ their head"; and his idea is, in the restoration of baptism where lost, that believers should first be knit together in fellowship and then proceed to set up a ministry and administer the ordinances by church authority. This does not exclude the theory of an unbaptized administrator baptizing in the extraordinary case of restoring the lost ordinance; but Lawrence would organize the church of believers first and then begin the administration of the rite of baptism, by commissioning a ministry for the purpose. Ordinarily, he says, this will be the case, any way, that is, after the ordinances are once restored.

There is another author quoted by Crosby, though not for the purpose, who witnesses nevertheless to the truth of history on this point. I allude to Thomas Grantham (Apology for the Baptized Believers, 1674), cited by Crosby (Vol. IV., p. xii., Preface). Grantham says:

"Thus we grant, that the Church of England is no less zealous for the doctrine of baptism than ourselves, yet it is apparent to us, that she has accidentally *lost* this holy ordinance, both in respect to the subject and manner of it, and in the due use and end of it, which was not appointed nor fitted to receive new-born infants into the church militant. And by this unwarrantable change, she has defaced the state, and lost the praise of a true church, because she has not kept this ordinance as it was delivered by Christ, and his apostles, but rather suppressed it, and much oppressed those that labor to *restore* it to its due *use* and *practice* in all the churches; which is a great aggravation of all these her errors in faith and practice concerning second baptism."

This testimony is in perfect keeping with Crosby's position that the English Church lost immersion, 1600 A. D., and that the Baptists restored it 1640–41, prior to which time it "had been for some time disused" in England—"so long disused," says the Bampfield Document, "that there was no one who had been so baptized to be found"—"none" says the Kiffin Manuscript, "having then so practiced in England to professed believers."

In this chapter I have not touched upon any witness employed, except by Crosby, who goes to establish the fact that the English Baptists restored immersion at a given time, and that that time must have been 1640–41. Crosby was a thorough believer in the fact that the English Baptists had wrought a reformation from 1609 to 1641 in the restoration of the church and in its ministry and ordinances; and he elaborately describes the revival of immersion by these English Baptists about 1640–41. He closes his account by showing that the Baptist "beginning" in England had been "well defended" by able Baptist writers "upon the same principles on which all other protestants built their reformation." (Vol. I., p. 107). On p. 299, Vol. IV., he refers back to the subject when, in 1691, the Baptists under Keach were trying to restore the ordinance of *"singing"* in the churches against great opposition, when he says:

" It must be confessed, that *reformation* is, and ever was, an hard and difficult work; and no easy thing to restore lost ordinances, especially such as have been for many years neglected, and strangely corrupted; which is manifest with respect to the ordinance of *baptism*."

Crosby refers (Vol. IV., pp. 292-294) to another controversy among Baptists about 1675 regarding the *"maintainance"* of ministers in which Keach took the affirmative against others opposed to reformation on this point; and Crosby says:

"Even from the very beginning of the *Baptist* churches in *England* several of their teachers had been tradesmen, and continued in their secular employment, after they were ordained to the ministry." "The pride and luxury of the clergy, &c." says Crosby, "did not a little contribute to their [the Baptist churches] running into this opinion, as it had the Lollards and Wyckliffeites *before them*."

On pp. 290 and 291, Vol. IV., about the year 1674, Crosby alludes to another controversy regarding the "laying on of hands" in baptism, opposed by Keach, in which he says:

"These things occasioned several treatises to be wrote on each side, and had been controverted among *Baptists* even since their *first* forming themselves into distinct churches."

On p. 207, Vol. IV., Crosby claims to "having traced the History of the *English Baptists* from their *origin*"; and he claims in the above extracts that their churches had a "beginning" in England after the "Lollards and Wyckliffeites before them," and that they wrought a "reformation" in the restoring of lost ordinances such as baptism, maintainance of ministers, singing in the churches and the like. He does not go beyond the year 1611-1633 to find the origin of Baptist churches; and all their reformation of ordinances which was gradual he refers to periods later than their origin.

With the Jessey Records and his witnesses, as the basis of his history, there can be no doubt that Crosby establishes the fact that the English Baptists originated their churches and ministry from 1611 to 1633, and that they reformed further in the mode of baptism and other things from 1640-41 onward. Vol. I., pp. 95-107, Vol. IV., p. 207, pp. 292-294, with Vol. II., Preface, pp. ii-liv. cannot be otherwise interpreted. Ivimey claims that the date of restoring immersion is unknown. He seems to think the movement did not apply to all the Baptists, especially the General Baptists. Nevertheless he is confused, and he does not change the plain affirmation of Crosby that this restoration of immersion did occur by "two" different "methods" by the English Baptists without distinction. Evans evidently agrees with Crosby. Armitage is only of opinion that all the Anabaptists did not practice affusion before 1641, and that some of them immersed; but he seems to base his proof only on Leonard Busher's definition and Featley's tract, neither of which sustains his thesis as we shall more fully see. With the Jessey Records, Hutchinson, Spilsbury, Tombes, Lawrence and Grantham, Crosby makes out his case; and with the Bampfield Document and the other testimonies already and yet to be examined the case seems established beyond contradition. It is hard to see how a more than probable case at least could be more fully settled than by Crosby's own witnesses and his own conclusions.

Dr. Toulmin in his Supplement to Neal's History of the Puritans (Vol. III., p. 543) says:

"In our Supplemental pages to the reign of James I. we have said that the first English Baptists, *on embracing their discriminating opinions*, sent over Mr. Blunt to Amsterdam to receive baptism [immersion] from the Dutch Baptists. This step was, however, looked upon by the more judicious, and the greater number of the *English Baptists* as a needless trouble and proceeding from an old popish doctrine of a right to administer the sacrament by an uninterrupted succession. For though the true practice of baptism [by immersion] was, in their opinion, *lost*, they judged that it might be revived, and a reformation begun, by an unbaptized person baptizing others." [Crosby, Vol. I., p. 148, 9.)

Toulmin's construction of Crosby's language is exactly correct. Not only does the Kiffin Manuscript declare the fact that Blunt was sent to Holland for immersion because there were none who so practiced in England, but the "greatest number and the more judicious of the English Baptists" restored baptism upon this theory also—that is, by an unbaptized administrator—because it was "*lost,*" as Toulmin construes Crosby who himself says that "immersion [in England] had for some time been disused." This is another historic opinion in confirmation of the fact that the Spilsbury method of restoring immersion, 1640–41, was the "*last method*" as distinguished from the Blunt, or "*former method,*" in the sequence of time.

Although Neal (Vol. III., pp. 173, 174) errs as to the date of the first secession of the Baptists from the Puritans, 1633, under Spilsbury and assigns it to 1638 under Jessey, yet he confirms the fact of the Kiffin Manuscript to which he refers (MS. penes me.) in the following statement that these Baptists renounced their former baptism and adopted immersion according to the "former method" of restoration mentioned by Crosby. Neal says of the Particular Baptists:

"They separated from the independent congregation [the Jacob-Lathrop] about the year 1638, and set up for themselves under the pastoral care of Mr. Jesse (as has been related) and having renounced their former baptism, they sent over one of their number [Mr. Blunt] to be immersed by one of the Dutch anabaptists of Amsterdam, that he might be qualified to baptize his friends in England after the same manner. A strange and unaccountable conduct! for unless the Dutch anabaptists could derive their pedigree in an uninterrupted line from the apostles, the first *reviver* of this usage must have been unbaptized, and consequently, not capable of communicating the ordinance to others."

Neal clearly implies that the Particular Baptists after renouncing their sprinkling received from their Puritan ancestors, sent Blunt to Holland for immersion which he says upon Blunt's return was communicated to Blacklock who "dipped the rest of the society, to the number of fifty-three" in "1644"—just six years after their secession under Jessey in 1638! As we have seen, Neal terribly blunders in his dates and in some of his facts, in his use of the Kiffin Manuscript; but he is clear in the main conclusion that immersion among the Baptists of England originated with the Particular brethren in 1640–41 which he carelessly substitutes by the date 1644. Neal and his editor Toulmin together (1817) properly relate the "two methods" of restoring immersion by the "English Baptists," according to Crosby; and they both agree in the fact that both methods were based upon the absence of immersion in England—that it was "lost"—and that the Particular brethren vainly sought to restore it by succession from Holland while the Baptists in general restored it by an unbaptized administrator.

Again, Neal is astonished at the attempt of the Particular Baptists to secure immersion by succession from the Dutch Baptists; for he implies the opinion that the Dutch Baptists had no such succession. He was right, since Blunt was sent to the Collegiants, who themselves had restored immersion in 1620, and to whom Crosby refers as having done so when he says: "Others were for sending to those foreign Protestants *that had used immersion for some time*"—exactly the reverse of his expression with regard to England, where he says that, since 1600, "*immersion had for some time been disused.*" By the phraseology, "*had used*" for "*some time,*" Crosby implies the opinion that the Dutch Baptists had lately restored immersion, just as now the Baptists were proposing to do in England, where "for *some time*" it had been "*disused.*" This no doubt was the opinion of the "greatest number and the more judicious of the English Baptists" whom Crosby represents, at the very time, as protesting against Blunt's deputation to Holland as "needless trouble" for the very reason that his movement "proceeded from the old popish doctrine of succession which neither the Church of *Rome*, nor the Church of *England*, much less the modern *Dissenters*, could prove to be with them." Hence Crosby represents this "greatest number" of the English Baptists as affirming the Old Smyth-Helwys principle (Persecution for Religion Judged, &c., p. 41) and practicing accordingly, "that after a general corruption of baptism, an unbaptized person might warrantably baptize *and so begin a reformation.*" It is here implied that the deputation of Blunt to Holland was a movement well known to the great body of the English Baptists, that they protested against it as "needless trouble," and that they rejected this "*former method*" of restoring immersion by adopting the second or "*last method*" of self-originating it by an unbaptized administrator. This is Crosby's testimony; and he is strongly confirmed by Neal (1722) who read the Kiffin Manuscript before Crosby wrote his history, and by his editor, Toulmin (1817), who infers that immersion was lost and so regarded by the "greatest number and the more judicious of the

English Baptists," who restored it by the method of self-origination through unbaptized administrators.

So far as my investigation of Crosby's witnesses, and of many other corroborating witnesses not mentioned by Crosby, goes, I find him correct. He seems to be thoroughly honest and unpartisan in his statements of Baptist history. He does not always give dates. He blunders sometimes in minor points. He deals summarily, if not evasively, in a few matters of embarrassing controversy; but upon the whole Crosby is thoroughly reliable with the material he had in hand. An article in the Dictionary of National Biography (Vol. 13, p. 212) regards Crosby as "trustworthy" in matters of fact; and all the historians, such as Brooke, Hanbury, Barclay, Evans, Ivimey, Toulmin and many others who touch upon Baptist history quote Crosby as authority. He was not a very learned man, and did not have all the facts of early English Baptist history now in hand; but he dealt honestly with what he had; and in the matter of restoring immersion by the English Baptists, 1640-41, he is being more and more thoroughly confirmed by every new investigation. We do not now need Crosby to prove this fact; but I have used Crosby at length because he is a *Baptist* historian—and the first.

ENGLISH BAPTIST REFORMATION.

(FROM 1609 TO 1641, A. D.)

CHAPTER XIV.
EDWARD BARBER AND PRAISEGOD BAREBONE.

The earliest Baptist author who wrote defensively on the subject of Dipping was Edward Barber, 1641 (O. S.) or 1642 (N. S.). His tract, entitled: "A Small Treatise of Baptisme, or Dipping," is the first polemic of the kind among Baptists; and this tract originated about the same time that the English Baptists restored immersion just at the close of a long imprisonment of the author for his utterances at a little earlier date upon the subject of "infant baptism." The Anabaptist contention before 1640–41 was believers' as opposed to infant baptism—inveterate and consistent; and the same determined contention was maintained after that date with the new phase of dipping added. Nowhere, with the exception of occasional utterances which taught that immersion was baptism, do the Anabaptists introduce any discussion or defense of immersion as the exclusive form of baptism until after 1640–41. Smyth, Helwys, Morton, Spilsbury and none of the rest—with the exception of the single utterance of Leonard Busher—contend for anything but baptism as a believers' rite without reference to mode, before that date; and it was not until Blunt restored dipping that Barber and such writers added immersion to the contention for believers' baptism as opposed to infant baptism. This fact could not have been simply due to the "yeare of Jubilee," 1641, by the abolition of the Star Chamber and High Commission Court. To be sure this event gave an enlarged liberty and impulse to Baptist growth and boldness of utterance, as never before; but the defense of dipping as the exclusive form of baptism among the Anabaptists, before 1641, would have been known in their written and oral utterances if the claim had ever existed. Crosby shows that the immersion issue was added 1640–41.

The truth is that the day had passed since 1600 A. D. and in fact long before that date, when immersion, even as an infant rite, could have been taken for granted as the universal practice of the English Church; and there is no evidence of the existence of adult immersion at all since about the beginning of the 16th century in the practice of any religious body in England. Pouring or sprinkling had almost completely supplanted dipping in any form; and if immersion had ever been an issue as the exclusive form of believers' in opposition to infant baptism, it would have been as squarely made and as publicly known in the contention before 1640–41 as after that date. The same records, whether civic or ecclesiastic, before 1641, which so clearly make known the teachings and practices of the Anabaptists in other respects would have revealed their practice in this respect. All that the records show is a long-sustained contention for believers' baptism against infant baptism without regard to mode; and it is solely upon this ground that persecution continuously raged against the Anabaptists before 1640–41. It is not until after 1641, in 1644, that the first case of civic persecution occurs against Baptists for the practice of immersion when Laurence Clarkson was imprisoned in the county of Suffolk, England, for that offense (Crosby, Vol. I., p. xv., Preface; Ivimey, Vol. II., p. 561). The second case was that of Henry Denne for the same offense, 1646, at Spalding, Lincolnshire, England—so far as I know. (Crosby, Vol. I., p. 305.)

Hence Edward Barber's Treatise would seem within itself a probable evidence of the recent restoration of immersion among the Baptists of England, 1641. The Tract does not primarily claim to have been written for the purpose of showing this fact; but it seems to imply that fact (1) from the date of its origin, (2) from some expressions in the treatment of the subject under consideration, and (3) from what is distinctly confessed in reply to Praisegod Barebone, in the latter part of the Treatise, with regard to the very recent adoption of immersion among the Baptists of England as charged by P. B. In the beginning of this tract (The Preface) Barber speaks of the *general ignorance* in the midst of the *abundance* of the knowledge of the *gospel*, especially among the *ministry*, "of that glorious principle, True Baptisme or *Dipping*," and then he speaks of himself as having been raised up, amongst others, "a poor Tradesman, to *devulge* this glorious Truth to the world's censuring."* He had not made such an utterance before, although imprisoned eleven months for his defense of believers' baptism against infant baptism—from which, in 1641–2, he had just been released; and it is just in the juncture with the restoration of immersion, 1640–41, that he makes another but a new divulgence, namely, that "Dipping" is baptism. He implies this further on in this introduction when he says:

"In like manner *lately*, those that profess and practice the dipping of Jesus Christ are *called* and *reproached* with the name of Anabaptists, although our *practice* be no other [not has been] than what was instituted by Christ himself, &c."

This Preface seems to imply the newness of the *practice*, not the *truth*, of "dipping" in the mind of Barber. The general ignorance of the ministry on this particular subject at this particular time—the specific emphasis of the fact that he was just raised up to "devulge" this "glorious truth" at this juncture—the peculiar reference to the certainty of the *censure* of the *world* then in the embrace of infant sprinkling—the allusion to the *reproach* that had *"lately"* fallen upon the Anabaptists for the profession and practice of dipping—all this has the appearance of something new in Barber's defense of "Dipping" as the *late practice* of an *old truth* among Anabaptists. The great purpose of Barber's Treatise is a defense of believers' baptism as opposed to infant baptism; but he adds "Dipping" as the exclusive mode to the contention with such fresh emphasis, and under such form of expression, as to imply something *newer* or of *later* practice among the Anabaptists, in his mind.

This fact is made much clearer in the conclusion of his Treatise in reply to P. B.'s "objections." In order that this fact may be made apparent—namely, that Barber probably had in mind the recent restoration of immersion when he wrote this Treatise—I will reproduce the "objections of P. B." which seem to explain the relation of Barber's tract to P. B.'s contention, and therefore to the recent introduction of immersion among the English Baptists. P. B., or Praisegod Barebone was an intimate

---

*This passage from Barber is in perfect keeping with Spilsbury, Cornwell, Jessey, King and others who claim that immersion was a "discovery," a "revelation" from God to the Baptists in the "latter age." Dr. Whitsitt has been unjustly criticized for the word "discovery" (invention), and yet this was the very word of the 17th Century Baptist writers.

friend of some of the Anabaptists. He was at the head of one of the divisions of the Jessey Church when the separation of 1640 took place under the agitation of the Blunt movement with which he was well acquainted. In the spirit of friendly remonstrance, as his Epistle Dedicatory intimates, he seems to have written his pamphlet (A Discourse Tending to Prove the Baptisme in or under the Defection of Antichrist to be the Ordinance of Jesus Christ, &c., London, 1642); and being held in the very highest historic esteem as a good and able man, his reliability as a writer cannot be doubted. Addressing himself to the nicknamed Anabaptists, as he calls them, he says (p. 3):

"But the way of new Baptizing, lately begun to be practiced by some, supposing themselves, and so others, not to have bin baptized with the Baptisme of Christ, hath no ground for its practice, but the cessation of the Church, and Baptisme with it, as not remaining in the world. That they are utterly ceased where Antichrist prevailed to exalt himselfe, their practice doth fully declare; and that it is so they take for granted and indeed."

On page 5 he says again:

"But now further Baptisme being lost and fallen out of the world and an Idoll and likenesse come in the roome of it, the Church being ceased, to whom *Christ* gave his power: persons not having their Baptisme of Jesus Christ, but being unbaptized, all which the opinion and practice of New beginning Baptisme supporteth to be most true and certain, and therefore do ground their proceedings. I infer hereupon, that it is, and ever shall be found unlawful and without warrant for any person, or persons whatever, to attempt, or goe about the raising, erecting up of it againe, unless the said persons have speciall and particular warrant from heaven and a Commission, as John the Baptist had. The Jewes (though blind) could see this, that none but a Christ, a Moses, or Elias, or Prophet from heaven might do this; so as there being none such to be found to restore and newly erect this Ordinance fallen out of the world, for any other to goe about the raising of it (as some please to term it) they shall but raise it from the bottomlesse pit—Commission being wanting in the actors of it, it shall be but only earthly and from beneath. And it being asked of these as the Jewes asked of *John* his Baptisme, *whether it were from heaven or men?* It must needs be answered of Men, for no commission can any shew to raise Baptisme thus fallen out of the world; nor to Baptize themselves or others, being themselves unbaptized."

Barebone states precisely the position of the Anabaptists of 1642; and he states precisely the objection of the Pedobaptists of his day. In principle and without regard to mode this was the controversy between Smyth, Helwys and Morton on the one side, and Robinson, Clyfton and others on the other side; from 1609-11 and onward; but now the controversy, since 1640-41, takes on an additional phase—the *way* and *manner* of new baptizing, as mentioned by Spilsbury. Hear Barebone again. He says (ibid, pp. 12, 13):

"But now *very lately* some are mightily taken, as having found out a *new defect* in the baptisme, under the defection, which maketh such a *nullitie* of Baptism, in their conceit, that it is none at all, and it is concerning the *manner* of baptizing, wherein they have espied such a default, as it maketh an *absolute* nullity of all persons' baptisme, but such as have been *so* baptized, according to their *new discovery*, and so partly as *before* in regard of the *subject*, and partly in regard of so great *default* in the *manner*. They not only conclude, as is before sayd, a nullity of their *present* baptisme. And so, but addressing themselves to be baptized a *third time*, after the true way and manner they have *found out*, which they account a precious truth. The particular of their opinion and practice is to *Dip*: and that persons are to be dipped, all and every part to be under the water, for if all the whole person be not under the water, then they hold they are not Baptized with the Baptism of Christ. As for sprinkling or pouring water on the face it is nothing at all as they account, and so measuring themselves by their *new thoughts* as unbaptized they address themselves to take it up after the manner of Dipping; but truly they want [lack] a Dipper that hath authority from heaven, as had John whom they please to call a Dipper, of whom it is sayd that it might be manifested his Baptisme was from heaven. A man can receive nothing, that is, lawful authority or power to Baptize, unlesse it be given *from heaven*, which I desire they would be pleased to mind, and they will easily see their *third baptisme* is from the earth and not from heaven, as John's was. And if this case be further considered it will appear at the most to be but a defect in the *manner*, and a coming short in the quantity of the Element. It is a wonderful thing that a *nullitie* should thereof follow forthwith, of which more may be seen in the *same case* before. Againe that the substance of an Ordinance of so high a nature and great concernment should be founded in the criticknesse of a *word* and in the *quantity* of an element is no less marvelous to say no more. Oh but Baptisme is a Buriall as it is written,

We are buried with him in Baptisme, etc., and we are raised up also to newnesse of life. This Buriall and resurrection only Dipping can import and hold forth."

On page 15 he adds:

"The Romanists, some of them, and some of the poore ignorant Welsh do use dipping [in their infant baptism], I thinke these will not say they learned this new truth of them, neither do I think they will hold their Baptisme ever the truer for their dipping . . . But inasmuch as this is a very new way, and the full growth of it, and setting is not yet known, if it be to themselves, yet not to me and others: I will forbeare to say further to it."

Barebone states precisely the fact, admitted by Spilsbury, that among Baptists immersion was the "new-found truth;" and he states precisely the fact that "very lately" the Baptists had discovered a "new *defect*" in their baptism under the defection of Antichrist. The former defect under that defection was the subject of baptism as discovered by John Smyth and his followers, and still urged as the principle upon which Baptists reformed, irrespective of mode; but the "new defect" under this defection was the mode of baptism which was sprinkling, and which they had recently changed to immersion—about "two or three yeares," Barebone says, in 1643, in his "Reply" to R. B. and E. B. (p. 18) which would properly fix the time at 1640–41. More than this, Barebone confirms the statement of Pedobaptist position by Crosby (Vol. I., pp. 96, 97), namely, that the adoption of immersion by the Baptists of England now nullified other forms of baptism as formerly the adoption of believers' baptism (without regard to mode) nullified the subject of infant baptism. Hence he calls it a "new discovery"—"partly as *before* in regard of the *subject* and partly [*now*] in regard of so great default in the *manner*." It was a "new discovery" of the *old principle* as Smyth and all the rest claimed "*before*" when they established believers' baptism by affusion; and it was now a newer discovery of the *old way* by which they continued believers' baptism by immersion. It was a "third baptism" with all the Baptists who had changed to immersion—first, having been baptized in infancy while in the embrace of Antichrist; secondly, having been sprinkled again when they separated from the Separation and became Anabaptists; thirdly, when in 1640–41 they restored immersion and became regular Baptists. Barebone is in precise accord with Barber, Spilsbury, Kiffin, the Jessey Records and all the rest who touch the subject—even to the word "discovery."

Under this quotation, as the other, Barebone continues his Pedobaptist argument for succession under the defection of Antichrist. Granting the Baptist assumption that the true church and baptism had been lost, they, the Baptists, could not restore them without a new commission, another John the Baptist, or Elijah, or Prophet; and granting that they had so lost immersion, the form of baptism, which they had *"very lately"* restored, they had no "proper administrator" to "raise" that up again. "Truly," says he, "they lack a dipper that hath authority from heaven, as had John."

Now we can understand Barber both in his Treatise as a whole and in his reply to Barebone in the latter part of his tract, where he says:

"Beloved, since part of this Treatise was in Presse there came to my hand a book, set forth by P. B. which could I have gotten sooner, I should have answered more fully."

He goes on, under the first head of his answers to P. B., to agree with him that Christ is not a Widower nor his church without a head, although the church, or is the ministry, is not always visible on the earth; and that for a time they were "hid in the Wildernesse." "Christ" could be "no Widower," nor his "Church without a head so long as his Spouse hath a being in heaven or earth." So much for the church and its ministry; but under the second head of his answer he says:

"2. We grant the *Ordinance* being lost, none but a *Christ*, a *Moses*, *Elias* or a Prophet from heaven can raise it; but believers having Christ, the Word and Spirit *have this*," that is, the authority of Christ, or the commission of a Moses, Elias or Prophet to *"raise it"* or restore it; and he cites the Scriptures, "Mat. 18:19, 20; 11:11; Luke 7:28; Rom. 10:6, 7, 8," in proof of such authority, or commission, to *"raise"* again or restore the *"Ordinance being lost."* He takes John the Baptist, who did not baptize himself—who, to begin with, was an unbaptized administrator; and just as Smyth, Helwys, Morton, Spilsbury, Tombes, Lawrence and others on this same question held, so Barber maintains that having Christ and his Spirit, believers are commissioned by the Scriptures which represent God to begin baptism anew when lost, without a baptized administrator, just as was John, who had God's authority to begin the ordinance at first. He goes on to show that the apostasy of Israel never raced the foundation of the constitution of the Jewish Church based upon the seed of Abraham and circumcision so long as they did this; and though circumcision was lost in the wilderness it was restored, as King says, by Joshua in the Land of Canaan, (Joshua 5:2–9), when the reproach of Egypt was rolled away. Barber's argument, however, is that "Antichrist" not only "changed all other ordinances both in the Church and Ministry, Worship and Government, but that he *"destroyed the true Apostolical institution"* of baptism both as to subject and mode—as seen in "the sprinkling of infants;" and that Baptists would never have *separated* from the Church of Rome or England, nor "removed this baptisme as false," if they had pursued the proper design and form, just as Kiffin holds.

Barber mentions an illustration of Barebone's in which he compares the ordinances of Christ in the hands of Antichrist to the vessels of the Lord's House in the hands of the Babylonians; and as the vessels were restored to Jerusalem and used again in the new Temple, so under the defection of Antichrist these ordinances were received by the Reformers, and were still pure gold and silver, and needed not to be *"new cast."* Barber replies that while this was true of Babylon, which had not "destroyed the Lord's vessels," nor made them of "Brass, Copper, Tin, or Lead," Rome had so done with the ordinances of Christ; and his argument is, under the figure, that they needed to be "new cast." "And thus it stands," he says, "in truth for the matter of Dipping of Christ, *destroyed and raced out both for matter and forme*, as hath been formerly shewed, the *matter* being a believer desiring it, the true *forme*, dipping them into Christ, &c.,"—precisely the position of Smyth, except that he uses the word "washing," as before 1641, while Barber uses the word "dipping," the usage after 1641. Hence Barber's previous assertion, in reply to Barebone, that the "ordinance being lost, &c.," believers have the Commission of Christ to restore the lost ordinance, not simply believers' baptism as opposed to infant baptism, but *now* the mode of baptism, as charged and not denied. What he held for the principle revived in 1609–11, he now held for the mode revived in 1640–41, without the slightest repudiation of Barebone's charge of recent introduction as contradistinguished from a former introduction. He grants that the ordinance which he defines by dipping had been "raced out and destroyed;" he defends the right of its restoration according to the Scriptures; and he tacitly admits its very late introduction by replying to the charge without denying it. Such a charge was too serious an aspersion, if it was false, not to repudiate; and the clear implication is that Barber took it for granted.

In his "Short Reply to the frivolous Exceptions of E. B.," 1643, at the close of his "Reply" to R. B., Barebone charges Barber with acknowledging this fact. He says, (pp. 55, 56):

"His second exception is to what I propounded, that if Baptism was lost and fallen out of the world none but a Christ, a Moses, an Elias, or at least a Prophet from heaven might restore, &c: To this he sayeth that he granteth that an ordinance lost and fallen out of the world none but a Christ, a Moses, Elias or prophet from heaven can raise it. Baptism was lost he acknowledgeth, when did Christ, Moses, Elias or any Prophet from heaven, come to raise it again &c; But this hee thinketh may serve, believers having Christ, the Word & Spirit, so he sayth may do it, &c."

Acknowledging this without denial, acknowledges Barebone's included charge of very late introduction—just as R. B. did in the same controversy.

Barebone charged that Christ was a "Widower" upon Barber's theory and advised him to wait 'till Christ came again to restore all things, as some held, for a proper administrator of baptism. "To which I answer," says Barber, "if the want of visibility of the church proveth Christ a Widower; then the state of the church of which P. B. is a member, was unheard of within these two hundred yeares, and so Christ a Widower, unlesse hee hold the church of Rome a true church, which if he doe, how dare they separate from her? If not, some of them, being loving friends, holding the same Principle: how dare *they* raise up a state before Christ come, as they say, to *restore* all things." Barebone in his "Reply" to R. B. and E. B., p. 61, retorts:

"Well two-hundred yeares is some Antiquitie, more then *two or three yeares, such as is the descent of the totall dippers in this Kingdom:* hee foolishly concludeth so Christ a Widower till then."

To this statement in 1643—made twice, once to R. B. and then to E. B., without denial from either or from any one else in the great controversy which then prevailed, is a thorough confirmation of the Jessey Records' date of 1640-41; and it goes without saying that Barebone was not only a friendly but an honest and capable witness who had every opportunity to know what he was talking about. In searching for the character of Barebone as a man and as a writer among the critical sketches of the British Museum, I never found an intimation against his ability or reliability, but the contrary; and with his bold and unchallenged statement, 1643, concerning the recent introduction of immersion, confirmed by the Jessey Records and the current teaching of all the Baptist writers of that day who touched the subject, I am constrained to accept his statements which are yet to be more fully confirmed.

The reference of Barebone to dipping among *some* of the Romanists and ignorant Welsh does not imply adult immersion among them in 1642, but their limited continuance of infant immersion down to that time. At that time we know that the Roman Catholics were nowhere practicing adult immersion; and only a few places, perhaps, like Milan —which has recently abandoned it—continued to practice infant immersion, sprinkling having been almost universally adopted by that church long before 1642-3. So of some of the Welsh who according to Sir John Floyer (Hist. Cold Bathing, 1722, p. 14) "had more lately left off immersion; for," says he, "some middle-aged persons have told me, That they could remember their dipping in baptism." Sir John Floyer was discussing the disuse of infant immersion, and urging its restoration; and he shows that the disuse of infant immersion in Wales followed later than in England. At the time Barebone wrote in 1642—though not at the time Sir John Floyer wrote in 1722— "some" of the Welsh still retained infant dipping. In 1650 Peter Chamberlen, in reply to Thomas Bakewell's book, "The Dippers Plunged in a Sea of Absurdities, &c.," says: "And the *Winter Baptizing* of Children in *Wales*, will sufficiently testifie that you foist in your own untruths, by the strength of your own distracted imagination." There was no adult immersion in Wales before 1641 since the first centuries; and Barebone was evidently alluding to the dipping of children among some Catholics and the ignorant Welsh. The very fact that Barebone referred to this continued practice among *some* of the Romanists and poor ignorant Welsh, both Pedobaptists, as not likely to be esteemed by Baptists as an example to them, implies that it was infant dipping to which Barebone was himself opposed, and which had been long ago abandoned in England. Even, however, if he had alluded to adult immersion among the Romanists and Welsh, it would not have altered the fact that the English Baptists had recently changed, in 1640-41, from sprinkling to immersion, Barebone himself being witness, and Barber and Spilsbury both agreeing thereto. Barebone makes his assertion, however, as broad as the "Kingdome" of England; and he declares, in 1643, that the "totall dippers"—exclusive immersionists—in that "Kingdome" were "only two or three yeares old." Hence he could not have alluded to the Romanists and Welsh as adult immersionists; and he concedes nothing by his allusion to partial dipping in warm climates.

Barebone's book was intended as a reply to Spilsbury who took up Smyth's old argument against the validity of baptism under the defection of Antichrist; and Barebone only takes up the old arguments and illustrations of Robinson, Clifford and others in defense of baptism under the defection of Antichrist. Barber copies largely the positions of Smyth, Helwys and Morton, and like Spilsbury and the rest, after 1640-41, adds the mode to the principle of believers' baptism, both of which had now been restored. In his reply to Barebone in the latter part of his Treatise he emphasizes the lost mode as brought in by Barebone; and what he admits of the principle as lost under the defection of Antichrist he admits of the mode, immersion, as being lost and the right to restore it according to the Scriptures. In 1643 Barebone, in reply to R. B., also answers Barber in the latter part of his book in the same strain that he had to Spilsbury in 1642-3, and as he again replied, 1644, to Spilsbury's Treatise Concerning the Lawful Subjects of Baptisme, 1652, but which must have been written in 1642, or else Barebone replied in 1654 instead of 1644. Barber makes no further answer, so far as I have seen, and although the purport of his Treatise is to prove that "Christ ordained dipping for those only that profess repentance and faith," as Dr. Newman says, yet he incidentally assents to the recent introduction of immersion by acknowledging that it was lost and by defending the right to restore it. His emphasis of baptism as dipping, in the light of the whole Treatise and in the light of history and current Baptist authorship, cannot presuppose, as has been claimed, "that dipping was at that time the commonly recognized usage, and presumably a usage of long standing," as well shown by Dr. Newman, (Review of the Question, pp. 203-4). There is not the slightest doubt that Barebone, 1642, affirms that the Baptists of England had "very lately" introduced immersion in England—within the last "two or three years" according to Barebone, 1643—fixing the time, 1640-41; and Barber is right along the line of all the rest of the Baptist writers of his day in acknowledging and defending the fact. This seems to be his implied conviction in the beginning of his Treatise; and it is the admitted conviction in the close. Nobody under the most strained sophistry can read Barebone's book and Barber's reply, and come to any other conclusion. Especially is this true in the light of so much concurrent testimony to the same effect at the same time from so many other sources. Barber's very boldness and exuberance—his almost ostentatious use of the word dipping as baptism—in the first defense of the mode, and as a fresh divulgence, has the aspect of a "fresh conviction;" and he is in perfect line with Smyth, Helwys, Morton, Hutchinson, the Jessey Records, Spilsbury, Kiffin, King, Tombes, Lawrence, Denne, Collins and all the rest who have likewise touched the subject.

ENGLISH BAPTIST REFORMATION.

(FROM 1609 TO 1641 A. D.)

CHAPTER XV.
SOME OTHER BAPTIST WITNESSES.

Having placed before the reader the evidence of Evans, Crosby, Hutchinson, the Jessey Records, the Bampfield Document, Spilsbury, Tombes, Lawrence, Grantham, Kiffin, Barber and Barebone and others, which prove that the English Baptists restored immersion about 1640-41, and that prior to that time they must have practiced sprinkling or pouring, I now present some other Baptist authorities whose testimony is quite as strong and valid.

1. The earliest of these Baptist witnesses is A. R[itor] in a work, entitled: A Treatise of the Vanity of Childish Baptisme, &c., London, 1642. On page 29, Part First, he says:

> "If any shall think it strange and unlikely that all the godliest Divines and best Churches should be deceived in this point of baptisme, for so many yeares together: Let them consider that all Christendom (except here and there one, or some few, or no considerable number) was swallowed up in grosse popery for so many hundred yeares before Luther's time which was not until about 100 yeares agone. Let them also consider how long the whole nations of England and Scotland have bin deceived in the point of the Hierarchy untill of late, and yet they now for the most part do see it to be Antichristian and abominable, and why may they not likewise be deceived in this point of the Baptisme of infants, &c."

Referring to the Second Psalm (Part II., p. 28), he says:

> "This may likewise teach us, to see and bewaile the great apostasie, both in faith and worship, that is brought into the world by this Childish Baptisme."

Part First (pp. 8-12), under the second head, is devoted to the proof that dipping only is baptism as opposed to sprinkling; and that whoever is not dipped is not baptized—all this in 1642, and soon after the introduction of immersion in England by the Baptists. According to his Preface to the Reader, A. R. was a recent convert from the Church of England, having been *sprinkled* in *infancy*, and must have been immersed in 1641-2. He writes in the same strain that Barber does regarding the ignorance of divines and churches—even England and Scotland in the darkness of the Hierarchy—"untill of late," and still deceived under the apostasy. S. C. (A Christian Plea for Infants Baptisme, London, 1643, II. P., p. 4) replies to A. R. in the same strain that P. B. does to Barber, or Spilsbury, and charges the Anabaptists with having taken up a "new baptism" by unbaptized administrators—with thus holding to a church of unbaptized members—and with claiming that otherwise "true baptism can never be had." No doubt this was the view of A. R., as it was of all other Baptists of his day; and his work is in line with all the other works then among Baptists, which claimed that immersion was "lost" in the apostasy—"swallowd up in grosse popery" —and that it must be restored by unbaptized administrators, according to the Scriptures.

2. In the next year, 1643, Praisegod Barebone answered a work written by R. B. (A Reply to the Frivolous and Impertinent Answer of R. B. [1642] to the discourse of P. B., London, 1643), and although I sought in vain for R. B.'s work, I find enough of it in P. B.'s "Reply" to make out the opinions of R. B., and to show that he was in the restoration movement. On pages 2, 3, P. B. represents R. B. as holding that the succession of baptism depended upon the "continuednesse of the church;" and he says:

"I confesse I know none, nor do I believe that any can show any such continuance." (Quoted by P. B. from R. B.'s Answer to his Treatise on Baptisme, &c.)

R. B. is also represented as using the phrase: "*perpetual interrupted succession*" and as denying any perpetual uninterrupted succession of the church.

"Baptism he saith (p. 15) may be obtained without any such special commission as had John, if an unbaptized person shall doe it."

R. B. squarely assumes that the church ceased and so baptism ceased, and that both had been restored. P. B. (p. 17) says:

"But it appeareth to be true that R. B. indeed holdeth so, that at sometime *lately* there were no baptized persons in the World: And yet Baptisme might be raised again well enough;"

and R. B. cites the Scriptures (2 Tim. 2:6) as the authority by which, having faith, baptism, "in an extraordinary case," could be restored by an unbaptized person—in precise accord with Spilsbury, who is here instanced (p. 18) as citing the case of David, though not a priest, eating shewbread in the Tabernacle.

Observe here that R. B., a Baptist, held that "sometime *lately* there were no baptized persons [Baptists] in the world;" and as he claimed that immersion had been restored, and tells us how it was done, therefore in 1642 "baptized persons" [Baptists] had only been "lately" in the world. P. B. (p. 18) holds that R. B. dissents, in this view, "from others of his judgment," and he claims that "there were baptized persons in Holland [alluding to the Mennonites] of a "hundred yeares discent."

"If R. B..," says P. B., "questions their baptisme, it is much: happily he may, because they practice not totall dipping: then sure it is likely, the restoration [of immersion] is but two or three yeares standing, a very rare business, and how rare are baptized persons [Baptists], he concludeth there needs no new commission to raise it againe, we may believe him if we will."

Of course, R. B. meant immersionists—not all Anabaptists. On page 19, P. B. continues:

"New things are very pleasing and many are much taken with them, as is R. B. with dipping, about which he taketh great pains, produceth many Scriptures, and would seem to be so strong, as nothing is able to withstand him . . . but sure the man is one that looketh through a greene glass, he seeth all the same color, all and every of the Scriptures, and examples are for total dipping the whole man in matter and burying him under water; and I appeal to the judgment of the indifferent Reader, whether there be any the least syllable to any such purpose: no marvell he should check me for not believing of it; and so confidently to further his fancie, and erroneous conceit, on the holy Scriptures, and which is more to hold all the churches, and Christians in the World to be unbaptized, but those two or three that have been thus totally dipped."

On page 30, he says again:

"What should be the cause R. B. hath labored so much in this matter of dipping and taken notice of every particular, I leave every man free to judge, for my part I take it to be as I said, It is new and the man is mightily taken with it." . . . "There is one thing in the end of this matter of dipping which he doth not declare himself about, Namely whether he learned this new way of dipping of the Romanists and Ignorant Welsh, and whether he count their Baptisme the Baptisme of Christ." . . . "I have spoken for the ordinance of Christ which he hath peremptorily condemned, and yet doth, denying the Baptisme of all the reformed Churches & separed Churches, & also of all other Christians either Reformed or yet in defection, only those two or three excepted that have within these two or three years or some such short time, bin totally dipped for Baptisme, by persons at the beginning unbaptized themselves."

I need not comment on these passages to show the recent introduction of immersion by the English Baptists in 1640–41 at the hands of both a Baptist and Podobaptist. This is but a specimen of the current controversy between Baptists and Pedobaptists from 1640–41 and onward to the close of the 17th century. The only question of importance now is: Who was R. B.? Back on pages 3, 4, Preface to the Reader, P. B. characterizes R. B. as a man of "often changes" in baptism—once "confident of his first baptisme" and "certainly of his second;" and he says:

"A man that had a mind to come to R. B. in his third Baptisme, before a year or two spent in serious wayghing of the matter, would find happily that R. B. had left his third baptisme, and by that time had taken a fourth, &c."

It is clear that R. B., having been baptized in infancy, had come out of the Separation as an Anabaptist by a second sprinkling, and had then adopted immersion in the 1640–41 movement. P. B. taunts him with his "often changes" and suggests that he might change to a fourth baptism, as many of the Anabaptists, still dissatisfied with their third baptism, did, or else abandoned it altogether, according to the confusion of conflicting sects, after 1641. There is no evidence here that R. B. had changed to a "fourth" baptism, though taunted by R. B. with the probability;

but it is difficult to determine who he was. It has been supposed that he was Richard Blunt; but this is improbable, unless Blunt who had sought regular baptism of the Dutch Collegiants, had changed to the Spilsbury theory that "baptizednesse is not essential to the administrator of baptisme." But neither P. B., in this discussion, nor R. B., makes any allusion to the deputation to Holland for baptism, a fact P. B. well knew in Blunt's case. P. B. does suggest that the Holland Mennonites had retained the descent of baptism for a hundred years, by affusion, which some of R. B.'s brethren still regarded as baptism and to whom the Baptists might have gone for succession, but of course R. B. and the new dippers rejected even Anabaptist affusion; and the intimation of P. B. is that some of the English Anabaptists had not yet come over to dipping—alluding, no doubt, to some of the General Baptists who had not broken from Mennonite affusion and relationship. At all events R. B. does not seem to be Richard Blunt; and he seems to have been a General Baptist "dissenting from others of his judgment" as to Mennonite baptism which Blunt and the Particular Baptists would not have considered at all.

There is another publication (A Briefe Answer to R. H., His Booke, Entitled, The True Guide &c., London, 1646) written by R. B.; but there is nothing in this work which indicates the R. B. above, or Richard Blunt. It seems to be an answer to a Quaker against the position that the "Baptisme of Water" signifies "by Scripture expression the Baptisme of the Spirit" and other propositions which make it a clear cut Baptist book characteristic of the times. On page 23, in answer to the charge of "schism," he replies:

"When the church of God is *restored* againe from under Antichrist to that primitive purity, and first patterne of Truth, he that maketh use of this Scripture [2 Tim. 2:2, cited by R. H.] is in a Church way, answering that patterne, and is infallibly assured of it, then he may infallibly make use of this place, to declare who they are that make divisions."

In his Epistle to the Reader (pp. 1, 2) after pointing to the collapse of faith under the Apostasy of Antichrist—and to those who thought restitution had come from Luther's time, or from Queen Elizabeth's time—he says:

"And yet we see much of that corrected of late; and must it needs be, there are no Truths left behind still undiscovered, Prophesyings in Saccloth? God is not bound to *restore* all Truth at once, nor to a multitude, but even to a few, and they perhaps despised ones, 1 Cor. 1:27, 28, even like those Fisher-men which Christ chose."

He goes on to assume that as the "decay of truth was graduall from the Apostles times, as may be sense," so the "*restitution* would likewise be graduall;" and he looks, as many Baptists and others did in that day, for the coming of Christ for the perfect "restoration of the truth from under Antichrist." Like all the Baptists of his day, he regarded the restoration movement as a "discovery" from God of the lost truth; and he believed that though much truth had been rediscovered—such as the true church, ministry and ordinances of Christ—yet there were other developments of truth to follow until the full restitution at the coming of Christ, which indicated him a Fifth-monarchy man. He has a little of the tone of the Seekers; and after all he may have been Richard Blunt after the dissolution of his church before 1646.

3. Thomas Kilcop (A Short Treatise of Baptisme, &c., London, 1642), after meeting Barebone's arguments regarding infant baptism, he proceeds to answer the charge concerning the Baptist claim that baptism had been "lost." He says (pp. 8-11):

"You deride us in your booke about the rise, matter, and manner of baptisme, the two last are clearely proved by Scripture already, the use of it being once *lost*, is the onely thing to clear; of that therefore a few words. Our baptisme received in our infancy (being corrupted) is notwithstanding true or false. If true, though corrupted (as you hold), then needs must the other ordinances be true, the church also true, for nothing (I conceive) is more corrupted (if so much) as baptisme, as in the first use; and then it followes that you doe ill in leaving true ordinances, and true church state, and should then returne againe. Ob. We shift off the corruptions only. Ans. Then should you goe to the root and strike at the greatest corruption first, which is I conceive the subject. Your onely course then would be to let your infants remaine unbaptized, and then such as you and others (upon triall) judge to be in covenant, and precious in God's account, you might safely baptize by virtue of your baptisme, if yours be true, though corrupted, as you hold it is; and not doing so, you go a wrong way to work to root out corruption. But for my part, I believe Christ will at no rate own the baptizing of infants for his baptisme, and therefore not true. And then it followes that it being false, is to be renounced as well as the church state being false, and true baptisme as well as true church state is to be erected; except we turn Familists and Libertines to let all alone and live loosely, which opinion is held out, for ought I know, only by such as are given up to their own lusts. Ob. But where is your warrant for so doing? I answer, That every Scripture that gives you warrant, or any of your judgment, to erect a church state, gives us the same warrant to erect baptisme, sith the one cannot be done without the other, for none can put on Christ (that is visibly by outward profession) but such as are baptized into Christ, that is into the way or profession of Christ, for so is the meaning. Gal. 3:29. [John Smyth.]

"So that as a certain company of you agreeing in one, may become a body with evry one's mutual consent: just so might we or you take up this ordinance, too, I mean if it be so that otherwise we cannot partake of it (AS ONCE IT WAS) and also know that Christ puts no impossibilities upon us, and we are nowhere so enjoyned that if we cannot know absolutely a people that have upheld it ever since John, then not to partake of it. But we are absolutely enjoined to be baptized. Mark 16:16. Which is an impossibility if that must needs be a tye. Againe, if Christ had so tied us, then would you be put to a great strait, to prove that baptisme that you have partakt of to be so upheld which thing I believe you cannot possibly doe; you must take the Pope's word for it or else some Historie or other which I dare not credit as I do the Bible."

Thomas Kilcop was one of the "fifty-three" baptized by Blunt and Blacklock, 11 Mo., Janu. 1641; along with Thomas Shepard and Thomas Gunne (baptized at the same time), and with William Kiffin (probably baptized the same year later) he was one of the signers of the 1644 Confession. He is one of the original parties mentioned in the so-called Kiffin MS., who introduced immersion in England upon the affirmation that *"none had then so practiced in England to professed believers";* and hence his very reply here to Barebone implies the recent introduction of immersion into England. Though a Particular Baptist he makes precisely the argument to P. B. that John Smyth did to Clifton—using Smyth's very language—namely, that the Baptists had as much right to erect baptism anew, as the Separatists had to erect a new church state; and just what Smyth, under the form of affusion, did in 1609, Blunt, Blacklock, Lucar, Shepard, Gunne, Kilcop and others, under the form of immersion, did in 1641. It is objected that Kilcop implies that it had not been necessary to restore baptism by the hypothetical clause, "*if it be so that otherwise we cannot partake of it;*" but the parenthetical clause "(AS IT ONCE WAS)" which follows, settles the question. Nothing could be plainer than his admission that baptism had been "lost" as Barebone charged that all Baptists held; and Kilcop's whole argument here is a succinct and vigorous effort in short to prove that Baptists had a right to restore immersion anew according to John Smyth's thesis. He does not pretend to contradict Barebone's charge, but defends it; and he here impliedly admits Barebone's further charge that "totall dipping in the Kingdome" was "only two or three yeares old," and that the Baptists lacked an original administrator. Kilcop is exactly in line with Barber, Spilsbury, Tombes, Lawrence and all the rest; and though baptized by Blunt with the regular baptism from Holland, he here utterly excludes the slightest idea of succession—planting himself like a true Baptist upon the Bible as his authority, and not upon history or tradition for the validity of his baptism. The Blunt movement or "persuasion" is well represented by the names of Shepard, Gunne, Kilcop and possibly Kiffin, as signers of the 1644 Confession; and by Kilcop, if not Kiffin, in the literature of the time

4. From an Anabaptist Sermon (The Arraignment, Tryall Conviction and Confession of Francis Deane, &c., London, 1643) I extract the following:

"Beloved, I am filled with much zealous joy to behold so great an Assembly gathered together in this Chamber to hear me discover unto you *new Doctrine* upon the receiving of a new member into our Assembly: who before had only the bare rags of Adam, and baptized by the ceremony of Antichrist, &c."

After having done with the text the preacher proceeded to baptize the new member, and said:

" Being come to this holy place, I desire all of you here present to take notice, that this our brother is received to the River Jordan called the old Foord neare Bow, and now the *new* Jordan or place of happinesse, for unless all be thus rebaptized stark naked, and dipped as well head as tayle as you are, none can be saved."

The preacher called his sermon on baptism ("Wash and be Clean") "*new doctrine;*" and he called the place of baptism "*new Jordan.*" The title of the tract refers to the incident as the Rebaptizing of a Brother at the *new holy Jordan*, &c.; together with the *manner* how they *use* to perform their "Anabaptisticall ceremonies"—referring no doubt to the oft repeated charge of naked baptism here reported and exaggerated as having been the custom of the Baptists. "The *new holy Jordan*, as they call it, neare Bow," is applied to the same river in the same vicinity by Mercurius Aulicus, 1643, the same year as follows:

"And the river Lee, which runs by Bow, wherein the *new* elect rebaptize themselves, and call it by the name of Jordan."

The preacher of this sermon from which I quote, if properly reported, was not a sound Baptist, either in doctrine or practice; but he is an illustration of the gross irregularities which, according to the history of the times, characterized the recent introduction of immersion.

5. The next witness is Francis Cornwell (The New Testament Ratified with the blood of the Lord Jesus &c., London, 1645). In his controversy with Whittle (p. 19) he says:

"Hence it is that we poor despised believers in Jesus Christ dipt, owne Jesus the Christ to be our eternal high Priest, that manifested his love to us in the Covenant of Free-grace. . . . This love *discovered*, caused us to hearken to the voyce of Jesus our Anoynted Prophet; for his voice is lovely: And when he revealed to us, by his word and good Spirit, that none was the subject of baptism; but such as believe in the Lord Jesus the Christ and repent of their *dead works*. When this truth was revealed, we harkened to the voice of Christ onely as his sheep ought to doe, John. 10. and regarded no more the voyce of a stranger, the Pope, the Bishop, the Priest. Nay when Christ was discovered to be our *King*, and that we were but as Rebells, untill we did obey his Command, when he by his good Spirit *discovered* what his commandments was, namely, that we which believe in Jesus Christ, must repent and be dipped in the name of Jesus Christ, the love of Christ our King constrained us to arise and be dipped in the name of Jesus Christ."

On page 22, in the addenda to Whittle's Answer, Cornwell says:

"The Nationall churches have trodden the holy citie of believers in Jesus Christ dipt under foot, *neere* 42 moenths; which reckoning a day for a year, may amount to *neer* 1260 years, Rev. 11. 2."

Cornwell takes the current Baptist position of his time, that the church of dipt believers (Baptist) had been lost in the Apostasy of Rome for "neer 1260 years;" that God of his sovereign purpose and love rediscovered the visible order of the church by immersion to the English Anabaptists; and that when they *discovered* God's purpose and heard the voice of Christ, they ceased to hear the voice of Antichrist and obeyed Christ. He clearly confirms the immersion movement of 1640-41 in the very terms of the ordinance restored; and emphasizes the fact that it was a *discovery* from God to his people—as all the rest so declare. Cornwell was one of the boldest and bravest leaders among the Baptist ministry, suffering imprisonment for his utterances, and he puts on record one of the clearest testimonies to the recent introduction of immersion by the Baptists of England.

6. Henry Denne (Antichrist Unmasked in Two Treatises, London, 1645, pp. 1, 2, 3). After an allusion to the Dragon of Revelation standing before the Woman clothed with the Sun, and after a reference to the fact that in every instance when the church had travailed in birth with any truth, the Ten-horned Beast had ever been ready to devour the child, he says:

"Our owne experience teacheth us in these our dayes, wherein the shadows begin to vanish, and the night to passe away, the *Sun* of Righteousnesse to draw neare unto the *Horison*. How many adversaries doe now bestirre themselves, with policy and force to keep us (if it were possible) in perpetual darknesse, and to hinder the rising of the Sun in our hearts. Among the rest the church is now ready to be delivered, and to bring forth the Doctrine of the Baptisme of Water, raked up heretofore in an imitation of Pædobaptism. The truth of the Ordinance or Institution of the Lord Jesus, lying covered with custome and Practice, and a pretended face of Antiquity. The Lord hath been pleased at this day, to put into the hearts and tongues of some, to stand up in defence of his truth (against the daring Face of Error) who doe now labor, ready to be delivered. But we see how many Champions ready armed, are come forth with reviling speeches and rayling accusations, to dash the countenance of this *new born Babe*."

The clear implication is that Denne here refers to the Baptist movement, 1640-41 and onward, to restore believers' immersion —the Doctrine of the Baptisme of Water; and he calls this movement a "NEW BORN BABE" just delivered amid the throes and agonies of the church—and still being threatened with destruction. This ordinance had been covered up, lost, under the "pretended face of Antiquity" by "Romish custom and practice;" but recently it had been restored and was still being restored in 1645. Hence he calls it *new*—"a new born babe;" and he is in perfect accord with Barber, Spilsbury, Cornwell and all the rest so far mentioned in this discussion. However different the phraseology of these writers on the subject, they all agree as to the facts of a recent restoration of baptism by the Baptists of England—"heretofore" practiced even by Anabaptists after the fashion of "Pedobaptism," by sprinkling or pouring!

7. Christopher Blackwood (Apostolicall Baptism: Or a Sober Rejoinder, To a Treatise written by Mr. Blake &c., 1645). On page 2, To the Godly Reader, he uses this phraseology:

"The true Baptisme of Jesus Christ, against the Innovation (to say no more) of Infants Baptisme."

Like Tombes, Blackwood regarded infant baptism an innovation of the early ages upon the baptism of Christ; and in the matter of giving it to the children of believing parents it was regarded as a late innovation—but not as late as the novelty of dipping among the Baptists of England. On page 12, he says:

"Now because the doctrine of dipping savors so of *Novelism;* not to instance in histories, without difficulty attainable; Peruse the book of Martyrs, Edition 7 [in which he refers Blake to Augustin and Paulinus baptizing in rivers] not in hallowed Fonts &c."

This is as near as he brings any example of believers dipping in England to the period in which he wrote; and he here speaks of dipping as a *novelty* in his time. In reply to Blake's claim that the ordinances have been retained under the defection of Antichrist and under the implied position that if this was not true there could be no restoration of baptisme, Blackwood (p. 77) says:

"I answer, suppose all Ministry and baptism were condemned, both theirs and yours (to use your words) yet is there no difficulty in setting up a right ministry and baptism, the way whereto is; 1. For believers to consider that they are the subjects to receive all ordinances in time of an apostasy, 2. That these believers gather themselves together, 3. That they make profession of their faith one to another, 4. That they consent and agree together, to worship God in all his wayes, that is or shall be *revealed* to them, 5. That they chuse out a Pastor (if he may be had) that may administer all ordinances to them. For Christ's promise of the gates of hell, not prevailing against the church or churches, against which in all ages the gates of *hell have prevailed;* but the body of Christ, or the *invisible*

Church, who only makes the same believing confession that Peter did: Against these the gates of hell cannot prevail to make them renounce that confession, which with heart or mouth, or both, they have made."

This is the clear Baptist ring of Blackwood's day. He is in perfect accord with Smyth, Helwys, Morton, Spilsbury, King, Barber and others. He admits the "*novelism*" of dipping at his time. He repudiates the Pedobaptist position that if the true church and baptism are lost they cannot be restored except by extraordinary commission; and he gives the analysis of the method of restoration according to the Scriptures—just as Smyth did and all the rest after him. He also repudiates the Pedobaptist doctrine of visible succession to the church and its ordinances; and he takes the uniform Baptist ground that while the gates of hell have never prevailed to destroy Christ's invisible body of believers and confessors, the gates of hell "in all ages" have prevailed against the visible churches and order of Christ. In all this Blackwood implies the recent adoption of dipping by the English Baptists; and he also implies their prior reorganization of the church anew—their separation and reformation after the rule and order of Christ.

8. Handserd Knollys' (The Shining of a Flaming fire &c., London, 1645). In reply to Saltmarsh's "Exceptions against the Grounds of New Baptisme" (Smoke of the Temple &c.) Knollys (p. 1) says:

"Paul's Doctrine was called *New*, although he preached Jesus and the Resurrection, Acts 17, 19. Also when our Savior preached with Authority, and confirmed his Doctrine with Miracles, they questioned among themselves, saying, What thing is this? What new Doctrine is this? Mark. th 1 & 27."

Knollys goes on to answer the "Exceptions" of Saltmarsh, but he never repudiates his charge of novelty to Baptist baptism. Like Spilsbury, Allen and others, he only intends to say that while Baptist immersion was a new practice, at the time, it was an old truth; and that while to Baptists, as Spilsbury puts it, it was a "new-found truth," it was to Pedobaptists a "new thing," as was Paul's doctrine to the Athenians, or as Christ's miracle to the Jews. No Baptist of that day ever denied that immersion was a new practice among Baptists; but they always retorted upon the Pedobaptists that it was the "old truth," the "good old way" and the like, though it was "new found."

ENGLISH BAPTIST REFORMATION.
(FROM 1609 TO 1641 A. D.)

CHAPTER XVI.
SOME OTHER BAPTIST WITNESSES—Continued.

9. Daniel King (A Way to Sion Sought Out and Found &c., London, 1649) is one of the most important and elaborate witnesses to the fact that the Baptists of England restored immersion in the "latter times." His work of 238 pages is devoted largely to the discussion of two propositions:

"1. That God hath had a people on earth, ever since the coming of Christ in the flesh, throughout the darkest ages of Popery, which he hath owned as Saints and as his Church.

"2. That these Saints have power to reassume and take up as their right, any ordinance of Christ, which they have been deprived of by the violence and tyranny of the man of sin.

"Wherein it is cleared up by the Scriptures and Arguments grounded upon the Scripture, who of right may administer Ordinances, and among the rest the Ordinance of Baptism with Water."

The Epistle Dedicatory is written and signed by Thomas Patient, John Spilsbury, William Kiffin and John Pearson, in which they fully endorse and earnestly urge the reading of the book by the Baptist people; and this endorsement fully covers the united sentiment of the then leading Baptists of England. In the preface "To the Reader," King indicates that his work is an apology for Baptist position in defense of the right to restore believers' baptism after it had been lost under the apostasy of Rome. It is an effort to allay the confusion created by the Seekers, Quakers and Pedobaptists, among Baptists and others with regard to recovering the church, its ministry and the ordinances *lost* in the apostasy of Rome; and to show that the Baptists had restored the visible church of Christ. The Seekers took the position that these had been lost and could not be recovered without an extraordinary commission from heaven, another John the Baptist, or an angel; and so they opposed Baptists and denied their power or right to recover them. The Quakers claimed that the ordinances were shadows and should not continue in the churches, and so fought the "new baptism" of the Baptists, as Saltmarsh and others. The Pedobaptists held that the ordinances had succeeded to them pure through the defection of Antichrist and so contended against the restoration claim of the Baptists upon the ground of the Seekers that if the church and its ministry or ordinances *had* been lost they could not be recovered except in an extraordinary way. To meet these varied objections and to rectify their confusion King wrote his book as endorsed by Patient, Spilsbury, Kiffin and Pearson; and it is one of the most elaborate and able defenses of the Baptist position that the ordinances had been lost and that the Baptists had recovered them according to the Scriptures.

In the first division of Part First of this book King establishes under the N. T., as under the O. T., a threefold sucession (1) of Believers, (2) of the Spirit, and (3) of the Word, without any reference to visible order, offices or ordinances, based upon the Covenant of grace which includes God's people, Jew and Gentiles, as his spiritual church against which the gates of hell should never prevail—such being "the church in the wilderness." On page 49 he says:

"From the time of Christ's coming in the flesh and revealing the New Covenant, throughout all ages to the world's end; there shall be a succession of Believers that shall have the Spirit of Christ, and the Gospel of Christ communicated to them, and they shall be enabled *in a measure* to hold the faith and publish it."

This was the Church in the Wilderness which King did not regard as having the visible order, offices or ordinances of Christ, but as only his spiritual Kingdom under the general title of the church, not the churches, in the wilderness; and this was the Baptist position of the 17th century.

After having established this position he proceeds (p. 5) to say:

"Now the next thing I would prove is, That this [spiritual] church, or these believers have power to *reassume* or take up any ordinance of God, and practice it among themselves (I mean any ordinance they see to be held forth in the Scriptures, and that they have been *deprived of* through the corruption of the times) whenever God *revealeth* to be his ordinance."

On p. 80 he says the same and adds these words:

"As to instance in the ordinance of *Baptisme*, I shall prove that a company of such Believers (when they see [discover] what is Christ's mind concerning that Ordinance, or the subject of it) take it up among themselves, though they know not where to have a rightly baptized person to dispense it upon them"—

the very principle upon which John Smyth proceeded to erect the first church among English Baptists. On page 82 he employs the expressions: "Since Baptism was lost"—"the Church corrupted"—"the Church hath lost her succession"—and the like. On pages 84, 85, he gives the reason why believers "ought to take up Baptism," and the method how, and says:

"And this is the very way to *reforme* what is amiss; yea and the people of God [Baptists] have *reformed*, and taken up ordinances upon this consideration; as of Israel's taking up circumcision in the Land of Canaan, Josh. 5:2."

King's argument is that as the Israelitish church in the wilderness lost circumcision and had it restored in Canaan, so the Gospel church in the wilderness lost baptism and it had now been restored by the Baptists in England. He then meets the usual Pedobaptist argument of the day based upon succession, namely, that, if the ordinances were lost, they could only be restored by a new Commission, and that therefore baptism could not, as Baptists held, be administered by unbaptized persons in order to recovery; and so he makes the usual Baptist argument of the time (p. 87, 89,) that a disciple able to preach and make converts is authorized by the Scriptures to baptize, though unbaptized himself, under the commission of Christ, Matt. 28:19, the apostles themselves not being qualified by their baptism, but by the Spirit. On page 95 he says again:

"Now then there having been a succession of Believers, and of Communicating of the Spirit and prophecying, enabling them in *some measure* to declare the Word; they may by vertue of Christ's Command and Commission, and by order of the Gospel take up *Baptisme*, elect and ordain *officers*, and set upon the use of any Ordinance that they may find in the Word of God to be theirs; for in the Scripture we may find the way of Christ: And when we have found the way, to shew a ground of keeping out of the way, &c., is the highest rebellion of all."

Preceding this on the same page he says:

"As soon as Believers see the Baptisme of Believers, according to the institution of Christ, to be their duty; They may, they ought (upon pain of neglecting their duty) take it up. Indeed when the ordinance is afoot to make use of those under the Ordinance to Administer it, is to goe on in an *orderly way:* But this that I have spoken, vindicateth him, whosoever it were, that *first* saw the Truth, and *recovered* this Truth from under Antichrist, to leave him out in doing his duty, in Baptizing those Believers that desire to so partake of the Ordinance."

King's position is that it was the duty of those who "first saw the truth" to restore the ordinance of baptism, lost under Antichrist; but when the ordinance is once "afoot" and the ministry re-established in the churches, we are to "make use of those under the ordinance" as administrators of it—and so "go on in an orderly way." This was the position of the leading Baptists of the 17th century; and strenuous efforts were made to check the indiscriminate application of the principle adopted in first introducing believers' baptism by unbaptized administrators, to a continuance of that method after baptism had been restored.

On page 109 King shows that baptism means dipping; and hence by the recovery of the lost ordinances he includes the revival of immersion which followed the adoption of the principle of believers' baptism by the Baptists of England, and which he takes for granted by all that he writes on the subject. The Third Part of his book which, under the title, Some Beams of Light, &c., London, 1649, was written in answer to the "Thirteen Exceptions" of Saltmarsh against the "New Baptisme" of the Baptists; and which is a Quaker argument against the continuance of the visible ordinances in the church, upon the ground that they are shadows of Gospel truths. King, without denying Saltmarsh's charge of "new baptism," ably and efficiently demolishes Saltmarsh and proves that the ordinances of baptism and the Lord's Supper were designed by the Scriptures to be continued visibly in the church; but this in no way contravenes his position in the first and second parts of his work that the ordinances had been lost under Antichrist and had been restored by the Baptists. He only argues here for the principle of continuance, and not for the fact that they had always, or would always, continue, when lost or corrupted. See Appendix (D).

I have only faintly gathered King's position from my notes; and his book deserves a more elaborate presentation. He is in precise line with Smyth, Helwys, Morton, Spilsbury, Kiffin, Barber and all the rest with regard to baptism as lost under the defection of Antichrist and restored by the English Baptists. Like all the rest, of his time, he denies a *visible* succession of Christ's churches, ministry and ordinances; and yet, like all the rest, he maintains a spiritual succession of believers through all the ages. The Baptist writers of the 17th century regarded the church in the wilderness as Baptists and as extending back to the apostles. They claimed the Anabaptist sects as their people and traced their pedigree, as a people, back to the New Testament churches; but, so far as I have read, they all confess to an oft broken succession of *visible* churches, ministry and ordinances. They all agree that Antichrist had been often revealed before their day by their Anabaptist brethren who had risen and fallen; but they regarded the reign of Antichrist for 1260 years as reaching down to their time and that the spiritual church had never come successfully and finally out of the wilderness until the English Baptists had recovered the visible church, its ministry and the ordinances.

10. Henry Jessey (Storehouse of Provision, &c., London, 1650). This book was partly written against the Seekers and partly in the interest of open communion and against the strict communionists of that day; but it tells the same story of immersion revival by the Baptists of England. On pages 12, 76 Jessey is very clear in the definition and uses of baptism as a "dipping in water;" and on pages 13-15 he squarely meets the Seekers' argument, namely, that baptism having been lost, could not be restored except by a prophet or an angel, or some extraordinarily commissioned person. Jessey agrees with Smyth that "two or three persons gathered together in Christ's name" may appoint some one, according to Christ's commission, to restore baptism; and contrary to the Blunt method of going to Holland for immersion, which was evidently in his mind, he says:

"Say not in thine heart, Who shall goe to Heaven, or to sea, or beyond sea for it? but the word is nigh thee. Rom. 10. So we may not goe for administrators to other Countries, nor stay [wait] for them: but looke to the word."

On page 16 he asks:

"Now must we tarry [as the Seekers say] in this Babylonish way, till such a mighty Angell come? Or must we reforme as farre as we see in all these, and all other things?"

The Seekers and others urged that the world was under the 1260 days of Antichrist's reign, that the church and ordinances were invisible or lost and that they could not be restored until Christ came in the restitution of all things; but Jessey, like Cornwell, takes the position that the spiritual church must come out of Babylon, had already come out, and must not wait for a "new commission," but obey the Scriptures as God *revealed* them to true believers (pp. 51–56). From page 57 to 76 he variously and elaborately discusses with his objector the question of a "proper administrator" of baptism, the fact of the ordinances having been lost under Antichrist, their restoration and the re-establishment of the ministry in newly erected churches, without any new commission but the Scriptures, just as Smyth, Spilsbury, Barber and the rest do, except in a more varied and versatile form; and it is clear that Jessey takes for granted the disuse of immersion in England and its recent introduction by the Baptists, defending their right to restoration upon the principle of *"reformation"*—as we shall more fully see.

On page 80 Jessey insists that the same necessity exists *now*, as in the days of the apostles, to respect the ordinance of baptism, though it had been *lost*. After its restoration he says that *some* had been "slack" towards its observance, while some longed to "enjoy" it. "Why tarry? said Ananias to Paul; while the Eunuch wanted to enjoy the ordinance"—is Jessey's argument to those who hesitated, as he had done, to receive the ordinance as restored by unbaptized believers. He represents himself as one that had *tarried*; and he says:

"Such considerations as these I had, But yet, because I would do nothing rashly; I would not do that which I should renounce againe: I desired Conference with some Christians differing therein in opinion from me; about what is requisite to restoring of ordinances, if lost; Especially what is essentiall in a Baptizer? Thus I did forbeare and inquired above a yeare's space."

In other words, after tarrying or forbearing for a year's space subsequent to the said "Conference," he received immersion without regard to the "baptizednesse" of the "baptizer," according to the Spilsbury theory. As already seen he disagreed with the Blunt method of sending "over the sea," as had been done, to Holland, for a regular administration of baptism. The Jessey Church Records show that in 1640 Jessey, with Blunt, was "convinced" that baptism "ought to be by dipping;" and although he *tarried* for several years, he declared his belief in immersion in 1642, and so baptized infants until immersed himself. His difficulty was about a "proper administrator"—about what was "essentiall in a Baptizer"—in the "restoring" of the "lost" ordinance; and hence "such considerations," rather than do anything "rashly," led him to "tarry" instead of hastening to "enjoy" the ordinance when it was introduced in 1641. In 1644 the "Conferences" in his church about "infant baptism" convinced him that that practice was wrong; and after a "year's space" of forbearing still, he, with most of his church, 1645, was immersed without regard to the "over sea" method of restoration. He uses the word "enjoy," found in the Records and in Crosby, characteristic of those who did not "tarry," in 1641, to receive the ordinance—or had not, like him, waited for it; and throughout the whole passage there is an apparent reference to the Blunt movement of 1641 for succession of baptism, with which he clearly did not agree. He regarded God's people in Babylon until they came out and adopted believers' immersion; and he pronounces the Seekers' theory of tarrying for the ordinances, until Christ or an angel come, a "Babylonish way," out of which the Baptists had *reformed*. Like Kiffin, he does not mention the Jessey Records; but the history and writings of both confirm them. See Appendix (A).

From page 93 to 103, again from 104 to 130, Jessey enters upon "A Question about the Warrantablenesse of Enjoying Communion together by Believers that differ about Baptism." This time his objector is a strict Communion Baptist. After various objections and answers with regard to the Scriptural ground of Communion based upon right baptism and New Testament order, the question is sprung about the comparative value of *restored* baptism as a prerequisite to Communion, which barred from the Lord's Supper those (such as the Congregationalists) not rightly baptized. On page 187 the objector urges:

"*None are to be owned as Disciples till they be baptized.*"

Jessey answers:

"If none but baptized ones are owned to be disciples; then the *first Restorers* of Baptisme were not owned to be disciples. And if the first were so owned, and others then and now have communion with or from the first; then disowne not others that want the same; disowne not communion with them."

Objection 28:

"*There was a Necessity for so RESTORING it at first: but no necessity of having communion with such now.*"

Jessey answers:

"Yet this necessity infringeth not the former Answers: But the same grounds hold firme."

This was substantially the argument of both the strict and open communion Baptists of Jessey's day; and both admitted that immersion had been restored "of late" by the Baptists of England. On page 111 Jessey speaks to his objector thus:

"If you must judge of your [Baptists'] *late* Baptisme, give leave to others to judge of theirs; and bear as you would be borne with in love;" and he speaks (p. 182) of all such in Queen Mary's dayes, or other times, that "loved not their lives unto death . . . we should not suggest, that such are not owned (according to the Scriptures) as Believers or saved Persons; for want of right Knowledge about Baptisme. Who are so much (if not more) owned in Scriptures for Believers, as those that are *now* Baptized, by deriving it from such a Baptizer," that is, unbaptized administrator.

It is clear that he includes, among those martyrs, the Anabaptists of Queen Mary's time as not having been baptized "as Baptists were *now* baptized," that is, now *immersed*, at the hands, originally, of unbaptized administrators, and who, he adds, were "rejecting Believers, differing about an Ordinance," from their communion. His position on this point was that Congregationalists and others who were not rightly baptized, but thought they were—who would do better if they learned more by affiliation and communion with the Baptists—had as much claim to communion upon their baptism as Baptists did upon theirs in view of the fact that they were only *lately* immersed, and that, too, at the hands of unbaptized administrators for which, strictly speaking, there was no *express* precept in the

Scriptures, but only the general principle embraced in Christ's Commission by which Baptists had restored immersion.

Jessey is evidently wrong in his premises for open communion, and his strict communion objector is right that, immersion having been restored, we must return to the New Testament pattern in all things; but he is a valid historical witness to the fact that the Baptists of England restored immersion about 1640-41. His testimony is stated in unmistakable terms, and he is evidently one of Crosby's authorities. By a different form of statement he is in exact line with the Jessey Church Records and Hutchinson touching the first method of restoration; and with Spilsbury, Tombes, Lawrence, Barber, King, Cornwell and others touching the second method.

11. Another strong Baptist witness is William Kaye (Baptism Without Bason, &c., London, 1653). He wrote against Infant Baptism in answer to Baxter and Lidenham; and he discusses several questions and answers about baptizing believers only. Probably a Fifth Monarchy man he regarded the time as being fulfilled for the return and reign of Christ as King; and in his introductory address (pp. 4, 5) he claims that the Baptists are the "heirs apparent to all the light which hath shined" at a time when the Law was "overturning both Church and State, because his far prophesied time is now fulfilled, to have a New heaven, or a reformed church, &c." He closes his introductory address (p. 6) with an appeal to "contend for the faith" and a submission to baptism, as Christ had, "to fulfill all righteousness," and with a benediction of grace "that calleth out of Babylon." Under the head of Questions and Answers concerning believers' baptism, we have the following:

"Quest. 9. *How comes it then to pass that this doctrine of baptism hath not been before revealed?*"

His answer is the usual Baptist reply, namely, that it had been "perverted and corrupted," by Antichrist, "till the Lamb's souldiers should procure the free course of the Gospel;" and although "Antichrist, before these times, hath been revealed, yet the Ordinances are but *beginning* to be cleared in *discovering* whereof the church *begins* to be *restored* to the purity of the primitive time of Christ and his Apostles." On page 33 the following question is also put:

"*What is the way of the administration of baptism?*"

The answer is:

"The Christian disciple that is to be baptized, must, Christ-like, upon profession of faith and obedience, descend to be covered or buried in water"—

in the name of the Trinity, and then be received into the church by the right hand of fellowship. In this discussion believers' baptism as opposed to infant baptism—immersion as opposed to sprinkling—is what is meant by the restored ordinance.

From page 34 to 37 Kaye asks and answers questions concerning the province of the magistry either to suppress or countenance this doctrine of baptism as established by the Baptist reformation, in conflict with the practice of the English Church; and he assumes, as a Fifth Monarchy Baptist, that as the magistry had cut down the Episcopal tree, it would be honorable still to continue their good work until Parochial sprinkling or infant baptism should be uprooted. From page 37 to 42 he appeals to the elect among the Reformers, still unimmersed and practicing infant sprinkling, to come completely out of Babylon as the Baptists had done. In spite of the great Reformation in which infant baptism "past muster," and has been defended by great names—

"yet behold the Lord makes the flock, or common people, to see the truth, when almost all public teachers were overvailed [Barber] . . . untill *at last* the Lord saw his time to trouble and thereby make the discovery of his light unto the public ministry, by calling some of them [Barber] to trim their lamps, that they may shine in the *discovery* of the mind of Christ in baptizing believers only."

Again:

"Did not the truth alwaies when it was *revealed*, and think you it shall not *now* as well as ever (if God intend mercy to England) marvelously prevail?"

On page 40, urging the elect Pedobaptists to come out of the darkness and ignorance of Pedobaptism, he says:

"We know, or may know, that believers themselves, which were really and fully baptized (Acts 19:1, 2, 3, 4) because they were ignorant at that time of the Holy Ghost, were upon that account (all the fundamentals being revealed without which baptism cannot be warrantable) rebaptized:

when *we* were *sprinkled* great darkness, in comparison of the light of the Gospel [Baptist] reformation that *now* shineth, was then as a cloud overvailing the Word."

Here Kaye refers back to the believers' baptism of the Anabaptists, before the introduction of immersion, which was sprinkling; and paralleling their first baptism as believers with the baptism of the twelve believers rebaptized by Paul, he says that they, like them, were at first under a cloud in comparison of the light which brought them into the Gospel reformation which was by immersion. On the same page, he says again:

"That they might be good and Godly men, and Martyrs, that were never more than *sprinkled*, it may be granted; but then it was a time when the smoak was in the Temple. Martyrs (Ten Martyrs in England, IIen. 8. Anno, 1553) have suffered for the profession of the baptizing of believers onely, but never any Martyrs have suffered in the defense of Infant pretended baptism."

The implication is that those ten Anabaptist martyrs were sprinkled, being under the smoke in the temple as to immersion, and included among the good and godly men whose good intentions did not relieve them of their error in this respect. This appeared by what follows after when Kaye says:

"If we would look on humane example, It is not for us to say as those obstinate unbelievers that the Martyr Stephen reproved, who said, *As our Fathers did, so will we do.*"

This point I will not press, however, and will leave the reader to judge in the light of what goes before as well as what follows after.

Kaye treats immersion as a new discovery from beginning to end; and he appeals to the elect under every form of Babylon. Having the light now revealed, if they see not, "in something newly discovered," such as this new baptism, then they are not the elect, and so he closes his appeal. He emphasizes, more definitely than the rest of the Baptist controversialists, his fight against "sprinkling" as the root of the Episcopal tree; and hence he means nothing but immersion, as believers' baptism, when he puts the question and answers it:

"How comes it to pass, that this doctrine of baptism hath not been before revealed."

Like all the rest, he regards immersion as a special revelation to the Baptists whom he regards in their separation from the Reformers as the true church of believers—the woman in the wilderness—having been called out from under the shadow of Antichrist and reformed.

12. William Allen, in two works (An Answer to Mr. J. G[oodwin], his XL. Queries, &c., London, 1653; Some Baptismal Abuses, &c., London, 1653). In reply to Goodwin's Querie III. (p. 34) he says:

"And if the first Church or Churches might not be constituted without baptism, then neither may those that succeed them, because the same reason that made baptism necessary hereunto with them, makes it necessary also unto us; for Gospell Order, settled by Apostolicall authority and direction, hath not lost any of its native worth, efficacy, or obliging virtue, by *disuse* or *discontinuance*, upon occasion of Papall defection, but ought to be the same now to those who are studious of a *thorough reformation* as it was unto them in the *first beginning* of Church Order."

On page 72 he answers Querie XXI., which calls immersion *"new baptisme,"* in these words:

"Though it should be granted, that many if not the generality of these that have entered into the way of the *new baptisme* (as the Querist calls it, it being the old way of Baptizing) have received their precious faith and other graces, under the dispensation of their Infant Baptisme, &c."

In his second work (p. 107), Allen, who, like Jessey, was advocating Open Communion, says:

"It is true (as I observed before upon another occasion) that it may fall out, that in undertaking a *reformation* and *restitution* of ordinances and worship from under their *corruption* and *decayes*, there may be an impossibility, precisely and in all things, to answer the original usage, but that through an indispensable necessity, there will be in these *reformers* some variation either in the *Administrator*, or in some conceivable circumstance of the *administration*, in respect of which indispensable necessity, God accepts men according to what opportunity they have, and not according to what they have not."

Allen regarded "gospel order" as having been *"disused or discontinued"* under the defection of Antichrist; and that they were restored under the Baptist *"reformation."* This included immersion revived by unbaptized administrators, as he implies in both works. He does not deny that immersion was "new baptism" in practice, but calls it the *"old way* of Baptizing," just as Spilsbury did, who calls it the *"old,"* but the *"new found,* way." Allen is with Spilsbury and Jessey on the communion question; and he is precisely with them and all the rest historically as to the disuse of immersion, and its restoration by the English Baptists.

13. Thomas Lamb (Truth Prevailing against the fiercest Opposition, &c., London, 1655). This is a reply to Goodwin's "Water Dipping, &c.;" and on page 44 he answers especially the charge of Schism preferred against the Baptists who separated from the Puritans. He asks:

"Why should our separating from you be counted Schisme more than your separating from the Parish Churches? Is not our ground the very self-same which yours *then* was? And what can you say to Mr. Baxter, who chargeth you with schisme for withdrawing from the National Church, which *we* cannot answer you with . . . As the *fatal Apostacie* from the pure Ordinances of Christ and the example of the Primitive Churches in worship, was graduall, so hath the *recovery* of primitive purity been ; now a little and there a little, as it hath *pleased God to communicate light* to his upright ones that he hath used in the *reformation*, but it hath been as it were by inches, and still been made costly to the names and Instruments, they all bear this burthen which now Mr. Goodwin charges us with schisme. The Pope crieth Schisme and Heresie after the Church of England . . . The Bishops cry Schisme after some of the Presbyterians. The Presbyterians cry Schisme after Mr. Goodwin and all the Separatists . . which withdrawings have been so many steps towards primitive purity. Now Mr. Goodwin crieth Schisme (pretty liberally) after us who have gone a few steps further in the same path (which as yet his heart serveth him not to proceed in) that we may reach the things we have heard from the beginning. 1 John 2:24 ; Coloss. 4:12."

Lamb squarely admits the charge of Baptist separation from the Separatists; and he argues their same right, at a later date, to separate from the Puritans, that they had at a still earlier date to separate from other Reformers. "Is not our ground [now] the very same which yours *then* was?" This is precisely Kiffin's claim in his Briefe Remonstrance; and it is what Barber and all who touch the question of Baptist separation admit. The English Baptists were chiefly Separatists from the Separatists, claiming their reformation upon higher ground—that is, the erection of their churches, after the rule of Christ, upon the principle of believers' baptism—and this is the contention of both Lamb and Kiffin. This claim of separation and reformation, however, fixes the origin and pedigree of the English Baptists, so far as they are *organically* concerned in their separation and not in preëxistent Anabaptist sects; and this agrees precisely with the history of the case. Lamb, as all the rest do, derives Baptist reformation from the "fatall apostacie;" but he locates this Baptist reformation as the last of a series of reformations gradually *recovering* primitive purity and order as they had been gradually lost. He nowhere denies Goodwin's oft-repeated charge of "new baptisme," and only says on page 61 in reply to the XVI. Consideration of Water Dipping:

"You have no need of Baptisme after Repentance and Faith (which you call new Baptisme) because your *old* sprinkling in infancy is effectual to all ends and new purposes of Baptisme which you reduce to three heads, &c."

"Water dipping" was what Goodwin specially called "new." No Baptist of the 17th century ever denied that the *practice* of adult dipping in England was "*new.*"

14. Hercules Collins (Believers' Baptisme from Heaven, &c., London, 1691). In reply to Thomas Wall's Baptism Anatomized and in answer to the charge that the Baptists had received their baptism from John Smyth, who baptized himself, on page 115, Collins says:

"Could not this Ordinance of Christ, which was lost in the Apostasy, be revived (as the Feast of Tabernacles was, tho' lost a great while) unless in such a filthy way as you falsely assert, viz. that the English Baptists receiveth their Baptism from Mr. John Smith? It is absolutely untrue, it being well known, by some yet alive, how false this Assertion is; and if J. W. will but give a meeting to any of us, and bring whom he pleaseth with him, we shall sufficiently shew the Falsity of what is affirmed by him in this Matter."

Collins indignantly agrees with Crosby that Smith's baptism never succeeded to the English Baptists; and Collins and Crosby agree in the position that believers' immersion "lost in the apostasy" was "*revived*" by the English Baptists—just as the Feast of Tabernacles was restored after being lost for a great while. Not only so, but Collins asserts that there were some living in 1691 who knew that Smith's baptism never succeeded to the Baptists of England. In other words, this points back about fifty years to 1641, when immersion was restored, and which was still a fresh fact in the memory of some old men. Last but not least, and down to the end of the 17th century, Collins is still in line with the long list of authors who agree, directly or indirectly, that believers' immersion did not exist in England before 1641, and that the Baptists of England restored it at that date fixed by the Jessey Records.

The controversial literature, from 1641 to the close of the century, between Baptists and Pedobaptists, was voluminous; and while reference to the recent introduction of immersion was occasional, there was no difference between them, express or implied, about the fact. The Pedobaptists charged it and the Baptists acknowledged and defended it, after 1641; and as said before, there is not the slightest hint of any such controversy before that date. The Baptist and Pedobaptist writers before 1641 stood on the border of the preceding century, and they must have known of the existence, character and customs of the sectaries of their day. Their writings have come down to us in sufficient volume to make plain the history of that period. The works of Smyth, Helwys, Morton and others set forth Baptist principles and practices in unmistakable terms from 1609 to 1641; and it would be marvelous if against the universal practice of sprinkling they had opposed exclusive adult immersion without a single mention of the fact by them or their opponents. This would be especially singular in the light of such a controversy from 1641 to the close of the century. More than this, if there had been any prior Anabaptist organizations in England succeeding to the time of Smyth and Helwys it would still be more remarkable that Smyth himself should have declared that down to his movement "never a one" of the *English* "at any time believed *visibly* in a true constituted church," that is, by believers' baptism; and this utterly excludes the succession of any Anabaptist church, or conventicle, to the English Baptists, prior to Smyth's organization. The Baptist and Pedobaptist writers of the 17th century sustain this position; and certainly so many of them from every part of the kingdom in a hundred years of controversy should have known whether or not there was any Anabaptist succession from the 16th century, and whether or not the Smyth-Helwys people immersed before 1641.

ENGLISH BAPTIST REFORMATION.

(FROM 1609 TO 1641 A. D.)

CHAPTER XVII.

WHAT THE ENEMY SAID—DR. FEATLEY.

So far I have considered, with the exception of Praisegod Barebone, only the testimony of Baptist documents and writers which establishes the clear probability that after the disuse of immersion in England, the English Baptists restored it in 1641. Praisegod Barebone seems to have written as a friend to the Baptists with whom he had been associated, some of them at least, before they separated from the Puritans, and with whom he must have been afterwards well acquainted; but I now come to notice the writings of enemies and to put them in evidence for what they are worth as corroborative of the testimony of the Baptists themselves. Our enemies do not always lie, nor do we always tell the truth in history; and the testimony of our enemies is at least valid when, unchallenged, it corroborates the facts of our history, "acknowledged and justified," as Crosby says, by Baptist writers themselves. In the citations from Barebone, and from those to whom I now refer, I see no conflict with the testimony of Baptists themselves. Hence it is not unfair to establish what seems to be clearly a fact that about 1641 the Baptists restored immersion in England—our enemies being in agreement with ourselves.

The first witness here produced is Dr. Daniel Featley, who, in 1644, wrote his "Dippers Dipt" (London ed., 1646). In his Epistle Dedicatory, after a very bitter arraignment of the English Anabaptists as heretics and schismatics, he says: "They flock in great multitudes to their Jordans, and both sexes enter the river, and are dipt after their manner, with a kind of spell, &c." This passage refers their practice to the time, in the present tense, when Featley wrote in 1644. It is objected that under the third head and at the close of this Epistle Dedicatory, Featley indicates that the Anabaptists had been so practicing immersion "for more than twenty years" near the place of his residence. He says:

> "As Solinus writeth, that in Sardinia where there is a venomous serpent called Solifuga, &c. This venomous Serpent (*vere Solifuga*) flying from, and shunning the light of God's Word, is the Anabaptist who *in these later times first* showed his shining head and speckled skin and thrust out his sting near the place of my residence for more than twenty years."

This passage occurs three pages after the one already quoted, and after a discussion of Anabaptist heresy with regard to majistracy, &c.; and it is written in the past tense with reference simply to the twenty or more years existence of the Anabaptists near his residence—not then flocking in great multitudes to their Jordans and dipping over head and ears—but Solifuga-like in a state of concealment. It is thus Featley proceeds to "enter into the lists of the ensuing Tractate" in the exposure of the Anabaptists, whom he here calls "*new upstart sectaries.*"

In The Preface to the Reader, and near the close, Featley indicates the later date of flocking in great multitudes and dipping in the rivers. After speaking of the Anabaptist fire not "fully quenched" in Germany and "soon put out" in the reign of Elizabeth and James, he proceeds:

> "But *of late*, since the unhappy distractions which our sinnes have brought upon us, the Temporall sword being otherways employed and the Spirituall locked up fast in the scabbard, this Sect among others hath so far presumed upon the patience of the State that it hath held weekly Conventicles, rebaptized hundreds of men and women together in the twilight, in Rivulets and some arms of the Thames, and elsewhere, dipping them over head and ears. It hath printed divers pamphlets in defense of their heresy, yea and challenged some of our preachers to disputation, &c."

The "unhappy distractions" and the otherwise employment of the temporal and spiritual sword, "OF LATE," point to the revolution of 1641, the "Yeare of Jubilee;" and it is distinctly here signified by Featley that it was at this period that these Anabaptists were openly and with impunity rebaptizing hundreds in the rivers. Yea they were "flocking in great multitudes" to baptism—a thing which could not have happened before 1641 without the intervention of civic and ecclesiastical proceedings which would have put on record the arraignment and punishment of the Anabaptists for such a practice. Such proceedings against the practice of immersion were had after 1641, as we have seen, when, in 1644, Laurence Clarkson was jailed in Suffolk and Henry Denne at Spalding, 1646, for this offense; and we may be sure that before 1641 when the temporal and spiritual swords were unsheathed against the Anabaptists, the baptismal demonstration described by Featley above would have been impossible without punishment and record. The twenty or more years of Anabaptist existence near Featley's residence do not include any reference whatever to Anabaptist immersion in England before the period *"of late,"* alluded to by the author, after 1641. As Dr. Whitsitt has demonstrated and as Dr. Newman well says:

" What Featley says about the practice of immersion refers definitely to the *present* (1644)."

Nothing is clearer than that Featley is speaking of Baptist dipping as they *"now practiced"* in 1644, and as they had not practiced before that date, 1641.

Again on page 118 Featley discusses the 40th Article of the Baptist Confession of 1644 on Dipping. He says:

" This Article is wholly sowsed with the *new leaven* of Anabaptisme. I say *new leaven*, for it cannot be proved that any of the ancient Anabaptists maintained any such position, there being three ways of baptizing, either by dipping, or washing, or sprinkling, to which the Scriptures alludeth in sundry places: the Sacrament is rightly administered by any of the three, and whatsoever is alleaged here for dipping, we approve of so far as it excludeth not the other two. Dipping may be and hath been used in some places *trina immersio*, a threefold dipping; but there is no necessity of it. It is not essentiall to baptisme, neither do the texts in the margent conclude any such thing. It is true that John baptized Christ in Jordan, and Philip baptized the Eunuch in the river; but the text saith not, that either the Eunuch or Christ himself, or any baptized by John or his Disciples, or any of Christ's Disciples, were *dipped*, *plunged* or *dowsed* over head and ears, as this Article implyeth, and *our* Anabaptists *now* practice."

Observe here that Featley stigmatizes *immersion* as the " new leaven of Anabaptisme" based on the definition of the 40th Article

and as the "*now* practice" of "our [English] Anabaptists," for two reasons :
1. Because it was *exclusive*. This was the new and added offense of the Anabaptists after 1640-41; and Featley implies the charge of Barebone and others that immersion as the essential form of baptism made a nullity of sprinkling and pouring. No other Anabaptists according to Featley ever made such a claim ; and he is in accord with Baillie, as we shall see, that "among the old Anabaptists, or those over sea, the question of dipping and sprinkling never came upon the Table." The English Anabaptists had made a new departure by making immersion exclusive, and this was the "new leaven of Anabaptisme" embedded in the 40th Article of the 1644 Confession and in the "*now* practice" of "*our* [English] Anabaptists."
2. Because it was not *essential*. Featley claims that immersion "over head and ears" cannot be shown as the practice of John, or of his or Christ's disciples. He yielded to the practice of immersion as indifferent with sprinkling and pouring—admitted the practice of trine immersion—but he insists that immersion is not essential to baptism at all, according to Scripture and old Anabaptist practice. He had a horror of this "over head and ears" business; and from this standpoint also he calls immersion the "new leaven," the tainted novelty, of the "*English* Anabaptists" who had recently adopted "totall dipping" as Barebone expressed it within the last "two or three yeares, or some such short time."

But it is objected that the phrases, "*new* upstart sectaries," "*new* leaven," respectively applied to the Baptists and to immersion in England, do not imply the recent introduction of dipping as something "new," nor that the English Anabaptists as a sect was "new," in 1644. It is claimed that Featley classifies the Anabaptists (pp. 19-22), such as the Novatians (250) the Donatists (380) and the Anabaptists of 1525 (all of whom he only identifies by the practice of rebaptism without reference to mode) in such a way as to imply only two sorts out of three sorts. These two sorts, it is argued, consist of the "ancient" and the "new" sort; the new sort including the 1625 and the 1644 Anabaptists as the same sort. Featley however does not apply the word "new" to any sort except the "new upstart sectaries" or "our [English] Anabaptists" of 1644, who are just 119 years younger than the 1525 Anabaptists; and he does not mean that the "*new* leaven of Anabaptisme"—now embedded in the 40th Article and which he calls the "now practice" of "our [English] Anabaptists"—was 119 years old. The only identification of the 1644 with the 1525 Anabaptists, according to Featley, consists specifically in rebaptizing those baptized in infancy, as well as all others, without any reference to mode; but the peculiarity of exclusive dipping, "the new leaven of Anabaptisme," is confined by him to "*our* [English] Anabaptists," the "new upstart sectaries," whose "*now* practice" was immersion, and who have now, in 1644, for the first time in history, put down dipping as a definition of baptism in a Confession of Faith.

Immersion, in the mind of Featley, was the "new" added to the old "leaven" of Anabaptism by any mode, whether among English or German Anabaptists; but immersion, especially *exclusive* immersion, was not then the leaven of Continental Anabaptism as such men as Featley, Baillie and Edwards well knew. The Anabaptists of 1525 and onward, as a rule, practiced sprinkling and pouring as sufficient and regarded immersion as indifferent with the other modes of baptism. They sometimes in some places practiced immersion; but as a matter of sufficiency, expediency or necessity they seem to have had no hesitancy in practicing sprinkling or pouring. According to Dr. Featley the Novatians (250) and the Donatists (380) practiced infant baptism and did not exclusively immerse, if they always immersed. Dr. Newman confirms Featley with regard to their infant baptism, (Hist. Antipedobaptism, pp. 17-20); and he is likewise clear that the Antipedobaptists of the 16th century generally sprinkled and that "immersion claimed a very small share of their attention," (Review of the Question, pp. 171-173). Baillie (Anabaptisme, &c., p. 163) says of them:

"As I take it, they dip none, but all whom they baptize they sprinkle &c."

But it is objected that Featley (Confutation of A. R., p. 49) shows that the Senate of Zurich decreed the drowning of the 1525 Catabaptists, because they immersed (*quo quis peccateo puniatur*) and for the same reason wished the English Anabaptists so punished "in some way answerable to their sin." Some of the English Anabaptists were burned, 1539, for the offense of Anabaptism. Therefore, it is argued, the English Anabaptists were immersionists, since they were punished for the same offense that those of Zurich were, and since Featley identifies the 1644 and the 1525 Anabaptists as the same by immersion. According to this logic, however, those English Anabaptists, burned in 1539, should have been drowned if punished in a form "answerable to the sin" of immersion; but drowning was a usual punishment for certain crimes in Switzerland and Germany long before the Reformation, and was specially applicable to women as being the easiest mode of death. It was the doom of the old Roman law to be sewed in a sack and cast into the sea for the sin of Sacrilege. Margaret and Agnes Wilson, of Stirling, the "virgin martyrs," 1685, were drowned in the Solway for their Covenanter's faith—this in Sprinkling Scotland. Felix Manz and other Anabaptists who sprinkled for rebaptism were drowned, while Hubmair, who poured, was burned and his wife drowned for the same offense of Catabaptism. The words *mergo, taufen, doopen=baptizo*, at that time, had attained the altered meaning of wash or sprinkle as well as dip; and hence the drowning of Anabaptists had no more reference to immersion than to other forms of baptism among the Anabaptists or Catabaptists whose crime was simply *rebaptism* without the slightest regard to mode. At the close of one of the public disputations at Zurich, Milner (Vol. II., p. 536) says that the Anabaptists went out and "*rebaptized the people in the streets*," that is by sprinkling, as in the case of Manz, Grebel, Blaurock and others, 1524. The Senate of Zurich, at the close of the several disputations, 1527, passed a decree that "whoever should *rebaptize* any person, should himself be *drowned*" (ibid., p. 538), according to a usual mode of punishment; and the celebrated words of Zwingle: "*Qui iterum mergit, mergatur*," are rendered by Milner: "He who rebaptizes *with water*, let him be drowned *in water*." These words had no more application to immersion than to sprinkling, according to the altered usage of *mergit* and *mergatur;* and Dr. Featley (p. 49) expresses the decree of Zurich in the same language when he thus renders it:

"If any presumed to rebaptize those that were baptized before, they should be drowned."

Whatever Featley's notion that those Anabaptists of 1525 who were drowned, immersed, he did not believe that they were drowned because they had immersed, but because they rebaptized; and he only expresses the formal fitness of drowning those who rebaptized by immersion. He does not in the slightest way intend here to identify the 1644 and the 1525 Anabaptists by immersion, or to imply that the English Anabaptists had been immersing all the while, or that any of them had ever been punished for immersion—the thing he seemed *now* to advise for the first time in England since they had added the new offense of *exclusive* dipping to rebaptism, the "new leaven" of their "now practice" and of their 1644 Confession, the new sin of "our (English) Anabaptists," and not of our "ancient" or 1525 Anabaptists, so far as *exclusive* immersion was concerned. Featley rightly expressed the sin and punishment of the 1525 Anabaptists, according to Gastius' Latin phrase above, when he says: "They who drew others into the whirlpool of error, by constraint draw one another into the river to be drowned;" but he does not mean that they were drowned simply for dipping when he says: "And they who profaned baptism by a second dipping, rue it by a third immersion." He really means no more than when he says of the Anabaptists (p. 135):

"Thousands of that Sect who defiled their first baptism by the second, were baptized a third time in their own blood."

The truth is that infant dipping which would be the first to be defiled by a "second dipping," was not in vogue in Zurich; and the "second dipping," with but little exception, was not in practice by the Anabaptists. The "third immersion," or drowning, was as applicable to sprinkling as to dipping; and Anabaptism or Catabaptism meant immersion into "error," rather than dipping into water, by what Featley calls a ";prophanation of the holy sacrament." If he believed the Zurich Anabaptists, 1525, immersed, he erroneously followed a tradition which still persists in spite of true history, and which grew out of the supposition that drowning was decreed as a form of punishment answerable to the sin of immersion. There were a large number of immersions at St. Gall, 1525, where the penalty was "banishment" for rebaptism, and where the practice seems to have been completely broken up; but at Zurich the penalty was drowning, where the practice of rebaptism was by sprinkling; and the first victim of the ordinary law was Felix Manz, a sprinkler, 1527, under the sentence of Zwingle himself: *"Qui iterum mergit mergatur."*

Zwingle in his Elenchus and Featley in his Dippers Dipt agree as to the meaning of Catabaptism which expresses the offense for which Anabaptists were punished without regard to mode of baptism—except in England after 1641, when dipping, as exclusive baptism, became an added offense to rebaptism, and was punished by law, as in the case of Clarkson, Oates and Denne. Featley says:

"The name Anabaptist is derived from the Preposition ἀνα and βαπτίζω and signifieth a rebaptizer; or at least such an one as alloweth or maintaineth rebaptizing: and they are called *Catabaptists* from the preposition κατα βαπτίζω, signifying an abuser or prophaner of Baptism. For indeed every Anabaptist is also a Catabaptist. The reiteration of that Sacrament of our entrance into the church, and seal of our new birth in Christ, is a violation and depravation of that holy ordinance." (Dippers Dipt., p. 19, 1646.)

He says again :

"An Anabaptist deprives children of baptism, a Catabaptist depraves baptism. A Catabaptist may sometimes be no Anabaptist, such as was Leo Copronymous, who defiled the Font at his baptism, yet was he not christened again: but every Anabaptist is necessarily a Catabaptist, for the reiteration of that sacrament is an abuse and pollution thereof." (Dippers Dipt., p. 124, 1646.)

Hence the crime of rebaptism did not consist in the mode of baptism. The word Catabaptist does not mean an immersionist any more than an affusionist or aspersionist in ecclesiastical literature; and hence drowning by the Zurich Senate, as already said, had no reference whatever to the mode of baptism. It was like burning or banishment, the punishment of Catabaptism which was regarded as the "prophanation" of baptism by rebaptism whether by immersion or sprinkling; and hence the Anabaptists burned in England, 1539, like those drowned at Zurich, 1527, were simply punished for Catabaptism without any reference to immersion, the practice of which in either case is without historic proof or inference. So of all the punishments inflicted upon Anabaptists on the Continent or in England until after 1641, when the offense of exclusive immersion was added to the crime of rebaptism, hitherto administered without regard to mode.

Whatever Featley's view then of immersion among some of

the Anabaptists of Switzerland, 1525, he must have known as Baillie did that immersion was not exclusive or general among them, and that sprinkling was their usual practice; and hence he did not call them "new and upstart," nor identify them with "our [English] Anabaptists" of 1644 upon the ground of immersion which he could not have called "new leaven," 119 years old. He identified them only upon the ground of rebaptism or Catabaptism; and he must have known as well as Barebone and others did that the practice of dipping by the English Anabaptists was of recent date. He lived in Southwark, and had known the Anabaptist Solifuga for more than twenty years; and what the so-called Kiffin Manuscript and the Bampfield Document, Crosby and his witnesses, say of the "disuse," of believers' immersion in England and its restoration by the English Baptists, 1640-41, must have been known to Featley and here taken for granted in his Dippers Dipt. Even, however, if he had identified the English Anabaptists of 1644 with the Swiss Anabaptists of 1525 upon the ground of immersion, he would have known the gap of "disuse" which yawned in the practice of immersion in England and upon the Continent; and his "new upstart," or "new leaven," stigma would have still been applicable only to "our [English] Anabaptists" and their "now practice" of exclusive immersion as now implied by the 40th Article of their 1644 Confession and "of late" exemplified in baptizing hundreds of men and women "over head and ears" and "naked" in their Jordans.

Let me repeat that if such had been Anabaptist practice before 1641 in England when the temporal and spiritual sword was unsheathed, such men as Featley and Edwards would have been engaged, not in controversy, but in prosecution, against the Anabaptists. The added offense of exclusive immersion greatly enraged the Pedobaptists already antagonized by rebaptism in other forms; and if the English Anabaptists from 1611 to 1641 had practiced and pressed their "new crotchet"—endangering the health and virtue of the people by naked baptism as claimed by Featley, Edwards, Baxter and others—we should have heard of it in the court records and history of that period as was to some extent true after 1641 in spite of the enlarged liberty of the Baptists. Featley does speak of the Anabaptist "fire" quenched in the reigns of Elizabeth and James, smothered under ashes during the reign of Charles I. down to 1641, now ablaze "of late" since the "unhappy distractions" of the revolution; but among all the charges of heresy and schism made in common to the prior period of Anabaptism in Germany and England he does not stigmatize any as "new upstart," nor with the "new leaven of Anabaptisme," nor with the licentiousness of naked baptism, except *"our Anabaptists in England,"* "*of late,*" nor does he imply it.

He compares "our Anabaptists in England" (p. 130) to a "*young* lion," who though not yet guilty, as might be claimed, of the crimes of their predecessors, yet he warns that when he is "older" grown and "knows his own strength, being hungerbit," he will run "roaring abroad seeking whom he may devour." Under the figure of the "Solifuga" (p. 5, E. D.) he refers to him as having "*first* shewed his shining head," "in these *later times,*" "neer his place of residence for *more* than twenty yeers;" and he here evidently points to the organic origin of the Anabaptists, 1633, and further back perhaps to 1611, as he knew them in and about London. Organically they were a "young," a "new upstart," sect; not yet arraigned or punished for the grosser crimes of former Anabaptists, but not to be trusted to older growth and strength in the heresy and schism of rebaptism to which they had now added the offense of exclusive immersion —the "new leaven of Anabaptisme"—endangering the health and virtue of the people by naked administration.

Featley regarded "our Anabaptists of England" not only as a "young," a "new upstart" sect, but, from the organic and exclusive standpoint, as a separate and distinct sect of Anabaptists. Upon the general principle of rebaptism and in some other respects he identifies them with the German Anabaptists and with the former Anabaptist elements in England, but he distinguishes them as *sui generis* with respect to their "new leaven" of exclusive immersion lately begun to be practiced in the Kingdom. Like Edwards (p. 133) he associates them with Brownists and other sects of recent origin whose errors were of recent date. To be sure, he points back to the foreign elements of Anabaptism as "chips" hewn from the German block, "Stock" [Stork,] some of which flew to England and kindled the Dutch Anabaptist "fire" in the reigns of Elizabeth and James; but he shows that this elemental flame was quenched, although the elemental embers lay under ashes until the fire broke out again under the organized form of "our Anabaptists of England"—English Anabaptists—at a later date under the "new" and distinctive peculiarity of exclusive immersion. "Our Anabaptists of England" were something "new and upstart" under the sun; and their exclusive immersion was the "new leaven of Anabaptisme" under the sun—not sanctioned by the teachings of Scripture nor by the practice of the old Anabaptists. Featley's "Dippers Dipt" is an implication that immersion in England was of recent introduction by the Baptists—a "splinter new practice" as Dr. Whitsitt puts it.

For a different but conclusive argument, geographically and critically considered, I refer the reader to Dr. Whitsitt's book on this subject. (A Question in Baptist History, pp. 70–74.)

Featley is in exact line with the Baptist documents and writers of his day. Cornwell, in 1645, positively affirms that the Baptists had *resumed* immersion under the "discovery" and "command" of Christ; and Featley, in 1644, affirms that immersion was the "*new* leaven of Anabaptisme" in the 40th article of the Baptist Confession. Barebone declares, in 1643, that Baptist dipping was only "two or three yeares old," and Edward Barber does not deny the fact while he defends the right to restore the "lost" ordinance. R. B. admits to P. B. that "until some time lately there were no baptized people in the world"—no immersionists; and if the Baptists, before and after Featley, make such admissions, then we know just what Featley meant, namely, that adult immersion was a "splinter new practice" in England. He could not, with the Baptist lights before him, have meant anything else; and he is only one of fifty or sixty writers in the 17th century, Baptist and Pedobaptist, who consistently confirm the 1641 thesis of the restoration of the "disused" practice of immersion by the English Baptists. Any other conclusion is utterly impossible.

ENGLISH BAPTIST REFORMATION.
(FROM 1609 TO 1641 A. D.)

CHAPTER XVIII.
WHAT THE ENEMY SAID—Continued.

Dr. Featley was one of the most learned and able enemies of the Baptists of 1640-41; and on account of his ability and prominence in the controversy which raged from 1640-41 onward, and since he is in dispute in this present discussion, I have given his testimony elaborate treatment. The other enemies whose testimony I here give, some of them at least, are quite as learned and able as Dr. Featley.

1. The first historic mention of Baptist immersion by the enemy is from John Taylor (A Swarme of Sectaries, and Schismatiques, &c., London, 1641), who puts in rhyme the following:

> "Also one Spilsbury rose up *of late*,
> (Who doth or did dwell over Aldersgate)
>   *   *   *   *   *   *
> He rebaptiz'd in Anabaptist fashion
> One Eaton (of the new found separation)
> A Zealous Button-maker, grave and wise,
> And gave him orders others to baptize;
> Who was so apt to learne that in one day,
> Hee'd do't as well as Spilsbury weigh'd Hay.
> This true Hay-lay-man to the Bank-side came
> And likewise there baptized an impure dame, &c."

This author gives the usual classification of the Baptists—and so claimed by themselves—as the "new found separation," that is, the latest separation among the Separatists. He makes it evident, also, that Spilsbury, who *"rose up of late"* to *rebaptize* Eaton, began to immerse about 1641, the year in which Taylor wrote. Eaton, it will be remembered, was in the secession from the old Jacob-Lathrop Church in 1633 and "with others," at the time, "received a further baptism." Baptized in infancy, he received another baptism when he became an Anabaptist in 1633, making two baptisms—both no doubt by aspersion. In 1638 he is evidently with Spilsbury, who was pastor of the 1633 secession; and now "of late," in 1641, he is rebaptized again by his pastor, Spilsbury, in "Anabaptist fashion," which was now immersion, this being Eaton's third baptism—a practice so often charged to the Baptists after 1641. Eaton, a layman, as instructed by Spilsbury, immediately proceeded to baptize others. All this accords with the date and detail of the Kiffin MS. and with Crosby's account. In 1641 Blunt by the "first method" of revival introduced regular baptism; and at the same time Spilsbury by the "last method" of revival introduced irregular baptism—that is, by an unbaptized administrator upon Spilsbury's own theory that "baptizednesse is not essential to the administrator of baptisme." See pp. 100, 101, 110, 111, this volume.

2. A Tract (The Book of our Common Prayer, &c., London, 1641), speaking of the growth and power of the sectaries, among whom the Anabaptists are mentioned, "swarming in every city," points to the discovery of a "base sect of people called Rebaptists *lately found out* in Hackney Marsh neere London." On page 8, it is said:

"About a Fortnight since a great multitude of people were met going towards the river in Hackney Marsh, and were followed to the water side, where they were all Baptized againe, themselves doing it one to another, some of which persons were so feeble and aged, that they were fayne to Ride on Horsebacke thither this was well observed by many of the inhabitants living thereabouts, and *afterwards* one of them Christened his owne Childe, and another tooke upon him to Church his owne wife, an Abominable Act, and full of grosse Impiety."

Although this does not favor Anabaptism on the part of "one of these" who "Christened his owne Childe," yet upon the whole it looks Anabaptistic and was characteristic of the disorder which immediately sprung out of the new movement; and this fact is characteristic of the irregularity of the movement at first as pointed out by Bampfield and as shown in the chapter on The Bampfield Document, to which I refer the reader.

3. S. C., in reply to A. R., in two volumes under the same title (A Christian Plea for Infant's Baptisme, &c., London, 1643)

says, in the second work, Preface to the Reader (p. 4), of the Anabaptists that they

"deny and disclaime the Ordinance of Baptism which they have received in the Apostacie. . . . Yea, they entangle themselves so in the bryars and thornes of the wildernesse that they are driven now to hold a Church all of unbaptized persons; and that though none of them be baptized, yet the said Church may set apart one or more of her unbaptized members, and give them authority to baptize themselves and others; and yet they grant that baptisme may be where there is no Church, and so (casting away the baptisme which they formerly received) they are driven (in taking up their *new baptisme*) to affirm that an unbaptized person or persons may and must baptize themselves, and after that baptize others, else true baptisme can never be had."

This is precisely the position held by Baptists at the time—except in all cases, self-baptism—as shown by Baptist authorities and especially by Bampfield. Against A. R.'s dipping, S. C. opposes "sprinkling or washing" as the Scriptural mode; and A. R. declares that the baptism of the Church of England was sprinkling, which he renounced in 1642 as having received it in infancy, showing that long before 1641 sprinkling was the Pedobaptist mode in England.

4. In a controversy between I. E., Pedobaptist, and T. L., Anabaptist, (The Anabaptist Groundwork for Reformation, &c., London, 1644), on page 23, I. E. asks T. L. this question:

"I ask T. L. and the rest of those Baptists or Dippers that will not be called Anabaptists (*though they baptize some that have been twice baptized before*) what rule they have by word or example in Scripture for going men and women together unto the water for their manner of dipping?"

Speaking of Christ washing the disciples' feet he asks why (p. 23) Baptists do not obey this command. "Is it because," says he, "it makes not so well for your planting of *new churches* as the others?" Again he says (p. 24):

"These [Baptists] and all other such like gatherers of people together, builders and planters, which comes so near their strain in framing and settling churches to themselves in their independent way, under the pretence of casting off all the abominations of Antichrist, and practicing to the state of the churches of the Apostles' times; let them and all others who in other kinds seem to endeavor a *reformation* take heed, &c."

The unchallenged charge of baptizing those "twice baptized before"—made by P. B. and others also—is proof that the Anabaptists before 1641 were sprinkled (1) in infancy, (2) when they separated, and (3) were dipped when immersion was adopted by the Baptists. Hence I. E. calls Baptist churches "new churches;" and he points out the current Baptist position of "having thrown off the abominations of Antichrist," and of having inaugurated a "reformation" of their own.

5. William Cooke (A Learned and Full Answer to a Treatise intitled The Vanity of Childish Baptisme [A. R.], London, 1644). On pages 21, 22, he says:

"Fourthly, will not this manner of dipping be found also against the Seventh Commandment in the Decalogue? For I would know with these *new dippers* whether the parties to be dowsed or dipped may be baptized in a garment or no? If they may, then happily the garment may keep the water from some part of the body, and then they are not rightly baptized; for the whole man, say they, must be dipped. Againe I would ask what warrant they have for dipping or baptizing garments more than the Papists have for baptizing Bells? Therefore belike the parties, must be naked and Multitudes present as at John's baptisme, and the parties men and women of riper years, as being able to make a confession of their faith and repentance, etc."

The objection that Cooke more fully quoted would show his ignorance and enmity regarding Baptists—his view of dipping, in the light of the 6th and 7th commandments, as dangerous and lascivious—in no way affects his characterization of Baptists as "new dippers." Many learned men of the time like Featley, Baillie, Baxter, Edwards, Goodwin, Cooke and others regarded dipping as dangerous to health, and often heard that it was naked and indecent in its performance; but their ignorance or enmity in this respect did not argue their ignorance of the fact that the Baptists had recently introduced it into England or had not practiced it in England before 1641. The Baptists themselves admitted the fact and defended their right to restore; and hence the Pedobaptists with their view of baptism, had no hesitation in calling them "new dippers." Cooke was contending with A. R., and knew all about the subject in controversy; and he is right in line with Featley, Barebone, Baillie, Pagitt and the Baptists themselves as to their "new baptisme"—that is, new in practice to the Baptists and new in fact to the Pedobaptists who had never seen or heard of adult immersion in England since infant baptism had taken the world.

6. Ephriam Pagitt (Heresiography, London, 1645) speaking of divers sorts of Anabaptist heretics mentions a new-crotcheted sort called "Plunged Anabaptists" as follows:

" Yea at *this day* they have a *new crotchett come into their heads*, that all that have not been plunged nor dipt under water, are not truly baptized, and these also they rebaptize; and this their error arizeth from ignorance of the Greek word Baptize which signifieth no more than washing or ablution as Hesychus, Stephanus, Scapulae, Budens, great masters of the Greek tongue, make good by many instances and allegations out of many authors."

It has been objected that Pagitt was not held in high esteem by his contemporaries—that he was "a good old silly body, of whom people make fun"—but the Dictionary of National Biography, Vol. XLIII., p. 65, speaks of him as a "great linguist," and says that his "accounts of the Sectaries are valuable, as he makes it a rule to give authorities." Whatever his views of baptism, or his ability as a critic, he was well acquainted with the Sectaries and with the fact that immersion had been recently adopted by the Baptists; and from his point of view he was correct in 1645 that they had "a *new crotchett* come into their heads &c." Like Featley, Baillie, Edwards and others, whatever identity he creates between them and the Anabaptists of Luther's time upon the common principle of rebaptism, he does not connect them by dipping. The "new crotchett" had come into the heads of the English Anabaptists at "this [his] day" embracing the late period of introduction, 1640–41; and he copies from Featley the significant fact: "They flock [now] in great multitudes to their Jordans &c." It is objected that Pagitt's assertion that both dipping and sprinkling were allowed in the English Church is an emphatic affirmation that dipping was then the practice of that church and was not new at that time in England; but although infant dipping was "allowed," then as now, it was not practiced and had been "disused" since the year 1600, with only here and there an exception. What Pagitt was criticizing, as a "new crotchett" lately come into the heads of the Baptists, was exclusive adult immersion—a thing unknown in England at the time it was introduced—contrary to the law of the English Church which "allowed" while it did not practice immersion even as an alternate form with sprinkling. This is the same position assumed by Barebone, Featley, Baillie, Edwards and all the rest against the exclusive form of Baptist immersion which *nullified* sprinkling and pouring as baptism—the great offense of Anabaptism since 1641, as rebaptism by any mode was the great offense before that date.

7. Josiah Ricraft (A Looking Glasse For the Anabaptists, &c., London, 1645) whose work is an assault upon Kiffin's "Briefe Remonstrance," says of Kiffin (p. 1, to the "Courteous Reader):"

"He pretends a *new light*, and takes upon him to set up a *New found Church*, and by this means seduceth and draweth away mens wives, children and servants to be his prosylites."

He charged Kiffin with "erecting new-framed churches" to which Kiffin replied as we have seen heretofore and upon which answer Ricraft (p. 6) thus retorts:

"For your Answr to this my secon Querie, instead of showing Scripture warrant for such a private man as you are, to erect a new framed Congregation; you allege your own practice, that your Congregation was erected and framed even in time of Episcopacy, and that before you heard of any Reformation; I pray you what answer doe you thinke in your conscience, this is to the Querie propounded; . . . I put the question againe more particularly, What Scripture warrant *private persons* have, to gather of themselves Churches, either under Episcopacy or Presbytery . . . That cannot help you that you say your pretended Congregations were erected before you heard of any Reformation; And if it should be granted *yours possible might be*, yet what shall we say to those multitudes of Congregations that have been erected since they heard of Reformation?"

This is but another confirmation of the fact that the English Baptists were Separatists from the Reformers, so confessed by Kiffin himself to Poole whose Queries were framed by Ricraft. Their churches were "new found," "new framed"—that is, lately self-organized under a self-originated baptism and ministry, whether before or after the Puritan or Presbyterian Reformation. Hence the Baptist ministry, in 1645, were called "private persons" because in the Pedobaptist view they had no ecclesiastical succession and no official authority to preach, baptize or erect churches. Therefore their separation was schismatical and heretical; and hence Ricraft presses the usual question of Scriptural warrant for self-originated baptism or the right to organize churches under a baptism, to begin with, which the Baptists had heretofore originated at the hands of men not baptized themselves. Kiffin does not pretend to deny this fact growing out of the recent introduction of immersion by the Baptists; but he defends Baptist separation and reformation from the charge of schism and heresy upon the ground that Presbytery was still in the hands of Antichristian heresy and corruption, and that the Baptists had erected their churches upon the principle of believers' baptism according to the rule of Christ and had made a better reformation, even before the Presbyterian movement of 1643-49.

Kiffin agrees, as seen heretofore, that when Ricraft's Reformation got rid of its abominations, that the Baptists who had separated from the Reformers, would *"return"* to them. This settles the question of Baptist origin and its late date in England— and that too at the hands of William Kiffin, than whom there is no better authority among the writers of the 17th century. He was confessedly a Separatist, and so of his entire church, in 1645; and he so speaks of Baptists in general as Separatists, and as having reformed upon the rule of Christ, and "before" the Presbyterian Movement, 1643-1649. Every Baptist preacher and church down to 1641 and onward, were Separatists. So far as I can find there were no original Baptists, or Baptist preachers, in England until towards the latter end of the 17th century. Smyth, Helwys, Morton, Spilsbury, Blunt, Barber, Kiffin, Jessey, Knollys, Tombes, Hobson, Lamb, Allen, Kilcop, Keach, Stewart, Owen—down to Collins, 1692—all came out from the Pedobaptists; and this is simply one of a multitude of proofs of the late Separatist origin of the English Baptists. Even the "intermixed" Anabaptists, 1633-38, who originated the Particular Baptists, were Separatists from the Puritans when they organized churches of their own persuasion.

8. Author of the Loyall Convert (The New Distemper, Oxford, 1645). The subject of this work is government or discipline, necessary in religion to the state. The Old Distemper was Romanism swept away by Episcopacy and Episcopacy substituted by Presbytery. The "New Distemper" is Separatism— especially Anabaptism. On page 14, among other disorderly things charged, it is said:

"Have not professed Anabaptists challenged our Ministers to dispute with them in our churches? . . . Have they not after their disputations retired into their Innes, and private lodgings, accompanied with many of their Auditors and all joyned together in their extemporary prayers for blessings upon their late exercise? How often hath Bow River (which they *lately* have baptized *New Jordan*) been witness to their prophanations."

Anabaptism was chiefly the "New Distemper" as the latest Separation of any importance; and a fling is here made at their *newness* by a reflection upon the river Bow as their "*New Jordan*"—"*lately*" so "baptized."

9. John Eachard (The Axe Against Sin and Error, &c., London, 1645), on page 8, says:

"For here is the cause of all the sects and divisions in Christendome; for when men have *lost baptism*, then one sect will devise to get remission of sins one way as by a Pope's pardon, by pilgrimage, or in Purgatory. The Anabaptists by a *new baptisme*, and by a *new church way*, not appointed by Christ, but *invented by themselves*, to make them more righteous, and holy, and clean than others, that are not of their way, and therefore will not communicate with others, &c."

This is the usual charge by the Pedobaptists of the 17th Century; and the charge is admitted and defended by the Baptists —except that their baptism and church newly erected were simply the old way "new-found," and *discovered* to them through the Scriptures by the Holy Spirit.

10. Nathanael Homes (A Vindication of Baptizing Believers Infants &c., 1645). In his Epistle to the Reader, (p. 2) he says:

"But the unsatisfactory calling of the Anabaptist-Administrators of their pretended better baptisme, upon a former worse-conceited-baptisme; being not extraordinarily called, or not having the first seale themselves; or being Sebaptists, that is, self-baptizers; or baptized with the old sort of Infant-baptisme: (in either of which they are most unlike to John the Baptist) hath justly caused many to hold off from them, and many to fall away from them. And many that are with them, to be at a loss where to rest. One congregation at first adding to their Infant baptism, the adult baptisme of sprinkling; then not resting therein, endeavoured to adde to that, a dipping, even to the breaking to pieces of their Congregation. Since that the Minister first dipped himself. Not contented therewith, was afterward baptized by one that had only his Infant baptism."

Here we have a clear view of Anabaptist transition from sprinkling to immersion; and we have here the fact revealed that not only before 1641, but even down to 1645 with some of them, sprinkling was their mode of baptism. On p. 193 Homes calls Anabaptisme, "*Catapaedobaptisme*, denying Baptisme to believers' infants." Homes also clearly shows the disorderly way in which, at first, many of the Baptist reformers, in adopting immersion, gradually proceeded to restore the lost ordinance.

11. John Saltmarsh (The Smoke in the Temple, &c., London, 1645). On page 14 Saltmarsh gives the heading: "Anabaptism So-Called; What it is, or What they Hold;" and then he goes on to state their position. Among their positions he gives the following: "That the Church or Body, though but of two or three, yet may enjoy the Word and Ordinances by way of an Administratour, or one deputed to administer though no pastour"—which is correct. On page 15 he makes the following heading: "Exceptions to the grounds of the *new Baptisme*"—that is, of the Baptists; and he speaks, on page 16, of their baptism as "*dipping them in water.*" The "new baptisme" he speaks of is *believers' dipping;* and he objects to the grounds upon which the Baptists established it by what he considered their novel view of Matt. 28:18 and Luke 16:16, namely, that "all administration of Ordinances were given to the Apostles as Disciples"—not as officials—and hence their theory: "That the Church or Body, though but two or three, yet may enjoy the Word and Ordinances by way of an Administratour, or one deputed to administer though no pastour." This was the Spilsbury thesis of beginning a Baptist church *de novo* where Baptism was lost—and so of Smyth before him and of all the Baptist authorities of the 17th century after him.

12. John Geree (Vindiciae Paedo-Baptismi, &c., London, 1645). After a long and vigorous reply to Tombes' twelve arguments against infant baptism, Geree concludes (p. 70) as follows:

"Anabaptists I conceive are of three ranks. First some in faction that embrace it because it is *new*, and different from the received doctrine, they affect singularity to be counted somebody."

Thus English Anabaptism was itself called *"new"* by this able and learned Pedobaptist.

13. Steven Marshall, B. D. (A Defense of Infant Baptism, &c., London, 1646). Comparing, on page 74, the English Anabaptist doctrines and disorders with those of Germany, Marshall says:

"Verily one egge is not more like another then this brood of new opinions (*lately* hatched in England and entertained among them who are called Anabaptists) is like the spawne which so suddenly grew up among the Anabaptists of Germany; and *ours* plead the same Arguments which *theirs* did; and if they flow not from the same Logicall and Theologicall principles, it is yet their unhappy fate to be led by the same spirit."

On page 75 (to Tombes) he says again:

"And for what you alledge out of the London Anabaptist Confession, I acknowledge it the most Orthodox of any Anabaptist Confession that I ever read (although there are sundry Heterodox opinions in it) and such an one as I believe thousands of our *new* Anabaptists will be farre from owning, &c."

Although Marshall charges similarity of doctrine and disorder among the English and German Anabaptists, he does not organically or ceremonially connect them. He calls the English Anabaptists, *"our new Anabaptists;"* and he says that their brood of *new* opinions were *"lately hatched in England."* No writer of the period, however he compares the English and German Anabaptists with each other, ever connects them by baptism or organization.

14. Robert Baillie (Anabaptisme the True Fountaine of Independency, &c., London, 1646). On page 53 Baillie states the Baptist position of his day accurately:

"This is clear of baptism, for they require in a baptizer not only no office, but not so much as baptism itself, *all* of them avowing the lawfulnesse of a person not baptized to baptize and as it seems, to celebrate the Lord's Supper."

On page 153, after stating the Baptist argument for dipping as against sprinkling, he says:

"However we deny both the parts of the proof, Sprinkling and Dipping are two forms of Baptisme, differing not essentially, but accidentally, circumstantially, or modally, so to speak, and till *very late* the Anabaptists [English] themselves did not speak otherwise."

On page 163 he says:

"The pressing of dipping and exploding of sprinkling is but a *yesterday conceit* of the *English* Anabaptists.

"Among the *new inventions* of the *late Anabaptists*, there is none with which greater animosity they set on foot, then the necessity of dipping over head and ears, then the nullity of affusion and sprinkling in the administration of baptisme. Among the *old Anabaptists*, or those over sea to this day so far as I can learn, by their writs or any relation that has yet come to my ears, the question of dipping and sprinkling came never upon the Table. As I take it *they dip none,* but all whom they baptize, they *sprinkle* in the same manner as is our custome. The question about the *necessity* of dipping seems to be taken up *onely the other year* by the Anabaptists in England, as a point which alone, as they conceive, is able to carry their desire of exterminating infant baptisme: for they know that parents upon no consideration will be content to hazard the life of their tender infants, by plunging them over head and ears in a cold river. Let us therefore consider if *this sparkle of new light* have any derivation from the lamp of the Sanctuary, or the Sun of Righteousnesse, if it be according to Scripturall truth, or any good reason."

On pages 178, 179, Baillie closes his discussion by asserting that the ancient testimonies in favor of dipping did not hold the form "unchangeable" or "necessary;" and he says:

"When any writer, either ancient or modern, except some few of the *latest Anabaptists* [English], is brought to bear witnesse of any such assertion, I shall acknowledge my information of that whereof hitherto I have been altogether ignorant."

Baillie is in perfect accord with the facts of history in the assertion that until very lately the English Anabaptists never adopted dipping as the exclusive form of baptism—making a nullity of sprinkling and pouring—just as Barebone and others declared and just as Crosby affirms as charged by all Pedobaptists at the time immersion was restored. Baillie is right also in affirming that such was never the position of the "old Anabaptists" of 1525, over sea—that the question of dipping and sprinkling never came upon the table of controversy with them—

and that at the time he wrote they dipped none, but sprinkled, as the Pedobaptists universally did. Of course, there was a small exception, at the time, the Rhynsburgers and Poland Anabaptists who had adopted immersion, respectively, in 1620 and 1574; but the great body of Mennonites and others of the "old Anabaptists" were sprinkling, and had so done from the first, with, here and there, some exceptions, in which, however, immersion was not exclusive or a matter of controversy. From Baillie's standpoint immersion was not only a matter of recent introduction among the "late Anabaptists" of England—"taken up onely the other year"—but it was a "late invention," a "sparkle of new light," and intended as a new and effectual device against infant baptism, by prejudicing parents against it, in pressing the fact that immersion was Scriptural. He seems to have forgotten that infant dipping was once the custom in England; but this is another evidence of the fact that, in 1646, infant immersion had long since fallen out of use.

On page 16 Baillie speaks of the "Mennonist dippers" who oppose the humane nature of Christ, according to Clopenburgh (Gangraena Theologiae Anabaptisticae, xlix., p. 63), but Clopenburgh, in this passage, does not call the Mennonites "dippers." I suppose Baillie was simply calling them by their name, "*Doopsgezinden*," notwithstanding which they are, and were then, sprinklers and not dippers—and always have been, according to the best Doopsgezinde authority. On page 30 he speaks of the "new-gathered Churches of rebaptized and dipped saints" among the German and Swiss Anabaptists at the "beginning of their rebaptization;" and while they actually began by sprinkling, some of them did dip, as at St. Gall and other places. No doubt Baillie here alludes to those who thus practiced; but he in no way contradicts himself in the assertion that, at the time he wrote, the "old Anabaptists, over sea," did not dip, but sprinkled, as Pedobaptists everywhere did, and as the "latest English Anabaptists" had done until "*the other year*," 1641, when they changed from affusion to immersion; and he claims it as a *yesterday conceit* among the *English* Anabaptists. He does not mention the date, 1641, as the Jessey Records actually do and as Barebone practically does, but he implies it. Baillie has been charged with prejudice and slander against the Baptists and therefore not a competent witness. So of Featley, Edwards, Baxter, and others who charge "naked baptism" and other gross irregularities upon our old brethren; but in all these charges they followed the common or general reports, and were no more bitter in their controversies with the Baptists than the Baptists with them. Both sides were equally harsh in what they said to each other.

15. B. Ryves (Mercurius Rusticus, London, 1646). On page 21, speaking of the state of things at Chelmsford, he says:

"But since this magnified Reformation was on foot, this Towne (as indeed most Corporations, as we finde by experience, are Nurceries of Faction and Rebellion) is so filled with Sectaries, especially Brownists and Anabaptists, that a third part of the people refuse to Communicate in the Church Liturgie, and half refuse to receive the blessed Sacrament, unlesse they may receive it in what posture they please to take it. They have among them two sorts of Anabaptists; the one they call the Old men or *Aspersi*, because they were but sprinkled; the other they call the New men, or *Immersi*, because they were overwhelmed in their Rebaptization."

Even down to 1646 the Anabaptists, all of them, had not given up their sprinkling, and they were called the "Old Men, or *Aspersi*," sprinklers. They were the *old sort* known before 1640–41; and the *new sort*, the "New Men, or *Immersi*," immersionists, were those who dated from 1640–41, and who, according to Evans, gradually cast the new sort into the shade. In this same year, Homes, as we have seen, gives us an insight into this kind of division among Anabaptists in England; but Evans says that after 1646 both bodies of the Baptists became entirely immersionists. The year 1646 gives us the last glimpse of sprinkling among the Anabaptists. The very fact of calling the immersionists of 1646 "*New Men*," as distinguished from the "*Old Men*," called aspersionists—*among the Anabaptists*—is a clear implication that, formerly, the Anabaptists sprinkled or poured for baptism. There was no such distinction down to 1641, when the Anabaptists began to immerse, and after which they were called "New Men" because they immersed—and because immersion was "*new*" among them. The "Old Men," or aspersionists, in 1646, were simply those of the Anabaptists, prior to 1641, who had not yet adopted immersion and were still persisting in this "old" mode of sprinkling—which, however, ceased among them after this date, as Evans says, with both bodies of the Baptists.

ENGLISH BAPTIST REFORMATION.
(FROM 1609 TO 1641, A. D.)

CHAPTER XIX.
WHAT THE ENEMY SAID—Concluded.

16. Thomas Edwards (Gangraena, London, 1646). From beginning to end, Edwards takes for granted the recent introduction of immersion in England by the Baptists. On page 1, Pt. I., he says:

"The first thing I premise, which I would have the Reader to take notice is, that this Catalogue of Errors, Blasphemies, Practices, Letters, is not of *old* errors, opinions, practices, of a former age, dead and buried many years ago, and now revived by this Discourse; but a catalogue now in being, alive in these present times, all of them vented and broached within these four years, yea most of them within these two last years, and lesse."

After enumerating 176 errors, blasphemies, &c., he says on page 36, Pt. I., as follows:

"Now unto these many more might be added that I know of, and are commonly known to others, which have been preached and printed within these four last years *in England* (as the *necessity of dipping* and burying under water of all persons to be baptized, &c.)."

Throughout his work he constantly assails "dipping" as the new mode of rebaptization and the "Dippers" as "new lights"— such as Oates, Hobson, Clarkson, Knowles, Patience, Denne, Kiffin and nearly all the rest known to the Anabaptist history of the time. On pages 138, 139, Pt. III., he repudiates the compliment "harmlesse" paid to the Anabaptists by Master Peters (1646) and calls it a "false epithete." "For what sect or sort of men since the Reformation this hundred years," he asks, "have been more harmfull?" After mentioning the tragedies, rapes, tumults, &c., charged against the old Anabaptists in "severall parts of Christendome," he says:

"If we look upon *our Anabaptists at home*, and consider what many things they have done and are doing; how can we call them harmlesse?"

Among other things they were doing (in 1646) he cites in the following words: "Who kill tender young persons and ancient with dipping them all over in Rivers, in depth of Winter;" and so he continues the catalogue of evils of which they were *now* guilty. He concludes by saying: "And yet Anabaptists of *our times* are guilty of all these and many more."

Edwards identifies the Anabaptists of 1646 with those of former times, even a hundred years before, upon the principle of rebaptism, schism, violence, &c., but not by "dipping." The error of dipping belonged only to *"our Anabaptists at home"*—to the "Anabaptists of our time"—in England; and nowhere in the Gangraena are the Baptists of 1641-46 organically or ceremonially related with the Anabaptists of 1525 and onward. Edwards (Pt. III., p. 177) like Featley wishes for a public disputation in England, authorized by Parliament, between the Anabaptists and Pedobaptists, to settle the question of baptism—as by the Senate of Zurich, 1525—but the opinion that the Zurich decree involved dipping which is wholly erroneous, does not imply that Edwards or Featley believed that the English Anabaptists had been dipping for 121 years, or that they were connected by organism or dipping with the Anabaptists of 1525. Edwards' idea was that the English Anabaptists like the Swiss would be defeated in debate and suppressed by law; and whatever Edwards' or Featley's notion about the punishment of drowning at Zurich as applicable to dipping, both of them refer exclusive immersion solely and only to the English Anabaptists after 1641. Featley calls it the "new leaven" of the English Anabaptists; and Edwards confines it within *"four years"* down to 1646, which would reach back to about 1641. On pages 188, 189, Part III., he says:

"There is one of the *first Dippers* in England, one of the *first that brought up the trade*, of whom I heard a modest good woman say that had observed his filthy behavior, &c., that it was no wonder that he and many had turned Dippers to dip young maids and young women naked, for it was the fittest trade to serve their turns that could be, &c."

Here it is clear that he points to one of the originators of immersion in England as a matter of knowledge on his own part, and in perfect consistency with his position that the dipping of the Anabaptists originated in the "four years past" back to 1641. He knew "one of the first who brought up the trade"—"one of the first Dippers in England."

However true or false Edwards' notion of the abuses of dipping among the Anabaptists, he is perfectly harmonious with the history of its restoration by the Baptists of England, 1640-41. He mentions no specific date except as comprehended in the expression "four past years" down to 1646, which is speaking either in round numbers, or according to the Puritan reckoning which would make 1641 to be 1642. He is in line with Barebone who claimed, 1643, that the total dipping of the Baptists was "onely two or three years old" and with Baillie who fixes it "onely the other year." Watts in 1656 put the date back as "13 or 14 yeare agoe," and so agrees with Barebone and Edwards; and they all have substantial agreement with the Jessey Records which accurately fix the date at 1641.

17. John Drew (A Serious Address to Samuel Oates, &c., London, 1649). Samuel Oates wrote a book (A New Baptisme and Ministry, etc., 1648, 4to), a Baptist production in conformity with Baptist position of his day, but which I have not been able to find. John Drew, however, so replies to it and quotes it, that we are able to understand precisely Oates' position as that the "Baptisme and Ministry" of the Baptist churches were "new" and based upon the current Baptist ground for restoration by unbaptized administrators—all of which Drew antagonizes upon the current Pedobaptist ground of succession under the defection of Antichrist. From page 6 to 18 he makes the usual argument against restoration by an unbaptized administrator, namely, that if the ordinances were lost they would have to be revived in an extraordinary way by a new commission and the like, and on page 14, he says:

"Thus in going a few steps backward, you must necessarily hang all the weight of your new Baptisme and calling either, (1) Upon one who was a Se-baptizer, Or (2) upon one who rested content with his owne infant baptisme [i. e., an unbaptized administrator]."

After trying to show the illogical and unscriptural position of establishing a new baptism and ministry upon the administration of a self-baptized or an unbaptized originator of the ordinance, he asks again:

"But suppose, Sir, you had a third maybe, and that a surer one whereon you might hang the weight of your *new Baptisme and Calling*, viz: An Administrator from some Church of Anabaptists beyond the seas, in Holland, or some other place. (I do but guesse sir, because I know not to what shelter you may take yourself) so that may be S. O.[ates] was baptized by Mr. Lambe, and Mr. Lambe by some rebaptized Minister of a foreign church; upon this account the matter would be a little better. For then I Querre:

"How came he to be your Minister? by what authority did he baptize that *first person in England* who baptized Mr. *Lambe?*"

Here according to Oates' theory of a new baptism and calling, or ministry, Drew argues that even if he should prove his succession from the Anabaptists of Holland who had no more right to begin lost baptism than the English, he would reduce his baptism and calling to a "nullity." The inference is that Drew had heard the report of Blunt's going to Holland for immersion, and that he, the first immersed person in England, had immersed Lamb; and he argues here that even if Oates had his baptism from Lamb, it would not help his claim to his "new baptism and ministry." The strong point in the testimony lies in the fact that not simply Drew, but Oates, a prominent Baptist preacher, takes the position that the "Baptism and Ministry" of the Baptist churches were "NEW." From page 19 to 38 he gives a "word of advice" to Oates' congregation in Lincolnshire, and urges them, on page 21, to look into the "warrantablenesse of that chiefe thing" which submitted them to Oates' "ministry," their "*second Baptisme;*" and he closes by saying:

"If therefore the Infant's right to that Ordinance be confirmed, I shall easily have the unwarrantablenesse of your *late dipping* granted me."

18. Nathanael Stephens (A Precept For The Baptisme of Infants, &c., London, 1650). This book includes a two-fold reply to Robert Everard, Baptist, by Stephens and William Swayne. On page 1, Epistle to the Reader, Stephens says:

"I found that the point which they [the Anabaptists] did bind very much upon was this; that there was no word of command for Baptisme of Infants in the New Testament. I found that this principally moved them to renounce the *old*, and take up a *New* Baptisme; to leave the *old*, and to joyne themselves to a *New* Church."

On page 2, speaking of Everard, his antagonist, he says:

"And therefore to a man who maketh it one of his chief designs to set up a *new church*, to erect a *new Ministry*, and to cast all into a new mould, what better principle can he have to begin withal than a *New Baptisme*."

From page 63 to 66 is an Appendix: "The Answer of William Swayne, &c., to Mr. Everard's book, &c." Everard had taken the position that Swayne, as all other Pedobaptists, was to be regarded as a heathen, because unbaptized, Matt. 16:18. In reply (p. 65) Swayne says:

"If Heathen, because not baptized after their manner, and consequently no church; then Mr. *Everard* and those of his judgment, were no church before they received their *new Baptisme;* but they were Pagans as well as others. If they were no true church, their first Administrator was no true Administrator, because there was no church to conferre an office upon him. Therefore they must say, he had his first Commission immediately from heaven, unless they will affirme that Heathens have power to make an Administrator of Baptisme. Now this is contrary to the Scripture, which saith, they ordained Elders in every church, Acts 14, 23. Therefore in the ordinary way the Church is before the Elders or Administrators. But if they shall say there was an Administrator before a church, as John Baptist; and therefore in like manner they may have such a one. If they say this they must prove from the Prophets that the Gospel-Churches must have two Baptists, be twice planted: which supposeth no Gospel Church in the world before the Second Baptist to plant a new church.

"Farther also they must say that there is a second Christ before whom the second Baptist must come as forerunner: And so new institutions, and foundations of Ordinances, Baptists, Apostles, Miracles; and whither will not this conceit come? But if they say that the Commission of Matt. 28:19, was their first Administrator's rule, then he must be a Disciple made by ordinary preaching and teaching, before he had any authority to Minister their new Baptisme, who ever he was. And was taught by some Heathen (think they), or by a Disciple? By a Heathen they cannot say. And if by a preaching Disciple, then Christ had a disciple before their new Baptisme. Therefore they that want [need] this New Baptisme, cannot be stated Heathens. And how foule then was their assertion at Withibrook, to call us Heathens out of their order? And yet have neither command nor example in Scripture for their Baptisme, in reference to their first Minister's Commission or Authority."

This extract needs no comment as showing the true position of Baptists and of the controversy between them and Pedobaptists. The Baptists held to the restoration of a new church and a new ministry by a new baptism, erected, after being lost, by the Scriptures; and here we see a specimen of Pedobaptist logic based upon Pedobaptist premises—succession.

19. John Goodwin (Water-Dipping, &c., 1653; Philadelphia, &c., 1653; Catabaptism, &c., 1655, London). In the first work Goodwin speaks, in the title, as follows:

"Considerations proving it not simply lawful, but necessary also (in point of duty) for persons baptized after the *new mode* of *dipping*, to continue communion with those churches, or imbodied Societies of Saints, of *which they were members before the said Dipping.*"

He uses the expressions "New Baptism," and "the Brethren of the New Baptism;" "Brethren of the New baptized churches;" "new Dippers of men and Dividers of churches;" "new Baptists" (pp. 8–26), repeatedly. On page 31 Goodwin says:

"To plead that a person unbaptized, may administer Baptism in case of necessity, is a sufficient plea indeed thus understood, viz.: 1. When God himself adjudgeth and determines the case to be a necessity; and 2. Authorizeth from heaven any person, one or more, for the work, as he did John the Baptist. Otherwise Uzziah had as good or better reason to judge that case of necessity, in which he put forth his hand to stay the Ark, then our *first* unhallowed and *undipt dipper in this Nation* had to call that a case of necessity, wherein the sad disturbance of the affairs of the Gospel, yea and of civil peace also, *he set up the Dipping Trade.*"

On page 36, he affirms "by books and writings" that the Baptists who "have gone wondering after dipping and Rebaptizing, have from the very first original and spring of them *since* the *late Reformation*, been very troublesome, &c." On page 39, he points out the fact that since immersion was introduced, there were "several editions, or man-devised modes of Dipping" invented, each succeeding edition rendering the former insufficient or irregular, and that some had been dipped three or four times. "For the mode of the *latest* and *newest* invention," he says, "it is so contrived and so managed, that the Baptist who dippeth according to it, had need be a man of stout limbs, &c." He evidently refers here to our present mode of baptizing a candidate backwards—the mode hitherto having been to press the head of the candidate forwards into the water. The backwards mode was adopted about 1653—showing the gradual progress of the late introduction of immersion.

Goodwin (p. 39) regards Nicholas Stork, or some one of the German Anabaptists of 1521 as the author of the practice of baptizing others without himself being baptized, after that *"exotique mode* in this nation," as he terms it in England. In other words it had been adopted lately in England, and was *"new"* and not indigenous to the soil; for he speaks of the "first unhallowed and undipt dipper in this nation," who "set up the Dipping Trade," and he affirms the origin of the Dippers, their very first and original spring since the *late* Reformation," and the mode *"exotique."*

In his Philadelphia, Goodwin deals in the same expressions about the "New Baptisme," "the way of the New Baptism," "the Brethren of the New Baptisme" and the like; and so he does repeatedly in his Catabaptism, where he calls it the "new mode of water-dipping." In his reply to Allen's complaint about his oft-repeated use of the expression, he says, (p. 8) Epistle to the Reader:

"Heretofore in discoursing with a grave minister of Mr. A.'s in the point of rebaptizing, and *the most ancient that I know walking in that way*, finding him not so well satisfied that his way should be stiled Ana-baptism, I desired to know of him what other term would please him. His answer was, *New Baptism.*"

On page 143 Goodwin answers Allen's evasion of the charge of "new baptism," and marvels that "Allen and his partizans can falsifie themselves touching the authentiqueness of their new Baptism." "For," says he, "all persons baptized in infancy, being judged by them unbaptized, and there being no other but such in the nation, when their new Baptism was first administered here, it undeniably follows that the first administration of it was a mere nullity." There is no mistaking Goodwin's understanding of Baptist position and the fact of the late introduction of immersion by the Baptists of England. He needs no comment.

20. James Parnell (The Watcher, or Stone Cut Out of the Mountain, &c., 1655, London). On pages 16, 17, 18, Parnell employs a long paragraph without a period in it which begins and closes thus:

"Now within these late years . . . one cries, lo here is Christ, if you can believe and be baptized you shall be saved; so they that can say that is the way, and that they believed Christ dyed for them, then they must be dipped in the water, and that they call baptizing of them, &c."

Parnell was speaking of the Anabaptists; and he not only clearly states their position, but he truly refers to their recent practice of dipping by the expression: "Now within these late years." He is in exact line with all the host of writers, Baptist and Pedobaptist, who touch the subject.

21. John Reading (Anabaptism Routed, &c., London, 1655). On page 100, Reading accuses the Anabaptists, by rebaptism, of crucifying Christ afresh. "How," asks he, "do they crucify him afresh to themselves, that is as much as in them is? Why I. They are said to do so, who iterate, or again do, or resume that which is a resemblance or similitude of Christ's sufferings, who died but once: for in reiterating it we make the first void; and so if we have a *new baptism*, we must have a new Christ, &c." On page 171 he says that the Anabaptists—

"obstruct and make void the holy ordinances of God to delude souls, by causing them to renounce their Baptism by taking another Baptisme under a vain pretense that they were not susceptive of Baptisme in their infancy, nor lawfully baptized, neither at all, if happily they were not dipped under water; for they say the institution of Christ requireth that the whole man be dipped all over in water: so that the Anabaptists *now* hold, that dipping the whole body in water is essential to Baptizing, &c."

By the phrase "new baptism" Reading does not simply mean rebaptism as distinct from infant baptism, and without reference to mode as was sometimes the case, but he especially meant dipping, by the word "*now*." "So that the Anabaptists," he says, "*now* hold that dipping the whole body in water is essential to Baptizing." In other words, he means that they did not formerly hold to that practice.

22. Jeffry Watts, B. D. (Scribe, Pharisee, Hypocrite, &c., London, 1656). This book was written by an Episcopalian to a

Baptist neighbor by the name of John Wele, who wrote him some very severe and abusive "queries." The work is divided into separate parts under different titles; and in his address To the Reader, under the head, "The Dipper Sprinkled," on page 3, Watts says:

"Yea this I have done, as for the convincing of the Anabaptists their dipping, or immerging Baptism (so called) to be a *Novelty*."

Just above on the same page he charges "upon that Dipping; that it was, and is, as I have said, a *New Business*, and a very *Novelty*." On pages 3, 4, he says:

"I wonder at the Iron-brow, and Brazen-face of *novel* [Baptist] Independency, and *New light*, that whereas it is every Seventh day at least, in the chimney-house Conventicles prating against the Old, Laudable, and Ancient Practices of this our, and other reformed Churches, it dares pretend to Antiquity (so contradicting itself), and glory of it in this point, of their *immersing* and Dipping (calling it the Good old way), &c."

Under the head of the Narration of the Dipping by a Baptist whose name is not given, the said Baptist, on page 3 of the Narration, says:

"I am sorry to hear you call it a New business, for it is older than your sprinkling of Infants, though indeed that hath been so long practiced generally, that this Old Good Way seems now a new Thing: And no wonder, for we read that the song the Saints sing for their deliverance once out of Antichristianism, is turned to be, as it were, a new song, Rev. 14:3. And no wonder though the old Practices of the Saints be, as it were, a new thing to the World, and unto their Leaders."

It is to this criticism that Watts now delivers himself under the head: "The Dipper Sprinkled," whom he styles the Hypocrite. On pages 1, 2, he replies:

"And you have as little cause to be sorry at my calling your Dipping a *new business* (unless with Heraclitus you can weep at everything you hear). I called it so indeed, and shall here now make the Calling true, as in word, so in deed; so far is it from being *older* then our sprinkling of Infants, that your self helpeth it forward, saying, That this hath been so long practiced *generally*, that your good old way (of Dipping) seems now a new thing. It seems so to you, it is so to me. You make me in the meantime no whit sorry but glad, to see you moved somewhat upon the charge of a *new thing or business*. Are not all your things now new? and your whole business, is it not new, or nothing?"

On page 2, he continues to say:

"Your Dipping, a new Business;" "your inglorious new Thing and Business, namely your *late* Dipping amongst us;" "your new Dipping."

In the case of the Much-Leighs dipping, given in the narrative above mentioned, Watts finds an additional novelty in the method of baptizing two women which he now goes on to discuss under several heads, namely: 1. Was not the person dipping a new thing? 2. The Persons dipped, a new thing? 3. The place where, a new thing? 4. The very dipping itself, in its action and manner, a new thing? (pp. 3-9.) The person dipping was a Lay-Brother and an unbaptized administrator; the party baptized was already baptized, according to Watts; the manner of dipping was in clothes which he claims was also new even among Baptists; he holds that the dipping of the person in a pond, and not in a river or a baptistery, was new; and he denies that the action of dipping in itself is Scriptural or customary in England. (p. 32.) On page 40 he says:

"*The Church of England hath been now of a long time, time out of mind, mind of any man living, in firm possession of baptism, and practice of it by sprinkling, or pouring on of water upon the face and forehead, and gently washing and rubbing the same therewith and pronouncing the word of Institution, In the name, &c.* It is your part to bring the *Writ of Ejection*, a word, or the example of the word sufficient to dispossess and eject us out of our baptism, and to invest yourself unto the same, by shewing your better title and plea of dipping and immerging the whole body in or under the water"

Here Watts settles the question, as an English churchman, as to the disuse of infant immersion and its substitution by sprinkling by the close of the 16th century; and he clearly affirms that the dipping of adults in England was only a late innovation upon the established rite of sprinkling in the Kingdom.

On page 63, Watts assumes that immersion had ceased for 500 years "in the purest and perfectest Western churches;" but he affirms the continental origin of "new men" (as compared with ancient) who were (in 1524) "the progenitors and predecessors" of the English Anabaptists and who, "against the constant and uniform custom of the Western church, were the first dippers and immersers in the West"—at which time, 132 years before, he regards immersion a "novelty," that is, as he says, *"in comparison of antiquity."* Then he adds:

"Nay, your Brother's dipping and immerging is not so *old* as theirs, for your Ancient Fathers Nicholas Stork, or Stock and Thomas Muncer, did not dip in your manner, [i. e. in clothes and ponds]; nor is it as old as your elder Brothers, who about 13 or 14 year ago, ran about the Countrey; for they did not dip in your manner, in their cloathes, but naked, nor in Ponds but Rivers; nor is it elder than yourselves were in the day that you and they practiced it and begot it in the Parish of Much Leighs upon the bodies of the two Sisters you dipt in June last past, and so is but a brat and brood of yours and theirs, not a twelve month old yet by a good deal."

In all this Watts regards the age of the dippers in England as only 13 or 14 years which preceding 1656 would go back to about 1641-2. The clothes and pond dipping he regarded as not twelve months old. Whatever be true or false with regard to naked baptism among the General Baptists at first—a thing the Particular Baptists repudiated—Watts fixes their beginning as dippers according to the history of the case; and he not only calls the dipping of the two women, but the whole thing, a "novelty" of but 13 or 14 years standing in England—a "new business." So he calls the immersion of 1524 a novelty as compared to antiquity, and so likewise the dippers of that date "new men" as compared with the ancient. He calls these dippers, as he supposed they all were, the Progenitors and Predecessors of the English Baptists; but he does not imply their connection by the succession of dipping, but only by a similar practice which in England was not simply a comparative "novelty" but wholly a "new business." The practice of sprinkling had beyond the memory of man been established by the English Church; and the Baptists may be regarded as lately come in with immersion as a Writ of Ejection to dispossess the English Church of its sprinkling by a better title.

23. Thomas Wall (Infants' Baptism from Heaven, London, 1692). Besides charging, on page 22, that the Baptists of Eng-

land received their Baptism from John Smyth—indignantly denied by Crosby and Collins—he says:

"For as Water Baptism is confessed by the Anabaptists to be a part of God's worship, see Mr. Keach's Book, Gold Refin'd, P. 47, in these words, Water Baptism is a part of Instituted Worship and service of God, without an express word drop'd from Christ or his Apostles, is Will-worship. Therefore by their own Grant, the way they come by their Baptism is Will-worship, and so Idolatrous, until they can prove it lawful for a man to Baptize himself, or that an unbaptized Person should Baptize another, and then that Person so Baptized, should Baptize him from whom he received his Baptism."

This is, away down to 1692, still the controversy between Baptists and Pedobaptists; and the above is the exact statement of Baptist position which no Baptist denied, except as to John Smyth. Even with him they did not deny their organic beginning, but with him they denied their baptismal origin, and hence put it somewhere this side of Smyth. The Jessey Records say 1640-41 and so practically say others.

I close the case with these witnesses among the enemy. I have more but these will suffice. In all, I have cited about twenty-eight Baptist and twenty-four Pedobaptist authorities, besides the Jessey Records—fifty-two in all—and consistent with each other and with the facts in the case, from beginning to end. There is not a discrepancy, of any value, anywhere to explain; and in all my search among the authorities of the 17th century, original sources, I never found a single contradiction of the thesis that the Baptists restored immersion in England about 1640-41. I have adopted Crosby's first history of the English Baptists, as the basis of my position; but I have not trusted him without an examination of his original sources of information. I find him correct; and I have only made this section of Baptist history more elaborate than he did, without evading the issue at any point. It is possible that my Pedobaptist authorities have been severe upon Baptist practice and have exaggerated the abuses of immersion in its irregular introduction; but in stating the position of Baptists and the facts of their history during the 17th century, they are perfectly consistent with the Baptists themselves. Smyth, Helwys, Morton, Hutchinson, Spilsbury, Tombes, Lawrence, The Jessey Records, Kiffin, Bampfield, Grantham, A. R., R. B., Kilcop, The Anabaptist Sermon, Cornwell, Denne, Blackwood, Knollys, King, Jessey, Kaye, Allen, Lamb, Collins, Barber, Crosby, Evans—all agree with Barebone, Featley, Taylor, The Tract on the Book of Common Prayer, S. C., I. E., Cooke, Pagitt, Ricraft, Author of Loyall Convert, Eachard, Homes, Saltmarsh, Geree, Baillie, Ryves, Edwards, Drew, Stephens, Goodwin, Parnell, Reading, Watts and Wall. It has been urged that the writer of the so-called Kiffin Manuscript was too sweeping in his main sentence that down to 1640-41 none had been immersed in England—that he did not know what he was saying to be true; but all these men ought to know what they were talking about. If there had been an immersion church in England prior to 1641, these authorities would have known something of the fact before the close of the 17th century, and we should have heard of it. They were all over the Kingdom; and their testimony cannot be offset by subsequent traditions and current opinions which have since originated.

There may have been sporadic cases of adult immersion, as in the case of infant immersion, between 1609 and 1641—or between 1500 and 1600—but they are historically unknown. Even if such cases existed, they count nothing in the great 1641 movement, in which the whole body of Baptists—unconscious of such cases—joined in the revival of immersion and claimed a self-originated "beginning" or "reformation." The traditions of Anabaptist organism or immersion before 1611-1641 are utterly exploded by the claim and practice of the "English Baptists" of 1641 and onward; and even if they then knew of any such traditions—as we *now* have—they regarded them as having no succession value and made them no factor in the revival or reformatory movement which originated their church, ministry and baptism, according to the Scriptures, as newly *"recovered"* and as having been *"lost."* So speak these witnesses, Baptist and Pedobaptist, whom I have put on the stand.

ENGLISH BAPTIST REFORMATION.

(FROM 1609 TO 1641 A. D.)

CHAPTER XX.
SIGNIFICANT FACTS.

Under this head I shall mention some corroborative facts which signify the introduction of immersion into England by the Baptists about 1640-41. I have touched upon these facts in the course of this work, but I wish here to emphasize them for the better recollection of the reader; and among them I shall include the "monuments" set up by Dr. Whitsitt in his book (A Question in Baptist History, pp. 99–100).

1. The first significant fact is the silence of history before 1641 regarding a single act of adult immersion among the English Anabaptists—especially between 1611 and 1641. It has been replied that there is no instance of sprinkling or pouring mentioned among them; but in the recorded facts of history it is clearly implied or taken for granted that they did sprinkle or pour if they baptized at all. Crosby says that, prior to 1640, immersion was "disused" in England; and, in his rendering of the so-called Kiffin Manuscript, he says if the Anabaptists had "*revived*" this "disused" ordinance it was not known—clearly implying that, down to 1640-41, the date of the Manuscript, they were sprinkling or pouring. The Bampfield Document implies the same thing; and Evans, Hutchinson, Spilsbury, Tombes, Lawrence and all the controversial writers of the 17th century who touch the subject confirm the plain implication. With the exception of the Collegiants (1620), the Dutch Anabaptists were practicing sprinkling; and not only is history silent as to English Baptist immersion before 1640-41, but it clearly implies that the English Anabaptists were sprinkling or pouring like their Dutch brethren across the sea. The very fact of reviving immersion in England—so elaborately recorded by Crosby—is proof that the English Anabaptists were sprinkling before the revival. William Kaye (see p. 197) undoubtedly

points to the period prior to the revival of immersion by the Baptists as a time when the Anabaptists sprinkled. He says:

"When WE were *sprinkled* great darkness, in comparison of the light of the Gospel [Baptist] reformation that *now* shineth, was then as a cloud over-vailing the Word."

He refers to this former sprinkling as believers' baptism like that of the twelve (Acts 19) in ignorance of the Holy Ghost, and rebaptized by Paul. So the Baptists, sprinkled under the cloud over-vailing the word, had now rebaptized under the light of the immersion reformation.

2. Another significant fact is that there is no evidence in 1640-41 that there was in England a single Baptist church, or Baptist preacher, or Baptist church member, of original Anabaptist origin apart from separation from the Puritans or other Pedobaptists. Such men as Kiffin, Lamb, Allen and others did not hestitate to acknowledge that the Baptists were separatists and reformers; and we know that the two original organizations, respectively of the General and Particular Baptists, were separatist bodies. So of many others known to history: Smyth, Helwys, Morton, Spilsbury, Jessey, Barber, Kilcop, Ritor, Blunt, Kiffin, Knollys, Tombes, Hobson, Lamb, Keach, D'Anvers, Owen, Blackwood, Cornwell, Powell, Stennett, Collins—all with but little exception of a later date down to the close of the 17th century, had been baptized in infancy, and had separated from the Pedobaptists. They lived all over the Kingdom, preached in every quarter, and such men must have known if there were any Baptist churches, preachers or people who antedated 1611 and practiced immersion before 1641. Cornwell lived and labored in Kent; and if Eythorne and Canterbury churches had been of the ancient Baptist origin and continuance claimed for them, and had come down to 1641 with a regular ministry and baptism, he would have known the fact, and he would have been the last man on earth to claim, as he does, that Baptists had but lately heard and obeyed the voice of Christ with regard to dipping. So of Powell in Wales. So of Kiffin, Tombes, Oates, Hobson, Lamb and others preaching and debating all over the Kingdom. Such men never would have admitted that Baptists were separatists and reformers— that their churches were newly erected under a baptism originated by unbaptized administrators—if there had been any

succession Baptist churches, ministry or immersion in England. There may have been old Lollard or Anabaptist elements in many places, having long retained some sort of conventicle existence, which sprang into Baptist churches and adopted immersion after 1641, and so continued to claim their ancient descent; but there were no Baptist churches in England before 1611, and there was no Baptist immersion in England before 1641. R. B. in 1642 (A Reply to the Frivolous and Impertinent Answer of R. B., &c., 1643), said "that at some time *lately* there were no *baptized persons* in the world"—that is, no *Baptists* so made by immersion. R. B. was a Baptist in controversy with Barebone, and he spoke advisedly, no doubt referring to the late introduction of immersion in 1641 to which Barebone alludes in 1643 when he declared that "totall dipping" in England was only "two or three years old or some such short time."

3. It is a significant fact that the first commitment to jail, so far as history shows, for the practice of *immersion* in England took place after 1641, in the year 1644, in the county of Suffolk, when Laurence Clarkson was imprisoned for the specific offense of teaching and practicing immersion as baptism. The second case was that of Henry Denne, who, in 1646, was imprisoned at Spalding, in Lincolnshire, "for having baptized some persons in a river there." (Crosby, Vol. I., p. 305.) Edwards (Gangraena, Pt. III., p. 117) inveighs against Baptist dipping and wishes for a public disputation, like that of Zurich, 1530, in order that Baptists found in "error" about immersion should be punished for dipping. If after 1641 such civic proceedings were desired or had against the simple practice of immersion, we may be sure that before 1641 the spiritual and temporal swords would have been employed with bloody severity if there had been any such practice among the Anabaptists. There were no such proceedings before 1641 in England, because there was no such practice; for if there had been such a practice among the Anabaptists the fact would have been known in literature and in the court records of the time. It is objected that before 1641 Baptists may have concealed their practice on account of persecution; but they are well known in other respects of their history during this period, aside from the fact that such a supposition is improbable, if not impossible, for thirty years. It is objected again that immersion was the normal mode in the English Church down to 1641, and therefore no

notice was taken of Baptist immersion until after 1641, when sprinkling had begun to obtain in the English Church; but history shows that sprinkling became general in the English Pedobaptist churches by the year 1600, and therefore the same objection to Baptist immersion would have obtained before as after 1641, if such had been the practice. The offense of Baptist dipping was that it was *exclusive* and *nullified* every other form of baptism; and Crosby (Vol. I., pp. 96, 97) shows that while Anabaptism by any mode which nullified the infant rite at the beginning of the Reformation was the previous offense of rebaptism, now (1640-41) the offense was *exclusive immersion* which *nullified* every other mode of baptism.

This was the offense charged by Barebone, Featley, Edwards, Baillie, Goodwin, and others; and hence they pronounced it a "very *novelty*," the "*new* leaven of Anabaptisme," only "two or three years old," after but never before 1641. If this offense which created such bitter controversy after 1641—resulting in several cases of persecution when liberty and light had been enlarged—had existed before 1641 when the Star Chamber and High Commission Court were in power, such men as Featley, who had been watching the Anabaptists for "twenty years," would have made the fact known both in literature and judicial proceedings, which would have multiplied by scores the case of Clarkson and Denne.

4. The baptismal controversy which followed the year 1641 is another significant fact which points to the introduction of immersion at that date. Crosby shows (Vol. I., pp. 96, 97) that this controversy began in opposition to the revival of the practice of immersion as the exclusive form of baptism; and on page 106 he shows that the introduction of this form of baptism at the hands of unbaptized administrators was the "point much disputed for some years." He says:

"The *Baptists* were not a little uneasy about it at first; and the *Pedobaptists* thought to render all the baptizings among them invalid, for want of a proper administrator to begin that practice: But by the excellent reasonings of these and other learned men [Spilsbury, Tombes, Lawrence and others], we see their [the Baptists'] beginning was well defended, upon the same principles on which all other protestants built their reformation."

Then the gigantic controversy raged from 1641 to the close of the century and onward for and against the introduction of immersion (1) on the ground that it was exclusive, (2) upon the ground that the Baptists had no proper administrator. Any one conversant with the literature of the period knows that Crosby states the truth in the case. In almost every discussion of the baptismal question after 1641 the Baptists, among other questions, were assailed upon the validity of their exclusive baptism restored by unbaptized administrators; and in almost every reply the Baptists defended their practice as based upon a Scriptural right to restore the lost ordinance through unbaptized administrators.

The question of believers' as opposed to infant baptism was always involved, and had been in controversy from John Smyth down to 1641. Not only so, but Smyth, Helwys and Morton had been charged with *self-baptism* and the want of a proper administrator to begin baptism, as they had instituted it; but as they had adopted affusion, which made no exclusive claim as to mode, but little warfare had continued against their self-originated practice. The controversy down to 1641 turned chiefly upon the question of believers' as opposed to infant baptism; but after 1641 the Baptists were constantly stung with the additional stigma of the invalidity and novelty of exclusive immersion restored by men who were not themselves baptized. By some they were stigmatized with Smyth's self-baptism; but this charge they always repudiated, and they invariably defended their restoration of immersion as legitimately accomplished, according to the Scriptures, by unbaptized administrators. The controversy on this question dates from 1641, and was never mooted by Baptists or Pedobaptists before that date. In fact, there never was any discussion between the Baptists and Pedobaptists of England on the mode of baptism until after 1641; and this controversy, as shown by Crosby, originated in the "revival of immersion," as the exclusive mode of baptism, by the English Baptists, at the hands of unbaptized administrators, about the years 1640–41. Hence this baptismal controversy which raged from 1640–41 and onward is a fact significant of the introduction of immersion at that date. The theory that immersion was the normal mode in the English Church down to 1641, and that therefore no controversy could take place as to mode until after 1641 when sprinkling came into practice among Pedobaptists, is absolutely contrary to all the facts of history in the case. Crosby declares that immersion ended in the English Church in 1600—that prior to 1640-41 "immersion had for sometime been disused"—that the controversy on the mode of baptism originated with the "revival of immersion" by the "English Baptists"—and all the facts in the history of the controversy absolutely confirm Crosby's position.

5. Another fact significant of the recent introduction of immersion by the English Baptists about 1641 is that the Anabaptists were never called Baptists, in England, until after that date, as in 1644 and onward. The word "Baptist" grew out of the usage which began with immersion when the Anabaptists were called baptized people, baptized churches and hence, finally, "Baptists," "Baptist churches," &c. The Baptists had always protested against the name of Anabaptist which implied rebaptism and which Baptists denied upon the ground that those baptized by them from other sects had never really been baptized at all; but it was not until after 1641 that they could the more effectively get rid of the odious name of Anabaptism by adopting immersion which "nullified every other form of baptism" and which gave them the claim of being the only people who baptized at all— and hence the only baptized people, *par excellence*, Baptists. The Pedobaptists, with but little exception, still stigmatized them as Anabaptists because, in their view, they still rebaptized those who had been baptized in infancy, and they so continued to stigmatize them down through the 17th and 18th centuries; but the Baptists, still protesting that they were "falsely called Anabaptists," gradually came into possession of the name "Baptist" —though often, at first, they spoke and wrote of themselves without any designation, or as the "people of God," or as the "gathered churches," or as the "baptized churches." The word "Baptist" was greatly offensive to the Pedobaptists also because it implied that none other than Baptists were baptized people; and hence they malignantly for this and the reason already specified kept up the stigma of Anabaptistry upon the Baptists after 1641.

The reason why the English Anabaptists were not called Baptists before 1641 is because they did not practice immersion— because they practiced sprinkling or pouring down to that date; and while they protested against the stigma of Anabaptism, the practice of the same mode with their opponents was only a repetition of the same ordinance. They made the same argument before as after 1641, namely, that believers' baptism was not a repetition of infant baptism—and that it utterly nullified infant baptism as no baptism; but it was not until 1641 when they adopted exclusive immersion which nullified every other form of baptism as no baptism, that they could be called a baptized people—Baptists. It is objected that the titles *Taufer*, *Baptistae* and *Doopsgezinden* had been applied to some of the Continental Anabaptists at an earlier date; but this fact in no way affects the history of the English Anabaptists who, for the reasons already specified, could not have assumed the title, "Baptist," until after the year 1641. So soon as they began to immerse they were called the "baptized;" and almost simultaneously with the title "baptized" came the designation, "Baptist"—a name given by no writer, Baptist or Pedobaptist, as a historical claim to the *English* Anabaptists before 1641.

6. It is a significant fact that, not until the year 1644, Oct. 16, (Thomason), baptism is defined as "dipping or plunging the body under water" in an English Baptist Confession of Faith (Article XL.)—prescribing, in the edition of 1646, the manner in which the ordinance was to be administered: "(yet so as *convenient garments* be both upon the administrator and subject *with all modesty*)." In none of the Confessions of Smyth, nor in the Confession of 1611 is the word *baptizo* rendered to dip, for the reason that the 1609-11 Anabaptists did not practice immersion; and this definition and the subsequent caution about clothing in the 1644-46 Confession presuppose the recent introduction of immersion and the unsettled manner of its administration about the year 1641—as indicated by the documents and writers of the time who pronounced it a "novelty" and who charged its administration with gross irregularities, such as nude or semi-nude baptism.

It has been variously objected that immersion was taken for granted by Smyth and Helwys because of its universal prevalence among the Dutch Anabaptists and in the English Church, 1609-11; or that hitherto Baptists had "scrupled" the use of "formal words" in order to evade persecution; or that the English Baptists were moved to insert immersion in their 1644 Confession, by the rejection of dipping on the part of the Westminster Assembly in 1643. These objections are all invalid (1) because at the time of Smyth and Helwys the Dutch Anabaptists were practicing affusion, and immersion had gradually ended with sprinkling in the English Church by 1600 and was "disused" in England; (2) if immersion was the "normal mode" before 1641, the Anabaptists had no need to fear persecution in the use of "formal words" by which to define baptism as immersion in their creeds; and (3) in the Preface to the 1644 Confession the signers make no reference to the Westminister Assembly and they declare their object, at this time, to set forth their position according to the word of God and to meet the misconceptions and misrepresentations of other people. They were still "falsely called Anabaptists," as of old," upon the theory that they repeated baptism; and they now put a "new" definition of baptism into their Confession, which not only nullified infant baptism as no baptism, as ever before, but which now nullified every other form of baptism, as never before. Hence Featley calls this definition the "*new* leaven of Anabaptisme," that is, "exclusive immersion," which none of the old Anabaptists ever maintained. Featley was precisely right as to the *newness* of the definition; and this XL Article of the Confession of 1644—with its caution about the manner of baptism—indicates the recent introduction of immersion in 1640-41. The first appearance of this definition, after several Confessions of the English Anabaptists, in the 1644 Confession—especially in company with the caution about clothing—is significant of its "novelty" which had already repeatedly been charged and defended with regard to immersion and the manner of its administration since 1641—never before.

7. The health and decency question (claimed in violation of the 6th and 7th commandments) with regard to immersion after 1641 is another significant fact which indicates its recent introduction at that date. Before 1641 there is no record of any antagonism to Baptists regarding baptism as dangerous to health or morals. Between 1641 and 1646 there was almost a panic among the Pedobaptists about the fatality of dipping people— especially in winter; and the charge was repeatedly made that the Baptists—some of them dipped men and women naked. Samuel Oates (Crosby, Vol. I., pp. 236, 238) is cited as being tried for his life at Chelmsford because Annie Martin died within a few weeks after she had been "baptized by him." Baxter and Cradock were prominent in their opposition to immersion on the ground of health; and Baxter, Baillie, Cooke, Edwards, Featley and many other prominent Pedobaptist writers con-

stantly charged the Baptists with naked baptism. Grant that there was no sense in all this furor, or that the charges were false, it does not alter the indication that immersion was something new, and never heard of before 1641 among the English Baptists. If they had been practicing immersion before that date, the same charges would have made the fact known, and their persecution would have been more prominent and effective; but history is as silent as the grave regarding the health or decency question charged to immersion in England before 1641. Various objections have been raised as explanatory of this health and decency furor on the part of the Pedobaptists who wanted to prejudice the cause of the Baptists, but they do not get rid of the fact that the furor indicates the newness of immersion among the Baptists after 1641—or that such a furor was unknown before 1641, when sprinkling or pouring was as universal among the Pedobaptists of England as after, and when the same fight would have been made upon exclusive immersion as after, if the Baptists had practiced it.

There are several other significant facts comprehended under the head of Dr. Whitsitt's Monuments which I can only briefly mention.

1. The historical fact heretofore mentioned at Chelmsford, 1646, (Mercurius Rusticus, p. 22) where there were "two sorts of Anabaptists; the one they call the Old Men or *Aspersi*; because they were but sprinkled; the other they call the New Men, or *Immersi*, because they were overwhelmed in their rebaptization." Here in 1646 aspersionists are called "*old* men" while immersionists are called "*new* men;" and since no such distinction ever existed among the English Anabaptists before 1641, it is reasonable to conclude that the "old men," or aspersionists, describe the Anabaptists who antedated 1641, while the "new men" or immersionists describe the Anabaptists who adopted immersion in 1641. The singular fact is that these "old men," or sprinklers, had continued down to 1646 and had not gone over to the "new" immersion lately adopted in 1641; but it indicates the gradual change of some of the Anabaptists who were slow to adopt immersion. Evans (Vol. II., p. 79), as already seen, refers the above distinction to the Anabaptists, or Baptists, some of whom still followed the Mennonite affusion; and he shows that after 1646 the *Immersi* "soon cast" the *Aspersi* "into the shade" and "their practice became

obsolete" when "immersion became the rule of both sections of the Baptist community." N. Homes, (Vindication of Baptizing Believers Infants, &c., p. 5, 1645) describes the state of Baptist division as seen at Chelmsford. He says:

"One Congregation at first adding to their Infant Baptisme the *adult* baptisme of sprinkling: then not resting therein, endeavoring to adde to that a dipping, even to the breaking to pieces of their congregation."

Here are the Old Men or *Aspersi* in conflict with the New Men or *Immersi;* and this revolution going on for several years after 1641 under the distinction of the Old and New Men, or the Aspersi and Immersi, in Baptist ranks, is a clear indication of the recent introduction of immersion in 1641.

2. As cited by Dr. Whitsitt, de Hoop Scheffer (De Brownisten, p. 156) points to the fact that after 1641 the relation between the Mennonites and the followers of Helwys and Morton who were so closely allied that in 1626 a movement (Evans, Vol. II., pp. 24-30) was set on foot to secure an "organic union of the two parties," was broken off. The fracture is traced only to the adoption of immersion by the English Baptists in 1641— the bond of union between the two parties down to that date having been sprinkling as the mode of baptism practiced by both. Henceforth the Mennonites would be regarded by the English brethren as unbaptized, and so the tie of fellowship was broken and correspondence came to an end in 1641. It is objected that the antagonism between the Mennonites and the Baptists regarding footwashing, civic oaths, war, magistry, the deity of Christ and the like; but upon these questions, according to Muller and Evans, we trace the most fraternal correspondence without any alienating difference down to 1631. Scheffer is probably right; and if so this is another fact significant of the introduction of immersion, 1641.

3. Dr. Whitsitt's seventh monument is the classic use of the word *rhantize* employed soon after 1641 to antithesize *immerse*, or to show a striking distinction between dipping and sprinkling. A. R. so employed the word in 1642 in his Treatise of the Vanity of Childish Baptism, p. 11. Also Christopher Blackwood (Antichrist in his Strongest Garrisons, &c., 1644) transferred the word to English and called it *"rantized."* Hanserd Knollys (Edwards' Gangraena, Pt. III., p. 241), in 1646, speaking to the Pedobaptists by the way of antithesizing *immerse*, said:

SIGNIFICANT FACTS. 249

"You were *rantized* but not *baptized*." Thomas Blake, 1645, contrasts *rantizing* not only with *dipping* but with *pouring*, the latter mode being his practice. This usage Dr. Whitsitt claims as another indication of the recent introduction of immersion in 1641; and it is certain that no such distinction obtained among the English Anabaptists before that date, although sprinkling was the settled practice of the English Pedobaptists from 1600.

It is objected that the word *rhantize* is not broad enough to antithesize *immerse*, and that the introduction of the word pointed to a conflict between Pedobaptists, some of whom preferred pouring but "resented the change to sprinkling just then introduced"—that is, in 1645, according to Blake, Wall and others. "The new word," says the objector, "was not derived to decide the departure from immersion to pouring [that is, among Pedobaptists], but from pouring to sprinkling." But the word *rhantize* was first introduced by the Baptists in 1642, in order to distinguish classically and perfectly—as never before—immersion from aspersion, and it indicates their new departure from aspersion to immersion.

There are other significant facts which point to 1641 as the date at which the English Baptists restored immersion, but these will suffice. Everything I have cited confirms Crosby's history of the revival of immersion at that date, and confirms the writings of the various authors I have cited and who confirm Crosby. There is no inconsistency at any point between these significant facts and the history of the case as established by Crosby, Evans and the writers I have quoted so elaborately. The truth is that the case is so plain that it amounts no longer to a probability, but to an established fact; and I cannot see how, with all this array of testimony direct and circumstantial, any one can escape the conclusion set up by history,

1. That immersion ended in the English Church in 1600.
2. That sprinkling which had already supplanted immersion, became general, if not universal, from 1600 onward.
3. That the Anabaptists restored immersion in 1641.
4. That these Anabaptists must have practiced sprinkling or pouring before they restored immersion, as their history goes to show.
5. That their subsequent history, according to the writers of the 17th century and the facts in the case, all points back to 1641 as the date at which they began immersion.

ENGLISH BAPTIST REFORMATION.
(FROM 1609 TO 1641 A. D.)

CHAPTER XXI.
WERE THEY BAPTISTS?

Baptists preceded the baptism of Christ. The great forerunner of the Redeemer was a Baptist. John was an immersionist and an Antipedobaptist. He practiced believers' baptism only; and in his refusal to immerse the Scribes and Pharisees without repentance, or because they were the children of Abraham, he repudiated the doctrine of federal holiness as a ground for either infant or adult baptism. He was also an anti-ritualist who, according to the Scriptures and Josephus, baptized with reference to righteousness immediately wrought in the soul through repentance and faith, and not mediately procured through sacramental efficacy whether with or without repentance and faith. John was, in every sense, a Baptist in principle and practice; and, ceremonially, he made the Redeemer a Baptist when he dipped him in the river Jordan. Christ made Baptists of his twelve Apostles, who were immersed and who were constituted an embryonic "church," with authority to settle personal offenses according to Matt. 18:17; and the first church at Jerusalem was a Baptist Church, including this apostolic college, which by its sovereign suffrage chose Mathias to take the place of Judas, and to which the Lord "added" by repentance and baptism 3000 souls on the day of Pentecost. This first Baptist Church subsequently elected its own deacons and elders according to its congregational sovereignty and independence; and all the apostolic churches, modeled after this first church, were Baptist Churches to whom the apostolic epistles were addressed as sovereign and independent bodies, with their bishops and deacons. These New Testament Churches were all immersionist, anti-pedobaptist and anti-ritualistic bodies, separate and independent of each other in polity; and while they voluntarily co-operated with each other in advice, missions, or benevolence, they knew nothing of organic union or ministerial office beyond the pale of a local church. They were neither Papal, Episcopal nor Presbyterial; but each church was a self-governing democracy under the law of Christ and the guidance of the Holy Spirit. Christ was the sole Head and Priest in these churches; and when the Apostles died they left no successors except the Scriptures as their authority.

It was thus that these Apostolic Churches entered the second century; but strange to say, they had already begun to apostatize before the close of the first century as indicated by the heresies of the Corinthians, Galatians and the seven churches of Asia. By the middle of the second century sacramentalism had become prevalent and infant baptism was its fruit. Congregational episcopacy had also popped its head above the clergy and laity of the local church; and before the close of the third century diocesan, provincial, patriarchal and papal episcopacy had developed. In the fourth century the union of Church and State had been consummated; and at the beginning of the seventh century the universal papacy of Rome was established over the world by the sovereign authority of the emperors. Anti-catholic sects began to revolt in the second century; and under different names they continued to separate and spread, survive and perish, until the 16th century Reformation. They were generally Antipedobaptists; and in the 16th century they became distinctly so in Germany, Switzerland, Holland, England, and in other countries of Europe. Before the close of the 16th century, however, with the exception of the Mennonites and a few fragments on the Continent, they were again practically crushed out of existence by the persecution of both Catholics and Protestants. From the fourth century the woman had been in the wilderness; and although she had struggled to get out and had revealed Antichrist a hundred times, she had as often practically sunk back under the cloud of papal darkness and despotism. Even the Mennonites and the Poland fragment of Anabaptists were Socinians and afflicted with other heresies. The Waldenses had been absorbed by the Pedobaptist Reformers; and it remained for the English Antipedobaptists, 1611–1641, to make the last grand effort which fully and finally brought the woman out of the wilderness. But for the Puritan revolution and the abolition of the Star Chamber and High Commission Court, 1641, in England, this Baptist reformation might have proved another failure; and instead of the triumph of 1611-1641, the church in the wilderness had had to wait for another step in the progress of human liberty, before coming out and up to the Baptist denomination as established in England and now dominant in the United States and other parts of the world.

Now with reference to these English Anabaptists, 1611-1641, according to their own testimony during the 17th century and onward, the following facts have been shown:

1. They claim to have been separatists from the Puritans, and there were no original Baptist churches, ministers or people, apart from separation, down to 1641 and later, known to history.

2. They admit that they originated their baptism and erected their churches anew, at the hands of unbaptized administrators.

3. They claimed to assume this prerogative under "discovery" from God and according to the Scriptures as authority for restoring Gospel order which they declared was "lost" in the "apostasy."

4. They adopted immersion, 1640-41, some thirty years after their separation and organization began.

5. They deny organic, baptismal or ministerial connection with prior Anabaptists; and while they all admit their origin by unbaptized administrators, they generally held that when the ordinance was restored, the necessity for restoration ceased, and that its administration should be regular, or go on in an "orderly way."

6. The 1260 years of Antichristian reign and of the invisibility of the church were regarded by them as reaching down to their time; and they held that they had come *visibly* out of the wilderness—all prior Anabaptists having failed to do more than reveal Antichrist and having sunk back under the "smoke in the temple" or into the invisibility of the spiritual church in the wilderness—having no Gospel order or baptism.

7. They all repudiated the doctrine of visible succession as the "mark of the beast"—whether of church, ministry or baptism.

8. They were divided as to whether the church was constituted by baptism or the covenant; as to close and open communion; as to particular and general atonement; but they seemed to agree that baptism introduced the believer into the general body of Christ, and not into a particular church.

9. In fine they claimed to have established a "Reformation" and to have had a "Beginning" of their own in England—based upon the principle of believers' baptism in 1609-1633 and upon the restored practice of immersion in 1640-41, including a newly erected church and ministry; and they claimed that their Reformation originated in Separation from the Puritans based upon a return to New Testament principles and practices which the other Reformers had not reached—not even the Puritans themselves whose reformation they commended as far as it went.

The question arises here: Were these people Baptists? According to historical usage the Anabaptists of England were called "Baptists" before they restored immersion in 1640-41. Crosby speaks of the "methods taken by the Baptists of England, at their revival of immersion;" and he speaks of the "difficulty which did not a little perplex the English Baptists" in selecting these methods. After treating of the Blunt method of sending to Holland for immersion, he speaks of the "greatest number of the English Baptists, and the more judicious" who regarded the Blunt method as "needless trouble" and of Popish "succession;" and he says:

"They affirmed therefore, and practiced accordingly, that after a general corruption of baptism, an unbaptized person might warrantably baptize, and so *begin* a reformation."

Evans likewise calls the Anabaptists of England "Baptists" down to the deputation of Blunt to Holland for immersion and at the same time represents the followers of Smyth and Helwys as practicing the affusion of the Mennonites—some of them down to 1646—after which he says "both sections of the Baptist community" adopted immersion as "the rule" without a "solitary exception." The Bampfield Document speaks of the "methods taken by the *Baptists* to obtain a proper administrator of baptism by immersion, when that practice had been so long disused, that there was no one who had been so baptized to be found." Robinson speaks of "the Dutch *Baptists*" as "*pouring.*" Here we have a number of Baptist authorities who call Anabaptists, "Baptists," at the very time they claim they did not practice immersion. Even the *Doopsgezinden*, the Mennonite Doopers of to-day, are so called, while they practice sprinkling. Dr. Jesse B. Thomas in his review of Dr. Whitsitt (Both Sides, p. 47) uses this expression "mixed Baptist churches," which indicates a greater looseness of usage than to speak of the Anabaptists as "Baptists" before their adoption of immersion, since some of the mixed churches in England retained not only sprinkled but Pedobaptist members.

Wherever the principle of believers' baptism has been maintained by any people, the earlier writers have always called them "Baptists;" and so we naturally do at the present time. The central peculiarity of the Baptists is believers' baptism as opposed to infant baptism; and the natural distinction is made by name between Baptist and Pedobaptist, without reference to mode. The Antipedobaptist is *essentially* a Baptist, other things being equal, even when he practices affusion, as the *Doopsgezinden* do—and as most of the Continental Anabaptists of the 16th century and all of the English Anabaptists in the first half of the 17th century, who were called "Baptists," did. Dr. Newman (Review of the Question, pp. 171–173), after showing that "immersion commanded a very small share of the attention" of the Continental Anabaptists of the 16th century—and after paying their martyr devotion to Baptist principles the highest compliment—closes by saying:

"*They were not regular Baptists, but they were thoroughly imbued with Baptist principles, and were, in a very important sense, the forerunners of all that was best in Puritanism and in the great modern Baptist movement.*"

All this was true of the English Antipedobaptists from 1611 to 1641. "They were not regular Baptists, but they were thoroughly imbued with Baptist principles." John Smyth founded a church upon the Baptist model, believers' baptism and a regenerate church membership; and, organically speaking, this was the "beginning" of the present denomination of Baptists, though begun with an unscriptural *form* of baptism. The principle, however, was right, and the form was corrected in 1640–41. The same was true of our Particular Baptist ancestors in 1633 who began upon the same principle that Smyth and his followers did; and while they were not afflicted with the Mennonite errors of the General Baptists, they had errors of their own which they inherited from their Puritan origin. So far as the mode of baptism was concerned—which was only one of their errors—they both abandoned the wrong and adopted the right; and we should give them credit for their reformation in becoming strictly Baptistic and count them our brethren.

The English Baptists, whether General or Particular, seem to be no sounder in Baptist principles and practices after 1641 than before, excepting the mode of baptism. They retained errors in doctrine and practice that were more vicious than the unscriptural mode of baptism, with but little exception—such as the Socinian and other peculiarities of the Mennonites among the General Baptists and the open communion and mixed church practice of the Particular Baptists—and they were well nigh as much in process of evolution towards modern Baptist perfection in this country after 1641 as they were before. But few if any of their churches after 1641, perhaps, would have been now received into the fellowship of one of our Associations; and with but a small exception of the English Baptist brotherhood of to-day, the great mass of English Baptists in some one respect or another could not organically affiliate with the larger body of American Baptists. Such men as John Bunyan, Robert Hall and Charles H. Spurgeon were open communionists; and even Spurgeon left the "Baptist Union" of England, at a recent date, because it was on the "down grade." The Baptist fraternity in England even to-day are very much mixed and divided and in error; and with the exception of a small body of them, perhaps, fellowship and communion would be impossible between them and the Baptists of this country.

Yet these people are Baptists who spring from their immersed ancestors who antedated the year 1641; and from them we of America also sprang. Therefore those old Anabaptists of 1611–1633 are our ancestors; and if we had no greater objection to our claim of kinship with them than their mode of baptism before 1641 we should have greater reason to congratulate ourselves upon our pedigree. Their aspersion or affusion was about their smallest offense; and yet above all their errors they were our heroic progenitors thoroughly imbued with our leading principles and peculiarities. They may not have been regular Baptists, but they were great and glorious in our principles and in their sacrifices and sufferings for our peculiarities. They were the English and American Baptist denomination in embryo; and they have evolved a history which has helped to shape the destiny of the world in the progress of Evangelical Christianity and in developing the cause of religious and political liberty. The Constitution of the United States has been pronounced by Dr. Griffis, the Congregational scholar, "an Anabaptist document;" and that production is the epitome and symbolization of Baptist history based upon the teachings of such men as Smyth, Helwys, Morton, Busher, Spilsbury and others who laid the organic foundation of the Baptist denomination of to-day. Blunt restored immersion to the Baptists; Keach restored ministerial support and singing in the churches; Andrew Fuller restored theology; Carey restored missions; our fathers of 1776 restored liberty; somebody must yet restore a plurality of elders to the Baptist churches; but our organic foundations were restored in 1611 and 1633 in England when the Anabaptist elements separated from the Puritans and organized churches of their own persuasion according to the model of the New Testament—based upon a regenerate membership and baptized upon a profession of repentance towards God and faith in our Lord Jesus Christ.

That there may have been a Dutch Anabaptist element in this foundation is possible. It is also possible that, in this foundation, there was a Lollard element. Baptist churches after 1641 sprung up most spontaneously and rapidly in sections where formerly these elements had existed in the eastern counties of England; and it is evident that in London and the sections indicated there was Anabaptist seed in the soil. If so, we have a spiritual vein of succession blood which connects us back with the old English and Continental Anabaptists who can trace an evangelical succession back to primitive times. Of any organic or baptismal succession we have no historical proof; and John Smyth and all the Baptist writers of the 17th century utterly deny any such a connection, especially as to the English. It would be a matter of denominational interest and history to be able to trace such a connection; but we are only historically certain of our Puritan origin, that as a denomination we organically sprang from the old English Anabaptists of 1611–1633, and that we became strictly Baptistic by immersion in 1641. We were essentially though not strictly Baptists before that; and it is with genuine pride and pleasure that we can point back to our heroic ancestry, however regretful for their many errors.

Neither circumcision nor uncircumcision—baptism nor unbaptism—*essentially* makes a Baptist. First of all, a regenerate heart is essential to a Baptist; and immersion cannot make a Baptist without previous regeneration. Our chief doctrinal peculiarity through all the ages is the *spiritual* as opposed to the *ritualistic* or *rationalistic* idea of Christianity: and our chief ceremonial peculiarity through all the ages has been *believers'* as opposed to *infant* baptism. If our people have ever failed in the baptismal *form* which more perfectly symbolizes the *spiritual* idea of Christianity, they have never failed in the *essence* of Christ's religion; and though they may have sometimes erred in the form they never erred in the principle or purpose of that form as a *believers'* rite. More than this, whatever their variation in the practice of that form, as a matter of expediency or sufficiency, they never denied its symbolism, and promptly returned to it when light and liberty changed their environment and afforded the opportunity. The greatest error on baptism that any Anabaptist can be charged with in history is that immersion was not the exclusive form of baptism; and the Polish Anabaptists (1574), the Collegiants (1620) and the English Anabaptists (1641) repudiated this error, and returned to the "ancient practice" of immersion as exclusive and essential to baptism. They thoroughly believed that immersion was a Scriptural form of baptism, and never lost sight of its burial and resurrection significance in their "washing with water" by the application of the element to the subject instead of the subject to the element; but their definition of baptism never implied or included sprinkling or pouring except as an alternate form which might be used as a matter of expediency or sufficiency. Hence in their zeal for the principle of believers' baptism they fell under the 16th century spell of indifference as to mode—a spell from which the Pedobaptist world has never awoke, though once immersionists.

One of the great distinguishing landmarks of these English Baptists of 1611–1641 was their anti-succession theory of the *visible* church, ministry and ordinances. They claimed a succession of faith and of God's Spirit and Word; and that when God so revealed his truth and moved true believers to obedience, it was their duty and right to "restore Gospel order." Blunt, 1640–41, made a departure from this theory, seeking regular baptism from Holland; but the great body of Baptists, both General and Particular, repudiated Blunt's "method" as "needless" and "Popish"—as a "succession" movement to restore immersion—and maintained that though baptism was lost, "an unbaptized person might warrantably baptize and so begin a reformation." This was the doctrine set up in principle by

John Smyth, Helwys, Morton and their followers, 1609-11, and this was specially the theory, both in principle and practice, of Spilsbury, Barber, Kilcop, and all the rest of the Baptists, General and Particular, with the exception of Blunt, 1640-41 and onward. Blunt's succession idea, if he entertained it, was purely Pedobaptist and utterly repudiated by every other Baptist of the Seventeenth century so far as I have seen; and as we have seen, the Blunt church, with the Blunt idea, probably became extinct before 1646, according to Edwards and Bampfield. Organic, ministerial or baptismal succession is not a landmark of the Baptists of the 17th century. Even if we could trace our baptism to Blunt who received immersion from the Collegiants, who may have received it from the Socinian Anabaptists of Poland, who may have received it from the Swiss Anabaptists, yet our foundation is insecure; for evidently the Continental Anabaptists of the 16th century, whether they sprinkled or immersed, originated their baptism by an unbaptized administrator, to begin with, as shown by their history. Our American succession, however, is from the English Anabaptists, or from Roger Williams, or both; and with but the Blunt exception, the English Anabaptists originated immersion by unbaptized administrators. The visible succession theory never originated among Baptists until about February, 1848, when it sprung up among our Southern (American) Baptists in opposition to the practice of receiving Pedobaptist immersions. Organic, ministerial or baptismal succession is purely a traditional fiction of recent origin, and the very opposite of original Baptist Landmarkism. The very first regular Baptist Confession of Faith, 1644, is an anti-succession document; and it presupposes by its very terms the restoration of immersion among the English Baptists by unbaptized administrators.

The great fundamental peculiarity of the Anabaptists of 1611-41 was that the Bible is the sole rule of faith and practice among Christians. This is one of the Baptist landmarks of every age; and it was upon the authority of God's Word that the English Baptists based their commission to restore gospel order—erect anew the church, the ministry and baptism as lost under the defection of Antichrist. They regarded "the church in the wilderness" as not a visible, but only a spiritual body—that the 1260 years of Antichristian reign reached down to their day—that the prior Anabaptist sects which successively rose and perished

Were They Baptists? 259

never brought the woman out of the wilderness—that God had peculiarly discovered to them, by his Spirit and Word, the duty of restoring Gospel order lost in the apostasy down to their day —and they invariably held that visible succession had been repeatedly broken. So far as I can discover, no English Baptist of the 17th century interpreted Matt. 16:18, to mean an unbroken continuance of visible churches, but such a succession as would imply a continual *reproduction* of such churches, under a perpetual succession of believers and of God's Spirit and Word. All of the English Baptists followed by the able and orthodox Gill interpreted Matt. 16:18 as simply referring to the spiritual body of Christ; and I now agree with those who took the position that the gates of hell should never so destroy Christ's visible churches that they should not be continually restored. Reproduction was the theory of the old English Baptists who never denied the facts of history as to a "broken succession" of visible churches, as they called it, and who never based their position upon the brittle thread of a sacramental or outward succession. They held to the strong and vigorous theory that the gates of hell might destroy the outward, but he could not touch the inward—that though you sweep every organism, and office and ordinance from the earth to-day, God's Spirit and Word through his believing people would reproduce them to-morrow. They regarded visible succession as the "mark" or "Character of the Beast."

It is certain that the Apostolic churches and those that succeeded them were lost in the Apostasy; and so of all the successive separatist sects of Anabaptists until the permanent restoration of Gospel order by the English Anabaptists, 1611-41. Like the typical people of God under the Jewish dispensation, Baptists in person and principle have *substantially* continued from John the Baptist till now; and as the Jew lost circumcision in the wilderness, the ark and the organism of the Temple service in Canaan, and restored them, so Baptists have continued to lose and restore their organism, ministry and baptism. The spiritual kingdom has never been broken, however often Gospel order has been interrupted or irregular; and our visible succession has been that of *continual* showers, but not that of a *continuous* flood. The gates of hell have never for one moment prevailed against God's Spirit, God's Word or God's People, whether in the typical or anti-typical wilderness; and although Satan has at various times made havoc of the external body of Christ, it has always succeeded again by reproduction or resurrection. The devil killed Christ on the cross, in the body, but not in the spirit; and as his body rose from the dead, so his visible churches, or bodies, have risen from the dead a hundred times. The present Baptist denomination would not be here, to-day, if Antichrist had not lost his power to destroy us in the English nation, as he did on the Continent; and if he had done with us in England what he did with the Anabaptists of Germany and Switzerland, there would have been the necessity for another reproduction in order to continue Baptist organism, office and ordinance. God alone restores and preserves Baptists; and this was the constant confession of the English Baptists of the 17th century. His Spirit alone is our Guide and the Bible alone our authority; and upon this platform we stand for doctrine and practice—for church constitution, ministerial function and ceremonial form and order. There is no church authority apart from Scriptural warrant; and our baptism, communion and ordination are regular only in a Scriptural church and at the hands of a Scriptural ministry, wherever set up, without regard to visible succession. The Anabaptists of the 17th century took the position that when the church, its ministry and its ordinances were once restored, then regularity should be resumed in any given community—that when the necessity for restoration ceased, then irregularity should cease—and I agree with those orthodox Baptists who took that position. Hence I am a close-baptism, close-communion and close-ordination Baptist—just as Kiffin and those like him were.

The Popish fiction of organic or visible succession founded on Matt. 16:18, as already said, was never adopted by Baptists until of recent date; and it has not only engendered a false Baptist ideal and spirit, but it has from the beginning been a source of strife and confusion among good brethren. No body of Baptists in the world, among themselves, has been more unhappy than where this fiction has prevailed, or since this notion began to be pursued among them. We have had more or less of strife for fifty years, based largely upon this difference of opinion among Southern Baptists; and there appears to be little prospect of peace until this Romish novelty shall be surrendered. I can remember, when affected by this ideal and spirit of high-church Baptistism, I was led to believe that such men as Fuller, Broadus, Boyce, Jeter and others were not *sound* Baptists; and for some years this fiction led me to feel that it was almost impossible for a Pedobaptist to be saved. The object of this volume is not only to sustain a historical fact, but to set up the old Baptist landmark of constant reproduction instead of visible succession; and if I can help to unite my brethren upon the Bible as the sole rule of authority, and the only basis of our continuance—under God—I shall think myself happy. In the fear of God, and in the light of Scripture and history, I dedicate this work to the peace and prosperity of the Baptist denomination; and I affirm my solemn belief that God never intended that his people should have a visible or organic succession, the claim of which has always engendered a traditional pride and persecuting spirit in those who have held it.

The charge will be made that the position of the English Baptists as Separatists and Reformers makes them the offspring of Rome—a daughter of the "Mother of Harlots." Such is not the case. In every age God has cried: "Come out of her my people"; and in every age they have come out and from under the shadow of the great Apostasy by separation or reformation. Every Anabaptist leader and sect of history was Separatist or Reformer; but they threw off the "mark of the beast," *infant baptism*, and other Romish heresies, and hence were never daughters of the old harlot of Rome. No Pedobaptist reformation or separation ever got out of Rome. The retention of infant baptism is *"the mark of the beast,"* and so of other Romish heresies which make every Pedobaptist denomination in some respect akin to Rome and like their mother or grandmother. Anabaptist separation or reformation generally went to the other extreme of Romanism; and hence their counter errors which, in many instances, helped to divide and destroy them. The only likeness which any Baptist has to Rome, is holding to *visible* succession, "Antichrist's chief hold."

APPENDIX.

(A)

THE CRITIC ON DOCUMENT "NUMBER 4."

CAPTION.

"An Account of divers Conferances held in ye Congregation of wch Mr. Henry Jessey was Pastor, about Infant baptism by wch Mr. H. Jessey & ye greatest part of that Congregation ware proselyted to ye opinion and Practice of ye Antipedobaptists.

being an old M.S.S. wch I received of Mr. Adams, supposed to be written by Mr. Jessey, or transcribed from his Journal."

"1643 ABOUT BAPTISME. QU: ANS:

"Hanserd Knollys our Brother not being satisfied for Baptizing his child, after it had been endeavored by ye elder & and by one or two more: him self referred to ye Church then that they might satisfye him, or he rectifye them if amiss herein which was well accepted.

"Hence meetings ware appointed for conference about it at B Ja: & B. K & B. G. & each was performed with prayer & in much love as Christian meetings (because he could not submit his judgment to depend on with its power—So yelded to)

"Elder ———The maine argument was from these fower conclusions

"I. Those in Gospel Institutions are so set down to us.—those not cleare

"2. Whatever Priviledg God hath given to his Church as a Church is still given to all Churches.

"3. God hath once given to his Church as a Church this privilege to have their Children in Gospel covenant, & to have its token in Infancy Gen. 17.7.10.

"4. Baptism seems to be in ye rome of Circumcision.

"Conclusion: to be now to Churches Infants.

"H. K. Ans:

"To ye third on wch ye weight lyes, that it wants ground and proof from Scripture. That Gen. 17 proves it no more to be given to a Church as a Church, for their Infants to have this token of Covenant in Infancy, than for the Churches Servants all bought with money &c without exception of Religion to be Baptized: and yt not only ye Chil: but Childrens Children to many Generations though neither Father nor Grandfather were faithful must be Members; for thus it was with Abraham's posterity: therefore this was not with it as a Church, but as Jewish or as peculiar to

Abrahams seed Naturall. Unless we may say of the Children of such wretches that certainly the Lord is their God and they his people, contrary to 1 Cor. 7.14.

"Elder.

"Ma: All such as we ought to judg to be in Gods covenant under promises should have ye token of ye Covenant

"Mi: Thus of ye Infants of Believers especially Church members.

"Ans. [B. K. Argumt]

"To ye first proposition or major its not ye Covenant yt interests to ye token of itselfe, but God's Insitution, proved thus

"I. The Lord's Supper is a token of the New Covenant, it must be to such children as being in Covenant, if Argument good

"2. Enoch, Methusala, Noah, Sem: ware in Covenant & to be judges so & Abraham at 75 years old & Isaac at two days old: these then must have circumcision if major be sound, but not so besides being in Covenant there must be a word on Institution touching the time & adjuncts &c.

"In Gospell times wherein all these are New there are now subjects, Gentiles: a new way of taking them in; new Ordinances, new time to them; as ye Lord's Supper so Bapt: As we must not goe to Moses for ye Lord's Supper, its time, Persons to partake &c but to New Testament so we must for Baptism. Now in New Testament is no Institution of Infant baptism.

"The being ye seed of Abraham would not qualify them for Baptism Matt: 3. This is the substance of what was discussed in all Love for many weeks togeather.

"Issue hereof was the conviction of Bro. Jac: & S. K. B. S. now against Pedobap: & ye stagering of more, whereof some searched ye Scriptures, some prayed earnestly for light, & had such impression on their Spirits against Pedobaptisme, as they told ye Elder on his enquiry, that he could not but judge there was much of God in it, yet still he then remaind in his judgment for it: though thus 16 ware in a weeks space against it, wth little or no speach each with other. This was about the 17th of Mo 1643-4. Having had weekly loveing conferance with prayer from ye midst of 11 Mo 1644. 1644.2,28. Concluded that to our friends yt then live in ye county (about 12) a letter should be writt from Church to each with tender care, exhortation & consolation.

"1644. 1st & 2 Mo. Haveing sought the Lord with fasting for those friends that left us, as not satisfied we ware baptized as a true Church & for our . . . . . And haveing by conference not satisfyed you.

"1644. 3.29. At Mr Fountains ye Church considered not further to do, some judged yt ye Church censure should pass, others not.

"Conclusion was to desire ye advice of ye Elders & Brethren of other Churches, wch was done 1644.3.27: at Mr Shambrookes where ware present these

"Mr Barebone, Rozer, Dr Parker, Mr Erburg, Mr Cooke, Mr Thomas Goodwin, Mr Philip Nye, Mr G. Sympson, Mr Burrows, Mr Straismere.

"These by enquiry not satisfyed that in these absenters was obstinacy but tender conscience & holyness & not disturbing in our proceeds advised us

"1. Not to Excommunicate, no, nor admonish wch is only obstinate.
"2. To count them still our Church & pray & love them.
"3. Desire conversing togeather so farr as their principles permit them, so waiting till either (1) some come in, or (2) some grow giddy & scandulous then proceed against them, to this we agrees and so parted.

"The names of some of our Dearly beloved Friends yt scrupled about ye Administration of Baptisme &c and in tenderness forbore ware these

B)
)Jackson
S)
B)
)Nowell
S)
S. Bayh
B. Berry
B. W. Hulls
S. Phillis Atkinson

S. Eliza Alport
S. Eliza Michael
S. Lydia Strachen
S. Kath Pordage
S. Cotheldy
S. Agnes Nadinam
B)
)Golding
S)
S. Kent (yt dyed)

S. Knollys
S. Keneston
B. Hen. Jones
S. Pickford
S. Dorrell
Eliza Phillips
S. Reves
B. Wade

and afterwards these
S. Wade

"After some time all these in ye 2nd Row were satisfyed vide in their scruple and judged supra yt such disciples as are gifted to teach & evangelise may also baptize &c &c and ware baptized

Some before H. Jessey and the rest of ye church ware convinced against Pedobaptism. And hence desired to enjoy it where they might, & Joyned also, some with Bro. Knollys, some with Bro Kiffin, thus These

B. S. Knollys
B. S. Wade
B. Couver
S. Jane Todderoy
S. Eliza Phillips

B. Ford
B. Potshall
S. Dormer
S. Pickford
S. Reves
B. Darel
B. Blunt

"After H. Jessey was convinced also, the next morning early after that wch had been a day of Solemne seeking ye Lord in fasting & prayer (That Infant Baptism were unlawfull & if we should be further bap-tized &c, thē Lord would not hide it from us, but cause us to know it) First H Jessey was convinced against Pedobaptisme & then that himself should be baptized (notwithstanding many conferences wth his honored Beloved Brethren Mr Nye,'Mr Tho: Goodwin, Mr Burroughs, Mr Greenhill, Mr Cradock, Mr Carter &c &c. with Mr Jackson, Mr Bolton &c). 1645 4 Mo Vul June 29. And was baptized by Mr Knollys, and then by degrees he baptized many of ye Church, when convinced they desired it.

APPENDIX. 265

"Then in time some of those before named returned to communion wth this Church as

S. Kenaston   B & S. Wade
B. Hen. Jones   S. Dorrell
S. Buckley   *S. Huddel als. Levill"

The hysteric effort of the critic to twist the Jessey Church Records into making Blunt a Baptist in 1644 and into fixing his deputation to Holland in the same year, is based upon a perversion of this document, No. 4, and upon the blunders of Neal. Crosby, who lent these MSS. to Neal, and who uses this document freely, makes no such reference to 1644; and he charges Neal with misrepresenting these Records in other respects, for instance, when he represents Jessey's church as becoming Baptist in 1638 instead of 1645 and laying the "foundation for the first Baptist congregation" in England, that is, in 1638. The "Blunt" mentioned in this document, No. 4, cannot be shown to be Richard Blunt of document No. 2 (1640–41). Perhaps, according to the Court Records, it would prove a "forgery;" and instead of "B.[rother] Blunt" it was S.[ister] Blunt!!
But grant for the sake of argument that it was Richard Blunt. It would only prove, as Barebone charged upon "R. B.," that, as many Baptists in that day did, he would receive a "fourth baptism;" and it would possibly identify R. B. with Richard Blunt as Barebone's antagonist, 1642–43. (See pages 178, 179.) Edwards, 1646, says that the church of one "Blount" (as Crosby spells Richard's name) had already gone to pieces. The regular or succession theory of Blunt's baptism had been repudiated from the start by the great body of the English Baptists. Even Kilcop, baptized by Blunt or Blacklock in 1641, held to the anti-succession theory; and so of Kiffin, who became a Baptist in 1641 and who was possibly baptized by Blunt or Blacklock in that year. Now whether the "Blount" mentioned by Edwards was Richard Blunt, or not—whether or not Blunt and his people were absorbed, in 1641, by Spilsbury—or whether or not he himself remained, as Kiffin and Knollys did, with Jessey—he likely at an early date abandoned his succession theory of baptism and fell in, as Kiffin, Kilcop and all the rest, with the great anti-succession party; and it would not be surprising to find him, in 1644, receiving a "fourth baptism," as intimated by Barebone of R. B. It was not only common with some of the Anabaptists at the time, but, as in Kent, the General Baptists sometimes reimmersed the Particular Baptists. In the controversy with Barebone R. B. was a strong anti-successionist, 1642–43; and if R. B. was Richard Blunt it would not be strange if by a "fourth baptism," he was reimmersed in 1644.
It will be observed, too, under the date of 1644, that after the withdrawal of sixteen members from Jessey, document No. 4 says: "After sometime all these in ye 2nd Row were satisfied (vide in their scruple and judged supra) yt such disciples as are gifted to teach & evangelize may also baptize &c &c, and ware baptized, Some before H. Jessey and the rest of ye Church ware convinced against Pedobaptisme." The document speaks of the first list of withdrawals as those who "scrupled about ye

---
*B. & S. in the above lists stand for Brother & Sister.

Administration of Baptisme &c;" and the document refers to those "in ye 2nd Row" as some of those who thus "scrupled" about the administration of baptism by unbaptized administrators as being "satisfied." If "ye 2nd Row" belongs to the last list "Blunt" is found in it; and this would indicate, if it was Richard, his conversion already to the anti-succession theory, and that he had gone with Knollys or Kiffin, both of whom were members of Jessey's Church and had left it—Kiffin in 1643 and Knollys in 1644 as this document shows in the last list as to "B. S. [Brother and Sister] Knollys."

The criticism, under this head, that Jessey was not convinced that immersion was the mode of baptism until 1645, is simply desperate. As already shown, in Ch. VIII., p. 103, according to the Kiffin MS., Blunt was "convinced" with Jessey, 1640, that baptism "ought to be by dipping"—and further convinced, in 1641, when, as Crosby shows, a "much greater number" seceded from the Jessey Church to the Baptists. Crosby (Vol. I., pp. 310, 311) affirms that Jessey's respect for the piety and solid judgment of many of these seceders—the "frequent debates" in his church on the subject and by a "diligent and impartial examination" of the "Scriptures and antiquity"—led him to the "conviction" that the "mode of baptizing" was immersion; and in the year 1642 he announced his conviction publicly in his church and declared that, "for the future," those who were baptized would be immersed—henceforth "dipping" the children until convinced that infant baptism was unscriptural. Crosby cites the controversy of 1644, as he found it in document No. 4, which finally led Jessey and the greater part of his church to renounce infant baptism; and when "convinced also the next morning early after a day of solemn seeking, fasting and prayer," that that practice was wrong and that he himself ought to be dipped, he was baptized, June 29, 1645, by Hanserd Knollys, who with his wife and others withdrew from the Jessey Church in 1644 and were immersed at the same time "B[rother] Blunt" did likewise. The controversy which primarily led to this step began in 1643 (Document No. 4) when the question of baptizing Knollys' child became an issue; and all this proves that Knollys and his wife were members of Jessey's Pedobaptist Church until early in 1644, when, as the result of the controversy over their own child, both withdrew and were immersed— more than twelve months before Jessey and his church became Baptists. In the early part of 1643 Kiffin, evidently, had withdrawn from Jessey and had become co-pastor of some church with Patient; but it was not until 1645 that Knollys had gathered a church and was pastor in London. Perhaps he immediately began this work in 1644 when with his wife and those who followed him he withdrew from Jessey's church. Though Kiffin became a Baptist and was perhaps immersed in 1641, Knollys delayed until 1644 to follow his conviction; and so far as documentary evidence shows, it is certain that neither of them were immersed before the year 1641.

APPENDIX. 267

(B)
THE CRITIC ON "THE 1641 THEORY."

The oft-repeated charge that the "copyist" or the "collector" of the Jessey Church Records forged into the Kiffin MS. the clause: *"none having then so practiced it in England to professed believers"* and that Crosby knew of no such clause in the manuscript he had, is so grossly absurd that it scarcely needs to be noticed. As repeatedly shown Crosby paraphrases and strengthens the clause in unmistakable terms when he says of the "dissenters" whom, on page 97, Vol. I., he calls "English Baptists:" "That they could not be satisfied about *any* administrator in England to BEGIN this practice; because tho' some [Anabaptists] in this nation rejected the baptism of infants, yet they had not, as they knew of, REVIVED the ancient custom of immersion," which he had just said (p. 97) "had for sometime been *disused*." This is Crosby's version and amplification of the clause in question; and he makes it clearer still, in the very terms of the MS., when he proceeds to detail the action of the "Baptists" in sending "Blount" to Holland for the "disused" ordinance. Why? Because there was no one "known," or to be "found," among the Anabaptists of England who had *continued* the practice? No, who had *"revived"* the *"disused"* custom; and the wildest vagary, in the light of history, is the desperate assumption that Blunt's deputation to Holland grew out of the "rumor" that Spilsbury had once gone to Smyth at Amsterdam for the same purpose! The very converse must have been the fact; for Spilsbury must have been a boy when Smyth died, and could have had no reason for going to Smyth. Blunt had a reason for going to Holland, and Crosby makes that plain also: because there they "had *used* immersion for sometime," as in England they had "disused" it "for sometime." But for the Collegiants who restored immersion in Holland, 1620, there had been no immersionists, at that time, in Holland, as in England, to whom Blunt could have been sent; and when Smyth was in Amsterdam and Spilsbury a boy, there were no Baptists in England, at all, of whom history gives any account—at least, so far as immersion makes Baptists. The Spilsbury "rumor" grew out of the Blunt deputation. There could have been no such rumor concerning Spilsbury before 1640-41, since Smyth died in 1612; and the Spilsbury rumor is a confirmation of the Blunt deputation.

The frantic effort to "explode" the "1641 theory" by trying to falsify the "Gould-Kiffin MS.," as distinct from the "Crosby-Kiffin MS.," is painfully pitiful. Never was there such an ado without doing anything in microscopic criticism. Not only is it claimed that Crosby does not mention "the famous ten words," but that he does not quote the date, "1641:" therefore the "Crosby-Kiffin MS." did not have that date, nor those ten words. I have shown that he paraphrased or amplified these ten words into a stronger statement than the words themselves; and I have shown that he not only quotes literally from the 1640 paragraph of the "Gould-Kiffin MS.," including the date, but he minutely details all the facts contained in both the 1640 and 1641 paragraphs of this MS. which follow the 1640 date and identify the 1641 date. It is absolutely certain that the

"Gould-Kiffin MS.," or its original, was before Crosby; and "a wayfaring man, though a fool," need not err in the fact.

But suppose that the date, 1641, could not be distinctively established, or that Crosby did not find it in the Kiffin MS. He affirms that immersion *ceased* in England in 1600; that it "had been for some time *disused;*" that the "English Baptists" *restored* it. When? It was either at or after their organization, 1609–1633; but according to Crosby's authorities, Hutchinson and the Kiffin MS., it was after 1633–38; and according to added authorities, such as Spilsbury, Tombes, Lawrence and others, the revival of immersion took place by two distinct methods, the *"former"* being the Blunt, and *"last"* being the Spilsbury, method. Blunt evidently went to Holland for the "former" method after 1633–38; and there is no way to escape the 1640–41 theory without overthrowing Crosby—albeit he does not mention 1641. The "English Baptists," according to Crosby, revived immersion in the 17th century, about 1640–41; and if we could fix no particular date at all between 1611 and 1641, the fact of *revival* is the same. All the writers of the 17th century, Baptist and Pedobaptist, either expressly or impliedly, declare this fact; and followed by Crosby they revolve around the date 1640–41, whether that date is mentioned or not. These writers demonstrate that the "English Baptists," as Crosby maintains, were Separatists—that they had a "beginning" of their own in England—that they wrought a "reformation upon the same principles on which all other Protestants built their reformation"—all in the 17th century. This is the history of the case; and nothing would be gained if the 1641 theory was exploded into atoms. The critics of Dr. Whitsitt's thesis have gone crazy about "1641." That date is no doubt the true one; but that date is the most insignificant consideration in the contention. The great question is: Did the Anglo-Saxon Baptists originate in the 17th century upon the principle of believers' baptism and independency—did they have a "beginning" as Separatists—did they introduce a "reformation" of their own—did they afterwards restore immersion and so complete their reformation? Crosby and the 17th century writers, as cited in this work, say they did; and the date at which they revived immersion is a small matter. The only way to get rid of the facts in the case is to explode Crosby; and in exploding him, the critics will have to explode fifty or sixty witnesses who sustain Crosby.

(C)

THE CRITIC ON THE FONT.

The critic cites Wall (Hist. Inft. Bapt., Vol. II., p. 403) as follows: "And for sprinkling, *properly called*, it seems that it was at 1645 just then *beginning*, and used by *very few*. It must have begun in the disorderly times of 1641." Wall is here referring to the change from *pouring* to sprinkling in the English Church, in 1645, on the part of a "very few," and which was resisted by such men as Thomas Blake, who favored and practiced pouring, and who said (Infants Baptism freed from Antichristianism, 1645, p. 4): "I have seen several dipped; I never saw nor heard of any sprinkled." Blake uses the word *"rhantize"* (which the

Baptists had used to antithesize immersion) to antithesize pouring; and Dr. Jesse B. Thomas (Both Sides, p. 31) says of the Pedobaptist use of the word: "It points rather to the rancorous opposition of the conservatives who reluctantly yielded to the force of public opinion so far as to accept pouring, but resented the further change of sprinkling, *then* [1645] *just being introduced.*" Affusion—a "washing" or rubbing "with water"—was and had been the practice of the Pedobaptists reaching back into the 16th century; and although affusion went by the general name of "sprinkling," it was not till about 1645 that the English Church began to practice what Wall says was "*properly called*" sprinkling—and then only by a "very few." The Jacob church is represented by the tract, "To Sions Virgins," as sprinkling from its organization; and it is likely the Independents generally practiced sprinkling instead of pouring—and so perhaps of the Presbyterians. From the time of Wycliffe and Tyndale pouring had begun in the English Church; and the Catechism of Noel, 1570, of sole authority then in the English Church, prescribed "sprinkling" as alternate with immersion. In spite of Queen Elizabeth's efforts to resist the Calvinistic innovation, she was not able to withstand the affusion movement; and Wall says (Hist. Inft. Bapt., Vol. II., p. 401): "In the latter times of Queen Elizabeth, and during the reigns of King James and of King Charles I., *very few children were dipped in the font.*" Affusion was the mode and "sprinkling, *properly called,*" as Wall puts it, never began to be practiced by the English Church until about 1645, and then by "*very few.*"

It is needless to follow the critic from Gough to Balfour against his chief authority, Dr. Wall. The "Stone Font," urged by the Bishops against the "profane bason," did not imply dipping between 1600 and 1645; for in the use of the same terms they forbid baptizing IN basons, which was by pouring, just as they require baptism IN fonts, which was in the same form. The Prayer Book of James I., 1604, meant no more as to dipping then than it means now, and with but little exception the English Church practiced then, just as it does now. The discovery of fonts and baptisteries sufficient to dip babies or adults in proves nothing for the practice of baptism from 1600 to 1641. We find them all over Europe as employed in earlier times for immersion; and there is a baptistery in a Nashville Episcopal Church for the use of any one who desires to be dipped in a sprinkling church.

Other witnesses employed by the critic are, like Wall, not touching the question as he supposes. Sir John Floyer, already quoted in Ch. V., positively declares that immersion, with a few exceptions, had ceased in the English Church from 1600 A. D. onward; and like Rogers, Downame and others, he was pleading for its restoration. Watts, in 1656, a learned Episcopalian, does not hesitate to say, at his time, that the "memory of man" did not run back to the period when the English Church was not in "firm possession" of sprinkling or affusion as against immersion. Such Baptist writers as Henry Denne and Thomas Crosby thoroughly agree with Sir John Floyer that immersion in England ended with the year 1600.

So far as *adult* immersion is concerned, as far as I have read, all the Baptist writers from 1641 to 1700 are against the critic at the font. In 1645 the learned Dr. Tombes defends the right to restore immersion by unbaptized administrators upon the sole ground that the ordinance had been "universally corrupted," and that the "continuance of adult baptism could not be proved." Cornwell, 1645, assumes that the Baptists had resumed "*dipping.*" R. B. in 1642 declares that "until *lately* there were no *baptized people.*" So expressly or impliedly of over fifty witnesses, Baptist and Pedobaptist, who wrote in the 17th century. Of what consequence then is it that Thomas Blake, 1645, had seen many (he says "*several*") infants dipped as exceptions to the rule of the English Church? Of course, Daniel Featley, like some Episcopalians now, might truly say: "Our font is always open"—that is, if anybody wants immersion. William Walker, 1678, truly said: "The general custom now in England is to sprinkle;" but in the light of Wall, Floyer, Denne, Watts, Crosby and others, I deny his other proposition: "So in the fore end of this centurie the general custom was to dip." Balfour (1827) says: "Baptizing infants by dipping them in fonts was practiced in the Church of England (except in the cases of sickness or weakness) until the Directory came out in the year 1644;" but he is only right as to the few exceptions which have been admitted by Wall, Floyer, Crosby and others. Affusion was the general mode of the English Church from 1600 to 1645, when, as Wall says, "sprinkling, *properly called*," began to be practiced, and then only by a "*very few.*"

(D)
THE CRITIC'S PERVERSION OF KING.

He quotes the following sentence from King's "Way to Zion, &c.:"
"1. That God hath had a people on earth, ever since the coming of Christ in the flesh, throughout the darkest times of Popery, which he hath owned as saints and as his people." The Critic then adds from King's Third Part which: "Proveth that Outward Ordinances, and amongst them *Baptism*, is to *continue* in the Church, &c." The Critic then adds his comment: "I think some people would have spasms if some prominent Baptist author were to put forth and prove the above propositions. But these words of Daniel King did not disturb William Kiffin, and those other Baptist preachers." He goes on then to quote further from King and Kiffin (who endorsed King's book) to imply the idea that they taught a *visible succession* of the church and its ordinances throughout all the ages. If he read King's book, he is guilty of one of the grossest pieces of garbling and suppression any writer ever perpetrated; and if he did not read his book, and only picked these sentences by scanning, then he is guilty of the grossest ignorance. No stronger book was ever written in the 17th century to prove that, while there had, in all ages, been a *spiritual* succession of "saints," the *visible* succession of the church, its ministry and ordinances, had been lost until restored by the Baptists; and while he maintained, as against the Quakers and Seekers, that the ordinances (including baptism) should upon principle continue in the church, he unequivocally declares the fact that they had not so continued until restored. Now that they have been restored he (endorsed by Kiffin and others) assumes against the Pedobaptists, Quakers and Seekers that the true

church and ordinances are in the world, according to the New Testament pattern; and they are defending their right to restore them and perpetuate them against the cavil and disturbance created by misrepresentation and opposition. For a complete refutation of the Critic's gross perversion of King, I refer the reader back to King's testimony on pages 187-191 of this volume, where he speaks for himself, and where he could have spoken more at length if I had had the space. I also refer the reader to my chapter on William Kiffin, pages 121-124, where he speaks as King does—and also to pages 107, 108, Objections To The Kiffin Manuscript.

The critic in quoting King's first proposition failed, or took particular pains not to quote his second which stands right under the first, as follows: "2. *That these saints have the power to reassume and take up as their right, any Ordinance of Christ, which they have been deprived of by the violence and tyranny of the man of sin.*" This is the point in controversy, and this is the point on which King lays stress in order to show that the Baptists had not only the right to restore baptism, under the Scriptures, but had restored it, and had re-established the churches of Jesus Christ on earth. This point and this part of King's discussion the critic suppressed, or else he overlooked it with a criminal carelessness next to the crime of garbling; and in either case he is not reliable as authority upon the discussion under consideration —especially so in seeking to make the false implication he does.

(E)
THE CRITIC AND THE WESTMINSTER ASSEMBLY.

It is not disputed that some of the "English divines between 1600 and 1641"—and long afterwards—opposed the innovation of sprinkling, defended and sought to restore the lost rite of infant immersion in England. This was true, as has been cited, of Daniel Rogers, George Downame, Joseph Neede, Henry Greenwood, John Mayer, Stephen Denson, Edward Elton, John Selden, Sir John Floyer, John Wesley and others; but the great mass of the English Church and clergy, between 1600 and 1641, were pouring for baptism, and only began to resent "sprinkling, *properly called*," in 1645, when the Presbyterian innovation began to be adopted, and then only by "a very few." As Wall says, however, very few infants were dipped from the latter part of the reign of Queen Elizabeth to the close of the reign of Charles the First. Pouring was the English Church fashion—improperly called "sprinkling."

If the Catholics of England were, according to Thomas Hall, like the Baptists of 1652, "great dippers," it does not appear from the author quoted. He only speaks of "*some* amongst us that have been dipped;" and it is not denied, in 1652, that "*some* of the Catholics" and the "poore Welsh" dipped their children—even in Winter.

It is well known that in the decision of the Westminster Assembly, 1643, immersion was excluded as an alternate form with sprinkling and not as a substitute for sprinkling; and it is also well known that the Presbyterians had introduced sprinkling in Scotland in 1539 and had consistently practiced it, with but little exception, in England, down to the date of the Westminster Assembly. It was also adopted by the Independents; and it was this innovation which was vainly fought by Queen Elizabeth and some of the Bishops in the latter part of the 16th century—not simply as against immersion, but as against pouring, which was not surrendered until about 1645 and then only by "a very few." Since the time of Wycliffe, Tyndale and Noel, pouring had been introduced in the English Church; and, so far as the English Church was concerned, it was pouring which supplanted immersion by 1600 A. D.—sprinkling, "properly called," being the mode, in general, among the Presbyterians and Independents.

(F)
THE CRITIC ON IMMERSION IN ENGLAND PRIOR TO 1641.

Under this head the critic's comment upon the 1644 Confession is characterized by the usual exaggerated inferences and exclamation points, but he says one true thing: "The makers of this Confession did not affirm the doctrine of church or baptismal succession." They imply the contrary for the reason that they had no such succession, as I have demonstrated in this work beyond controversy. Among other things, however, the critic affirms one thing wholly untrue : "None of the signers of this Confession avow that immersion was lost." Besides the admissions of Kilcop and Kiffin, Spilsbury positively shows that not only baptism was lost and that the visible succession of the church had been repeatedly broken, but he shows that the Baptists had recovered them—and *how*. See Ch. XII., pp. 144–151. But what of immersion before 1641?

1. The oft-repeated citation of Thomas Fuller (Ch. Hist. of Britain, Vol. VII., p. 97) with regard to the expression: "Donatists new dipt," applied, "for the main," to the Dutch Anabaptists, 1524, I have already noticed in Ch. II., p. 23. Fuller wrote in 1656, just 132 years after this Dutch immigration to England, and so far as I can find he cites no data by which to show that they were dippers. He evidently followed tradition or took his idea from the custom of the Anabaptists of his day, 1656, as the basis of his dipping phraseology; or else, according to the usage of his day, he employed the word "dipped" in the sense of *christened*, and so alliteratively characterized the 1524 Anabaptists as "Donatists new dipt" under a new name. They were evidently of the Hoffmannite type and their practice, at that date, was sprinkling. In 1653, Goodwin speaks of the "first *undipt dipper*" who originated immersion among the Baptists since "the *late* [Puritan] reformation." The Anabaptists of England, before 1641, did not dip. The quotation from Reading (The Anabaptists Routed, 1655), which says: "Anabaptists not only deny believers' children baptism, as the Pelagians and Donatists did of old, but affirm, That dipping the whole body under water is so necessary, that without it noné are baptized," proves nothing except that the Anabaptists of 1655 were practicing exclusive immersion, and that, like the Donatists and Pelagians of old they denied "believers' children baptism." Reading was one of the writers of the 17th century who charged Baptists with "new" or self-originated baptism. See Ch. XIX., p. 233.

2. The quotation from Turner (1551) I have cited also in Ch. II., pp. 24-27. The controversy between Cooke and Turner regarding the practice of "*baptysm*" administered to the "Catechumeni" of the early church on "Easter and Whit Sunday," involved only the *subject* but not the *mode* of baptism; and Turner, an English Church immersionist, uses his own language in reply when, insisting that the *passive* act of baptism, as contradistinguished from the *active* form of the Lord's Supper, should not be deferred with children, he says: "Childes may as well be dipped in the water in the name of Christ even as olde folke." The mode was not in question; and as for the word "Catabaptist" which Turner applies to the Anabaptists, it cannot be shown, in the ecclesiastical use of the word, that it ever means *immersionist*, but only a "prophaner" of baptism by "reiterating that ordinance." Sophocles' Greek Lexicon of the Roman and Byzantine period, gives as the ecclesiastical meaning of the word: "*travesty of baptism.*"

3. The Critic cites John Man (1578), but there is nothing in the short phrases of the fragmentary quotation to prove that the Anabaptists in *England* dipped at all. Some of the Swiss and German Anabaptists had dipped about 1525, and the Poland Anabaptists had resumed dipping in 1574. The tradition that the Anabaptists had generally dipped was common then as it is now; but it cannot be historically shown that the Dutch Anabaptists, then in England and becoming extinct, practiced dipping. Whether of the early Hoffmannite, or later Mennonite, type, they practiced sprinkling; and it is certain that the *English* Anabaptists from 1609 to 1641 did not immerse—as I have abundantly shown.

The citation from Man is the best the Critic has so far done; and yet like all his citations, so few and far between, it is too indefinite as to *whom* and *where* to prove Anabaptist immersion in England before 1641—or rather down to 1578—against the testimonies of so much history which know nothing of adult immersion in England from the earliest times to 1641. The learned Baptist, Dr. Tombes (1652), as cited on page 152 of this volume, shows that "*no continuance of adult baptism* [*immersion*] *can be proved*," prior to 1641, among Anabaptists.

(G)

THE CRITIC ON FOXE, FEATLEY AND OTHERS.

The critic cites us to a work of the time of Henry VIII. and Edward VI., brought out by John Foxe about 1571, which refers to infant baptism as immersion, the general though not universal custom of that time; and which also refers to the "cruel ungodliness of some," which (cruel ungodliness) rushes headlong into baptism which they "without reason" were "unwilling to bestow upon infants." Not one word is here employed to signify the Anabaptist mode of baptism; and the charge of "baptismal regeneration" in the passage does not refer to the Anabaptists at all, but to "*others*," I suppose the extreme ritualists, who imagined that the "Holy Spirit" emerged from the external element of baptism, and that his "grace swam in the very font of baptism." Never was a passage so misrepresented. The critic formerly quoted Fox's Book of

Martyrs for a similar purpose and had to abandon his mistake; and it would have been infinitely better for him to have steered clear of Foxe altogether.

The critic refers to Leonard Busher's definition of baptism as dipping and to Prof. Masson's opinion that the practice of the "Helwisse folk" was immersion—for an answer to which I cite the reader to my Ch. IV., and especially to pp. 52, 53. The Helwys people did not immerse, but the critic cites us to "contemporaneous evidence" from I. H., 1610, as proof that they did so practice, as follows: "For tell me, shall any one that is baptized in the right forme and manner (for that ye stand much on) upon the skinne be saved?" How he gets immersion by a baptism "*upon the skinne*" is hard to see. Evidently the sprinkling Puritan referred to the pouring or washing (often accompanied by rubbing) of the "Helwisse folk" who followed the custom of the Mennonites, and about which there was sometimes controversy between the aspersionists and affusionists. Immersion gets the subject into the water, but it was the washing of affusion that applied the water to or "upon the skinne."

The critic cites John Robinson as declaring that John Morton and his congregation practiced dipping, in the following words: "In the next place they come to baptism in which they think themselves in their element, as filth in water. And beginning with John's baptism, &c." Morton himself is quoted as declaring his belief that John himself baptized "in Jordan," adding that "this indeed was the practice of the primitive churches." Robinson evidently refers to the contention for believers' baptism by the Anabaptists—always "beginning with John's baptism—in which, without any allusion to their mode, he represents them "in their element" of controversy "as filth in water." Smyth, Helwys, Morton and other Anabaptists, before 1641—yea, Mennonites and Pedobaptists—who practiced affusion or aspersion, believed that John baptized in Jordan, and they regarded immersion as a mode of baptism. Hence in the light of history these quotations prove nothing as to the practice of Anabaptists before 1641. I. G[raunt] is cited as showing, in 1645, that Morton, thirty years before, practiced dipping; but I defy the most microscopic criticism to show, in that quotation, that Morton ever dipped—by the remotest inference.

Edmond Jessop (A Discovery of the Errors of the English Anabaptists, 1623, p. 62) is cited as stating an Anabaptist error in his version of Col. 2:12; but his exegesis of that text is in perfect keeping with the Anabaptist and Pedobaptist view of the time, namely, that the burial and resurrection symbolism of baptism, whatever the mode, was spiritually synonymous with the circumcision or washing of the heart. See my Ch. IV., pp. 49-51.

The Critic, under this head, cites Dr. Featley's "Dippers Dipped," &c.; but for a complete answer to all he says on this point, I refer the reader to my Ch. XVII., pp. 202-212. Only one point here needs to be noticed. He cites as a fact (Tanner MS. 67.115. Acts High Court of Commission, Vol. 434, fol. 81. b., Bodleian Library) that "Barber was before Featley in 1639 for being a *dipper*," but he gives no quotation. This was very close to 1640-41, but there is no historic evidence that Barber or any of the English Anabaptists were dippers—even if they had been traditionally so called—in the year 1639. Barber was imprisoned in that year for his opposition to infant baptism—was confined for fifteen months and released about 1641, but he was not punished as a "dipper." His Tract and controversy with Barebone, 1642, imply his admission that the Baptists had reassumed immersion very recently—as Barebone shows, about 1641—and he could not have been a "dipper" in 1639. I should be glad to see the quotation to this effect from the authority cited. The Critic often assumes to cite authorities upon his own statement without quoting their language; and most of his quotations, to say nothing of their strained impertinency, are merely fragmentary and phraseological. On Barber I refer the reader to my Ch. XIV. pp. 163-174—especially to pp. 166-171.

(CONCLUSION.)

I have carefully followed the criticisms, so far afloat, against the Jessey Records, or the Kiffin MS., based upon the theory "*forgery*." The going to press of this volume prevents, here, further notice of what may yet be offered; but, in my judgment, these criticisms are not only microscopically hypercritical and unscholarly, but thoroughly disingenuous and partisan, in their treatment of the subject. In some of them criminal ignorance as to facts which might have been known, is displayed; and if it is not ignorance, then the more culpable crime of garbling, suppression and misrepresentation must be charged. Even where these criticisms had some slight advantage as to minor details which in no way affect the main facts of history," a mountain is made out of a molehill;" and they have the appearance of a determined stand in favor of a pet theory, right or wrong, without regard to the history of the case. Hence the Jessey Records, or the Kiffin MS., must, at all hazards, be proved a "forgery," which is an unwarranted slander of the documents; and in order to this a still hunt through the literature of the 17th century is instituted for the purpose—the sequel of which, up to date, is an ignominious failure. These criticisms may gratify the partisan spirit of some and flatter the ignorance of thousands who will not investigate further, and who will be misled into deeper error; but they will forever be the sport and the contempt of scholars and historians. In characterizing these criticisms I do not charge any *deliberate* design to be dishonest; but they fairly illustrate the reckless and unfair methods of discussion so often developed by the hysteric weakness and feverish excitement engendered by partisan warfare in religion—in all ages characteristic of traditionalism and sacramentalism. God forbid that, for any reason, we should, intentionally or unintentionally, be led to suppress, or misrepresent, the truth.

Further criticisms of the Jessey Records and the Kiffin Manuscript will be considered in this Appendix in the future issues of this volume—if necessary; and in the meanwhile I refer the reader especially to the testimonies of the 17th century writers contained in the foregoing pages, which forever silence the theory of "forgery" applied to the documents in question.

INDEX.

Act of Uniformity,.................. 20
Adams, Richard, ...108, 113, 130
Adshead, Joseph A.,.............. 52
Affusion, Practice of General Baptists, 1609 to 1641, ... 59
Ainsworth, Henry,...........37, 44, 130
Allen, William,..............38, 198, 199
Allute, G. W.,.................... 47
Anabaptism, without reference to mode, the crime before 1641,..... 59
Anabaptists,
    English—no organization before 1611,.................... 68
    First notice of in England, 1534,..................... 18
    Foreigners,................... 19
    Position at beginning of English Reformation,............ 80
    Their Doctrines,...........18, 19
Ancient Records, Epworth—Crowle, ... 51
Angus, Dr. Joseph, ...86, 52
    Dates origin of English Baptist churches, 1611-1633,..... 36
Antipedobaptism, not charged to the Ancient British Christians,.. 12
Aquinas, Thomas,................. 152
Armitage, Thomas,..............13, 44
Ashton, Robert,..........33, 45, 47, 52
    Probability of Smyth's affusion,....................... 45
    Smyth and Robinson Controversy, ...33, 34
Aspersion, Practice of Particular Baptists before 1641,.............. 59
Austin, Invasion of England (596, A.D.),....................... 70
    Demands of British Christians,...................9, 10
    Massacre of British Christians,....................... 9
Baillie, Robert, ...17, 41, 216, 222
    Testimony, ... 222
Bampfield, Francis, a Se-Baptist,..
    ....66, 130, 131
    Document, ...128-139
    Prof. Vedder's testimony on, 139
Baptism of Anabaptists, 16th century,........................ 23
    From 1609 to 1641, Separation, 57
    After 1640-41,.............79, 80
Baptism of the Romanists and Welsh,................168, 172, 178
Baptists, British Christians, first 800 years,................... 9

Baptists,—
    Antiquity of churches before 1611-41 traditional, ... 22
    Church of, in Chester Co., Wales (1422), unknown,.... 18
    Dutch, poured for baptism,.. 75
    English, difficulties in way of restoring immersion, 80, 81, 87
    General, Origin of,........29- 54
    Growth of, to 1644,...41, 58
    Literature and errors, 42, 43
    Mode of baptism before 1641,................44- 49
    Relation to the Mennonites to 1641,.......... 43
    No trace of their principles in England for 558 years,... 9
    Particular, Origin of,......55- 57
    First church,........... 57
    Growth from 1633 to 1644, ...41, 58
    Mode of baptism before 1641,................... 57
    Reformation of, in England, founded in Puritanism,.... 17
    So-called, before restoration of baptism, ... 75
    Supposed traces of elements in Wales to 16th century,.. 12
    Witnesses to restoration of immersion,........163-201
    A popish fiction,....260, 261
    A. R[itor],.........175, 176
    Anabaptists since called "Baptists" before adopting immersion,. 255
    Baptists not the daughter of Rome,.......... 261
    Baptists antedate the baptism of Christ,.... 250
    Barber and Barebone,..
   163-174
    Christopher Blackwood, ...185, 186
    Daniel King, ...187-190
    Francis Cornwell,..183, 184
    Francis Deane, ...182, 183
    Hanserd Knollys, ... 186
    Hercules Collins, ...200, 201
    Henry Denne, ...184, 185
    Henry Jessey.......191-195
    R. B.'s reply to P. B., 176-180
    Thomas Kilcop's reply to P. B.,.......180-182
    Thomas Lamb, ...199, 200
    William Allen, ...198, 199

INDEX. 277

Baptists,—
  William Kaye, ...195-198
  Separation began,...... 251
  Succession a recent doctrine among Baptists, 160
Baptists, Were they? 250-261
  Believers' baptism central peculiarity,...... 257
  Summary of the 17th century Baptist position,..... ....252, 253
  Reproduction, not visible succession,........ 257
Bakewell, Thomas, Catabaptism,. 26
Barber, Edward, 88, 63, 126, 150, 163-174
  Tract and Testimony, ...163-174
Barclay, Robert,..........41, 44, 59, 78
Bards, Welsh,.................. 13
Barebone, P.,....58, 97, 166, 171, 176, 180
  Brownist and not a Baptist,. 97
  His reply to Barber,......166, 167
  His reply to R. B..........176-180
  His reply to Spilsbury, ... 148
Barrowe, Robert,..............17, 19
Bastwick, Dr.,..................... 21
Batte, John,................61, 100, 115
Baxter, Richard, ...9, 216
Bede, Venerable, ... 9
Bishops, Early British, at Council Nice, Arles, etc.,................ 11
Blackburn, William,.............. 52
Blacklock, Samuel,............61, 65
Blackwood, Christopher,
  ....149, 150, 185, 186
  His testimony,............185, 186
Blunt, Richard,........61, 62, 63, 65
  Deputed to Holland, 1640, .62, 68
  His church probably disbanded,..................65, 66
Boucher, Joan, burned,.......... 20
Bocking, Church, ...22, 54, 63
Brinsley, John, Catabaptism, ... 26
Burnet, Bishop,..............72, 80
Burrage, Henry S.,............... 44
Busher, Leonard,............42, 53, 163
  Definition of baptism,....... 42
Caerleon on Usk, Bishop of........ 11
Calamy, Edmund,................
Canne, John,..............63, 64, 124
  Baptized man, 1641, ... 64
Canterbury, Church,.............. 54
Catabaptism,.....................24- 27
Cathcart, William,..........10, 14
Clarkson, Lawrence, in prison for immersion,..................... 164
Clifford, Dr. John,..............52, 106
Clyfton, Richard,..............29, 130
Cobham, Lord, Lollard Martyr.... 15
Collegiants, ... 73
Collier, Jeremy,.................. 20
Collins, Hercules,..........38, 200, 201
  His testimony,............200, 201
Columba, St.,..................... 12
Confessions of Faith, ...48, 49, 51
  Of John Smyth,.............. 49

Confessions of Faith,—
  Of 1611, ... 48
  Of 1644,..................245, 246
  Of 1641, an anti-succession document,................... 258
Conventicles, Dutch-English, at close of 16th century,.......... 21
Cornwell, Francis,......38, 149, 182, 183
  His testimony,............183, 184
Crosby, Thomas, Historian,......
  ....9, 14, 20, 29, 37, 41,
  55, 56, 59, 62, 64, 67, 69, 72, 74,
  81, 83, 85, 92, 96, 116, 132, 140, 222
  His account of the origin of the General Baptists, ... 29
  His account of the origin of the Particular Baptists,.... 55
  His account of the disuse of immersion,................. 68- 78
  His account of the restoration of immersion, ...79- 90
  His Witnesses, ...140-163
    Hutchinson, ...142-144
    Spilsbury, ...144-151
    Tombes,...........152-156
    Lawrence,............. 156
    Grantham,............. 157
    Toulmin, ... 159
    Neal, ...160, 161
  Reliability as an author,..... 162
D'Anvers, Henry,................. 10
Dean, Francis, Anabaptist Sermon, ...182, 183
Denne, Henry,.........38, 71, 184, 185
  Imprisoned for dipping,...... 164
  Testimony,................184, 185
Dexter, Henry M.,................ 44
Dippers Undipt,................... 231
Donatists, ... 11
  "New Dipt,"............. 23, 271
Doopsgezinden, ...23, 224, 245
Downame, George,................. 73
Drew, John, his testimony........ 228
Eachard, John, Author, The Loyall Convert, ... 220
Easter, Time of Keeping by Early British Christians, ...9- 11
Eaton, Samuel,.................
  .. 56, 57, 59, 100, 111, 150, 213
Edwards, Thomas, Gangraena,....
  ....53, 66, 216, 236
  His Testimony,.............. 236
Elizabeth, Persecution of the Anabaptists,......................... 20
Emmes,........................... 66
Enemy, The, What He Said,....213-228
  Author of The Loyall Convert, ... 219
  Book of Common Prayer,.... 214
  B. Ryves,..................... 125
  Ephraim Pagitt, ... 217
  I. E. to T. L.,................ 215
  John Drew,................... 228
  John Eachard,................ 220
  John Geree,................... 221

278 INDEX.

Enemy,— PAGE
  John Goodwin,................ 231
  James Parnell,................ 233
  John Reading,................ 223
  Josiah Ricraft,............... 218
  John Saltmarsh,.............. 221
  John Taylor,.................. 213
  Jeffrey Watts,................ 223
  Nathanael Homes,............ 220
  Nathanael Stephens,......... 229
  Robert Baillie,............... 222
  S. C.'s Reply to A. R.,........ 214
  Stephen Marshall,........... 222
  Thomas Edwards,............. 226
  Thomas Wall,................. 236
  William Cooke,............... 216
Episcopacy, of Early British Christians, ... 12
Fabian,........................... 9
Facts, Significant,............239-249
  Baptismal controversy after 1641,..................... 242
  Health and Decency question, ... 246
  Immersion not punished before 1641,................. 241
  Immersion put into the Confession of 1644,.............. 245
  Never called Baptists until after 1641,................ 244
  Old Men and New Men after 1641,......................... 247
  Relation between General Baptists and Mennonites broken off, 1641,............ 248
  Silence of History,........... 239
  17th Century Baptists Separatists,...................... 240
  Use of the word *rhantize* after 1641,......................... 248
Familists,......................... 66
Featley, Daniel,..25, 41, 53, 117, 202, 216
  Baptist Dipping (1644),....202-204
  Catabaptism,.............25, 209
  "Dippers Dipt,"............202-212
  New Leaven of Anabaptisme,......................204-206
  "Our Anabaptists in England,"...................211, 212
  Zurich Decree of Drowning, ...204-210
Floyer, Sir John,..............71, 72
Font in Place of Baptistery, ... 70
Foxe, John,.................19, 70, 273
Fuessli, J. C.,..................... 26
Fuller, Thomas,...............19, 70
Geree, John, Testimony........... 221
Gieseler, J. C. I................... 26
Goodwin, John, Catabaptism...25, 216
  Testimony,..................... 213
Gould, George,..............91, 117, 118
Green, "Feltmaker," Brownist,... 58
Gunne, Thomas,................... 62
Hanbury's Memorials,............. 111
Harrison, Robert,..............17, 19
Henry, Dr. Robert, ... 13

PAGE
Helwys, Thomas, 32, 38, 41, 42, 51, 83
              140, 149, 150, 168
  Antagonizes Smyth and the Mennonites,................ 40
  Definition of Baptism,....... 50
  Maintains Smyth's Position, ...82, 33, 37, 39
  The Joshua of the First Baptists, ... 39
High Commission Court, ... 79
Hill Cliffe Church,...............22, 63
Hobson, Paul, not a Baptist before 1641,...........................63, 64
Hollanders, Persecuted at Oxford 1158.......................... 13
First revolt from Rome in England,..................... 13
Homes, Nathanael, Testimony.... 220
Hoveden, Roger,.................. 14
Hutchinson, Edward,..60, 61, 63, 84, 124
  Account of Revival of Immersion,................142-144
  Immersion: Word never put into an English Baptist Confession until 1644,............. 51
  Account of its Disuse in England,......................68-70
  Account of its Restoration, 79-90
  Adult first 300 years,......11, 68
  Agitation 1640,............... 60
  Anti-succession Method,...85, 86
  Armitage's Admissions,..... 90
  Called the "new way" after 1641,......................... 147
  Conclusion from Crosby's Account,..................... 88
  Crime after 1641,............. 59
  Did not Succeed from John Smyth,...................... 83
  In Disuse prior to 1640,...... 60
  Its restoration a Particular Baptist movement,......... 59
  Ivimey's Account,.........88, 89
  Not among Baptists from 300 A. D. to 1641,.............. 74
  Purely a Baptist Movement, 82
  Regular Method,............. 84
  Revived,...................... •61
  Subject changed 400 A. D., Crosby,..................... 69
  Succession through the British churches from 300 to 1600,........................ 68
  The Discussion, a digression of Crosby,................. 80
  Three Methods of Restoration proposed,.............. 82
  Two Methods of Restoration adopted,.................... 83
Infant Baptism: Probable practice of the early British Christians,....................... 9
  Ground of Separation 1633,.. 56
  Practice of the Novatians and Donatists,............. 206

INDEX.

	PAGE
Iranaeus,	12
Ivimey, Joseph,	9, 14, 52, 53, 58, 88, 96, 116
Account of restoration of Immersion,	88, 89
Jacob, Henry,	56
Jacob-Lathrop Church, Secession 1633,	56
Secession 1638,	57
Secession 1639,	57
Jessey, Henry,	58, 65, 66, 67, 97, 150, 191-195
Became Baptist in 1645,	58
Confirming the Kiffin MS.,	102
Convinced of Immersion in 1640-41,	61
His church Baptist in transition,	58
His testimony,	191-195
Mixed-church Communion,	58
Practiced Infant Immersion from 1642,	103
Jessop, Edmond,	37, 44, 180
Johnson, Francis,	37, 44
Kaye, William, Testimony,	195-198
Kiffin, William,	38, 62, 63, 64, 218
Account of,	116-127
Endorsed Daniel King's Way to Sion,	123
Not immersed before 1641,	124
Kiffin Manuscript Examined,	91-103
Confirmations,	100-103
Objections,	104-115
Part of the Jessey Records,	91
See Appendix, A,	266
Used by Crosby as valid history,	98
Kilcop, Thomas,	38, 62, 63, 181, 182
His testimony, reply to P.B.,	180
King, Daniel,	38, 124, 150, 151, 187-191
His testimony,	187-191
See Appendix, D,	264, 265
Knollys, Hanserd,	21, 63, 64
Became an Anabaptist in 1636,	22
Fled to America, 1686,	22
Never became a Baptist before 1641,	64
Pastor of a Baptist church in London in 1645,	22
Perhaps not a Baptist till 1634,	263
Reply to Dr. Bastwick,	21, 22
See Appendix. A,	262
Lamb, Thomas,	88
His testimony,	199, 200
Lathrop, John,	56
Lawrence, Henry,	88, 63, 122
His testimony,	156
Lechler, Gothard,	16
Lewis, John,	69, 104
Llewellyn, Prince of Wales conquered 1282, A. D.	12
Lollard, Walter, in England 1315, A. D.,	14
Lollard Movement crushed in 16th Century,	16

	PAGE
Lollard Movement,— Forerunner of the Reformation,	16
Lollards, Baptist principles of,	68, 71
Lost Ordinances—Baptism,	31, 82, 86, 94, 121, 128, 145, 152, 156, 158, 166, 170, 171, 176, 177, 180, 183, 187, 188, 189, 192, 197, 198, 200
Lucar, Mark,	61, 62, 67
Luther, Martin,	68
Marshall, Steven, his Testimony,	222
Masson, Dr. David,	52, 53
Mennonites, New Fryelers,	40, 41
Milton, John,	21, 52
Morton, John,	32, 38, 40, 41, 42, 43, 50, 83, 140, 150, 163
Defends Smyth's Position,	84, 85
Mosheim,	10, 36
Muller, S.,	44, 45, 46, 52
Muncer, Thomas,	236
Munster, not the Origin of the Baptists,	68
Neal, Daniel,	41, 52, 64, 65, 109
His Blunders, see Appendix, A,	265
His Testimony,	180
New Baptisme,	147, 166, 167, 176, 178, 182, 183, 184, 185, 190, 194, 195, 199, 204, 215, 216, 217, 220, 221, 223, 225, 226, 228, 230, 231, 235, 236
Newman, Dr. A. H.	15, 19, 23, 24, 25, 26, 44, 50, 67, 125
New Men, or *Immersi*,	47, 225
Noel's Catechism,	72
Nonconformity of Early British Christians,	12
Novatians,	11
Oates, Samuel,	38, 223
Olchon, No evidence of a Baptist Church there before 1641,	13
Old Men, or *Aspersi*,	48, 225
Orme, William,	96, 120
Ottius, J. H.,	26
Pagitt, Ephraim, Heresiography,	217
Parnell, James, his testimony,	233
Patient, Thomas,	88, 119, 157
Patrick, St.,	11
Payne, John,	21
Pearson, John,	157
Pelagius, on infant baptism, 5th century,	10
Penry, John, not an immersionist,	17, 21, 24
Perkins on Galatians,	141
Petiers, Jan, burned,	20
Powell, Vavasor, not a Baptist before 1653,	124
Price, Thomas,	52
Propagandists of Early Christianity in England,	9
Rapin,	70
Rauschenbusch, Dr. A	45
Reformation, Baptist,	82, 87, 107, 122, 189, 192, 198

Index.

Revival of Immersion, ...61, 80, 81, 82, 83, 84, 86, 88, 94, 114, 125, 128, 132, 139, 140, 143, 144, 145, 148, 149, 152, 154, 155, 156, 157, 159, 160, 166, 170, 171, 176, 177, 179, 183, 184, 185, 187, 189, 191, 192, 194, 195, 198, 200
Ricraft, Josiah, Anabaptist Looking Glasse, ... 218
Ritor, A., ...175, 214, 216
   Testimony, ... 216
Robinson, John, ...32, 37, 44
   Assails Helwys' baptism,..32, 33
Robinson, Robert, ... 108
Ryves, B., testimony, ... 225
Saltmarsh, John, testimony, ... 221
Sawtry, first Lollard martyr, ... 15
Saxon Invasion and Massacre, ... 70
Scheffer, de Hoop, J. G...42, 44, 46, 52
Schyn, Herman, Catabaptism,..23, 25
Seekers, ... 66
Separation, Baptist,...121, 199, 213, 218
Shepard, Thomas, ...61, 62, 67
Shute, Giles, ... 52
Smyth, John, ...29, 38, 44, 47, 52, 59, 60, 149, 150, 163
   Baptized by Affusion, ...45, 46
   Death, 1612, ... 45
   Definition of Baptism, ... 49
   Organization of first Baptist Church, ...29, 36
   Reply to Clyfton, repudiates visible succession, ...31, 32
   Retraction of his Errors, ... 37
   Self-baptism, ...29, 31, 43, 44, 82
   Separation from the Brownists, ... 29
Some, Dr. R., ...20, 53
Spanhemius, Fredrick, Catabaptism, ... 25
Spencer, Captain, Brownist,....57, 58
Spilsbury, John, ...38, 57, 59, 60, 61, 63, 65, 66, 67, 124, 157, 163, 213
   One of Crosby's witnesses, ...144-151
Sprinkling, General, from 1600 to 1641, ...72, 73
   By Anabaptists before 1641,.. ....28, 59, 61, 196, 197
Stephens, Nathaniel, testimony,.. 229
Stork, Nicholas, ...211, 232, 236
Stovell, Charles, ... 64
Strype, John, ...20, 108

Succession, Visible and Spiritual, ...31, 69, 78
   Visible succession repudiated by the Baptists, ...31, 32, 146, 150, 185, 189
Taylor, Adam, General Baptist Historian, ... 37, 52
Taylor, John, ...100, 111, 114
   Testimony, ... 213
Terwoot, Hendrik, burned, ... 20
Thomas, Joshua, ... 12
Tombes, Dr. John, ...38, 63, 126, 151
   One of Crosby's witnesses,... 152-156
Tookey, Elias, ... 42
To Sion's Virgins, definition of baptism, ... 50
Turner, Dr. William, Catabaptism, Immersion, ...24, 26, 27
   See Appendix, E, ... 271
Tyndale, John, ...16, 17, 72
Usher, Archbishop, ... 14
Vedder, Henry C., ...20, 22, 44, 138
Van Braght, Tileman,, ... 23
Waldenses, ...13, 14, 70, 78
Wales, under the darkness of Romanism down to 16th Century, ... 13
   First Baptist church in, 1649, 13
Walker, Williston, ... 112
Wall, Thomas, ...44, 52
   Testimony, ... 236
Waterlanders, Aspersionists,....45, 46
   John Smyth sought admission among, ...38, 46
Watts, Jeffry, on Sprinkling in England, ...72, 225
   Strong Witness, Novelty of Immersion, ... 223
Welsh Protestantism in England finally destroyed, 1282, ... 12
Welsh lately left off immersion, .. 71
Wesley, John, ... 72
Whitsitt, Dr. Wm. H., ...15, 44, 99, 165, 212, 239
Wilson, W., ... 52
Wrighters, became a Seeker, ... 66
Wyckliffe, John never left the Romish Church, ...15, 68
   Baptist Principles, ...68, 71
Zanchius, ... 152
Zwingle, Ulrich, Catabaptism, ... 24

www.ingramcontent.com/pod-product-compliance
Lightning Source LLC
Chambersburg PA
CBHW031929230426
43672CB00010B/1866